MW00826759

Stigmatized on Screen

Stigmatized on Screen

How Hollywood Portrays Nonstandard Dialects

Lindsey Clouse

LEXINGTON BOOKS
Lanham • Boulder • New York • London

Published by Lexington Books
An imprint of The Rowman & Littlefield Publish Group, Inc.
4501 Forbes Boulevard, Suite 200, Lanham, Mar nd 20706
www.rowman.com

86-90 Paul Street, London EC2A 4NE, United K dom

Copyright © 2022 by The Rowman & Littlefield blishing Group, Inc.

All rights reserved. No part of this book may be roduced in any form or by any electronic or mechanical means, including informatio torage and retrieval systems, without written permission from the publisher, except by eviewer who may quote passages in a review.

British Library Cataloguing in Publication Inforn ion Available

Library of Congress Cataloging-in-Publicatio ata

Names: Clouse, Lindsey, 1981– author.
Title: Stigmatized on screen : how Hollywood pc ays nonstandard dialects / Lindsey Clouse.
Description: Lanham : Lexington Books, 2022. | ludes bibliographical references and index. | Summary: "This book analyzes th 00 top-grossing films of the last 20 years to show how speakers of traditionally gmatized dialects are represented, underrepresented, misrepresented, and mocked ltimately, the author demonstrates how Hollywood reinforces long-standing nega beliefs about the languages of marginalized communities"— Provided by pul her.
Identifiers: LCCN 2022023364 (print) | LCCN 2 023365 (ebook) | ISBN 9781793647412 (cloth) | ISBN 978179364742 epub)
Subjects: LCSH: Motion pictures and language. | nguage and languages in motion pictures. | Motion pictures—United States—H ry—21st century. | English language—Dialects—United States—In motio ictures.
Classification: LCC PN1995.4 .C5856 2022 (pri | LCC PN1995.4 (ebook) | DDC 791.43/64—dc23/eng/20220519
LC record available at https://lccn.loc.gov/20220 64
LC ebook record available at https://lccn.loc.gov 22023365

™ The paper used in this publication meets the inimum requirements of American National Standard for Information Sciences—Pe nence of Paper for Printed Library Materials, ANSI/NISO Z39.48-1992.

Contents

Acknowledgments

So many teachers, colleagues, and friends have had some part in this journey. In particular, I would like to thank Jenny Kluck and Jeremy Rud, without whose constant support, encouragement, feedback, and friendship, this book literally would not have happened. Thank you to Cristina Tovar for her patience with my ignorant questions about Spanish. This project also could not have been possible without the Rapid City Public Library and their stellar staff. I am also grateful to editor Jessie Tepper for seeing the potential in this research and for giving me this opportunity. And, of course, to my mother, Terri Clouse, who has always been my biggest supporter.

Finally, thank you to all the creators whose art I have so callously dissected in these pages. You keep us all going.

Chapter 1

"You Know Something, You're Smart, if You Would Just Deign to Speak English"

Introduction

At the time of its release in 1994, Disney's *The Lion King* was unusual for the degree of racial diversity in the casting of its voice actors. About half of the named characters with speaking lines—both heroes and villains—are voiced by people of color, though notably both the young and adult versions of title character Simba are played by White actors (Jonathan Taylor-Thomas and Matthew Broderick). But despite the diversity in its casting, *The Lion King* nonetheless reinforces a different, perhaps less obvious pattern of discrimination that was pervasive throughout Hollywood prior to its release and remains so today—dialect discrimination.

Though the hero characters Simba, Nala, Mufasa, and Sarabi are voiced by both Black and White actors, they all speak so-called "standard" English. A new viewer who was unfamiliar with the actors behind the roles might not realize that some of these characters are, in fact, people of color; their speech—which lay audiences would perceive as "unaccented," unmarked—is coded as White. The villains, on the other hand, speak a range of other dialects. Scar, brother of Mufasa and mastermind behind the plot to murder the royal family and assume the throne, is voiced by White English actor Jeremy Irons and speaks Received Pronunciation (RP), better known to lay audiences as the King's or Queen's English, the dialect of the upper class in southern England. Hyenas Shenzi and Banzai are voiced by Whoopi Goldberg and Cheech Marin and use Black English (also called African American Vernacular English or AAVE) and Chicano English, respectively, including grammatical structures that most audience members would consider "nonstandard," "incorrect," "bad English." Shenzi uses singular *was* ("It's not exactly like they was alone, Scar”), *ain’t*, and mult le negatives, which linguists call *negative concord* (“There ain’t no way I’m oin’ in there!”); Banzai also uses *ain’t* and negative concord (“We ain’t got stinkin’ entrées!”). Finally, Ed the hyena is voiced by White American a r Ed Cummings, though in the film Ed never actually speaks; he only la ns and grunts. The three hyenas are goofy, bumbling, and stupid, often ser g as the film’s comic relief, and they ultimately cause Scar’s downfall whe they fail to kill Simba as a cub, then later turn on Scar himself.

The association of “standard” English h intelligence, competence, and heroism and “nonstandard,” stigmatized ialects such as Black English, Spanish-influenced English, and Southern .S. English with humor, stupidity, incompetence, and villainy is a patter that appears again and again in mainstream film. Gendered dialects such a “Valley Girl” are often similarly used to depict women—especially youn women—in stereotypical ways: silly, self-absorbed, ditzy, and dumb.

The 2019 remake of *The Lion King* had opportunity to correct this pattern, an opportunity to elevate the stigmat d dialect-speaking characters to the same level of dignity and competence the “standard” speakers or perhaps even cast a stigmatized speaker in a e role. And it does have an even more diverse cast than the original, with ack people providing the voices for nearly all of the speaking roles inclu ng young and adult Simba (JD McCrary and Donald Glover). But rather n push back against the practice of relegating stigmatized dialect speakers roles as comedic or incompetent characters, the remake elected to erase th completely. Scar—now voiced by Chiwetel Ejiofor—is still intelligent, l evil, and still speaks RP, but Shenzi is now the leader of the hyenas and also portrayed as intelligent and conniving. She’s voiced by Florence Kas nba, who was born in Uganda, grew up in Germany, and speaks RP with r native fluency. Banzai and Ed have been eliminated altogether and repla d by two new hyena characters, Kamari and Azizi, voiced by Keegan-M ael Key and Eric André, who again provide comic relief but are marked more competent than their 1994 counterparts. They speak “standard” Engli In fact, the only character in the 2019 version who does not speak a “stand d” American or British dialect is Rafiki the baboon, voiced by South Africa actor John Kani.

It seems as though Disney filmmakers r ized that the 1994 depiction—in which the only characters whose speech s coded as non-White were the dumbest and most bumbling—was unam guously racist, but the alternative—placing speakers of stigmatized diale s in serious or heroic roles—was untenable. Speakers of Black English, Ch no English, and other similarly marginalized dialects, with stunningly fe exceptions, simply *do not play serious heroes in serious films*, especially mily films. Rosina Lippi-Green first pointed out the problems with dialect representation in *The Lion King* and other children's films in her book *English with an Accent: Language, Ideology, and Discrimination in the United States*, released first in 1997 and again in 2012. In animated Disney films in particular, she notes, main characters speak "standard" English without exception, while "nonstandard" dialects and foreign accents are used to Other the sidekicks and villains. In *Beauty and the Beast* (1991), which takes place in France, title characters Belle and the Beast speak "standard" American English while sidekicks such as Lumiere the candelabra and his love interest Featherduster have French accents. In *The Hunchback of Notre Dame* (1996), the Romani woman Esmeralda, main character and love interest to the White hero Phoebus, again speaks "standard" American English while the other Romani use an "inconsistent and unidentifiable" foreign accent.[1] In her discussion of the 1994 *Lion King* in particular, Lippi-Green summarizes what she calls the "familiar message": "AAVE speakers occupy the dark and frightening places, where Simba does not belong and should not be; he belongs on the sunny savannah where [standard English] speakers like his father live."[2] Black English and other stigmatized dialects, along with foreign accents, it is clear, are markers of the villainous and the humorous, not the heroic or the serious.

As the 2019 *Lion King* demonstrates, measurable progress *has* been made in casting diversity in American film over the last several decades. But representation in speaking roles and especially top-billed roles still lags behind representation in the U.S. population at large. A major 2016 USC Annenberg study of gender, race, and sexuality in front of and behind the camera in film and television found that in 2014, 28.3% of characters with speaking roles were people of color, almost 10% less than their proportion of the U.S. population.[3] And though these numbers are gradually improving, even as more Black and brown faces appear on our screens, the depiction of Black and brown voices remains stagnant and, in cases like *The Lion King*, has arguably taken steps backward.

The chapters that follow will examine the most widely spoken stigmatized dialect groups in the U.S. and their representation in the 493 top-grossing films (U.S. and Canadian domestic box office) from 2000 to 2019. Each chapter will explore the features that characterize the dialect group and analyze the representation of the dialect in the 493-film dataset. This will include discussions of the depictions of the speakers in stereotypical ways. We shall see, for example, that speakers of Southern U.S. English are frequently represented as racist or unintelligent, that Black English is treated as inherently comedic and unsuitable for serious characters in serious films, that speakers of Spanish and Spanish-influenced English are regularly relegated to roles as domestic servants and drug dealers, and that young women who use gendered speech patterns are often portrayed as du and ditzy. These patterns apply even to nonhuman characters in animated, ience fiction, and fantasy films. In some ways, the picture of stigmatized akers in modern film is also the picture of minorities and women in film in neral—underrepresented or, too frequently, represented in stereotypical w s. However, this picture is even more problematic for stigmatized speake than for minorities and women broadly. It's important to note that, for exa le, not all Black characters speak Black English, and those that do are far re likely to fall into stereotypical representations than Black characters o use "standard" English. This holds true for Southern White characters o use Southern English, Latinx characters who speak Spanish or Spanish-i uenced English, and women and girls who use gendered speech patterns. I fact, a number of popular films quite clearly employ intentionally diverse asts—*The Matrix* trilogy (1999, 2003, and 2003), *Big Hero 6* (2014), *Th* *artian* (2015), the most recent *Star Wars* trilogy (2015, 2017, and 2019), *ider-Man: Homecoming* (2017) and *Far From Home* (2019), *Shazam!* (20)—and yet include no linguistic diversity whatsoever. The message is cle there is a place of prestige for Black, Southern, Latinx, and female cha ters on our screens, but only if they conform to White, Northern, upper-c s male linguistic standards.

Media both influence and reflect our liefs about various groups, and these stereotypical depictions of stigmati l dialect speakers reflect enduring beliefs about the dialects and the peo who speak them. Furthermore, in our still highly segregated society, for " ndard" English-speaking White Americans, media are a major—often *t* major—source of exposure to speakers of other dialects. As Nikolas C pland puts it in "The Mediated Performance of Vernaculars," "Quite sim , mass media are the main contemporary means of constructing and con ning 'difference,' including linguistically indexed difference, and that is ficient reason to treat mediation as a core sociolinguistic domain."[4] In si ler terms, it's worth examining dialect diversity in film because it's one f the primary ways that people learn about "nonstandard" dialects and t r speakers. We'll also examine the impact these depictions have on audie es, including both speakers and nonspeakers of these dialects. And in the nal chapter, we'll explore ways to address the problem of dialect discrimi ion both in film and in society.

HOW THE FILM SET WA DETERMINED

The 493 films examined in this book repr ent the top-grossing films at the domestic box office (U.S. and Canada) fro 2000 to 2019, adjusted for inflation. This list was obtained from Box Offi Mojo by IMDbPro (an Amazon subsidiary), which "receives data from a riety of sources, including film studios, distributors, sales agents, and others from around the world."[5] It's the most comprehensive source for American box office data.

Box Office Mojo allows the user to sort top-grossing film lists by highest total gross, approximate number of tickets sold, or inflation-adjusted gross using average ticket prices from any year since 1910. The number of tickets sold is determined "by taking [the film's] box office gross and dividing it by the average ticket price at the time it was released. To adjust it for inflation (or see what it might have made in the past), the estimated number of tickets sold is multiplied by the average ticket price of the selected year."[6]

Box Office Mojo lists the top 1,000 grossing films of all time but does not enable users to see the top-grossing films from a given time period. Thus, our film list was created by omitting all films that were released prior to 2000 and after 2019 from the list of 1,000 films, resulting in a total of 493 films. The list in Appendix A[7] is ordered by approximate number of tickets sold and displays both total lifetime gross and gross adjusted for inflation using 2019 average ticket prices.

Readers will notice that two nonfiction, documentary-style films—*Fahrenheit 9/11* (2004), an actual documentary, and *Borat: Cultural Learnings of America for Make Benefit Glorious Nation of Kazakhstan* (2006), a partially unscripted satirical documentary—were included in the final set of 493 films. These two films were analyzed in the same manner as the other films, because, as with any scripted film, documentary directors, writers, and editors make conscious choices about narrative construction, which footage to cut and which to keep, and how to depict the individuals seen and heard on screen. Through their choices, documentary filmmakers can construct positive or negative portrayals of these individuals, and, as with fiction filmmakers, they're influenced by the same types of cultural stereotypes and internal biases when they make these choices; thus, in the analyses that follow, these individuals are counted the same as any fiction character.

WHY THESE FILMS?

The focus of this book is the depiction of stigmatized dialects and speech patterns in popular film and its impact on viewers' perceptions of these dialects and speech patterns and their speakers. As such, the films chosen were those that sold the most tickets and therefore reached the most viewers in American theaters between 2000 and 2019. Home video sales, rentals, and streaming data are far more difficult to track and no comprehensive source currently exists that compiles data for all of these home-viewing options.

The films were limited to those released from 2000 to 2019 because these films represent the most modern examples of these depictions for which data are available; thus, any stereotypes or other negative depictions cannot be dismissed as out-of-date nor attributed to archaic attitudes which are no longer held by a majority of Americans.

METHODOLOGY

Each of the films in the set of 493 was viewed at least once and all uses of the stigmatized dialect groups Black English, Southern U.S. English, and Spanish and Spanish-accented English (SAE), as well as gendered speech patterns were noted. We'll discuss the characteristics that define these language groups in their respective chapters. Only characters whose audible speech clearly and unambiguously meets the criteria for the stigmatized dialect group in question are counted as data. Characters who used a stigmatized dialect were then classified as protagonists, secondary characters, and minor or background characters. Protagonists are defined as those characters who have the most screen time in a film regardless of the actor's billing. While most films have only a single protagonist, if two or more characters have roughly equal screen time in a given film, all were classified as protagonists. Secondary characters are defined as those who appear in more than one scene and/or have more than three lines and/or whose presence has a significant impact on the plot. Minor and background characters are defined as those who appear in only one scene and/or have three or fewer lines, whose presence does not impact the plot, and who are usually not given names in the film credits. All uses of stigmatized dialects were then counted and analyzed for patterns. Musical performances including singing and rap were not included in the analysis because they don't represent natural, unmonitored speech. Additionally, dialogue in which a character quotes another piece of media was not included. For example, in *I Am Legend* (2007), protagonist Robert Neville (Will Smith) recites some dialogue from the 2001 film *Shrek* as it plays on his television; this dialogue was not included in the analysis because it does not represent Neville's own natural speech. Individual characters who appear in multiple films are counted as separate characters. For example, Puss in Boots (Antonio Banderas) appears in four films (*Shrek 2* [2004], *Shrek the Third* [2007], *Shrek Forever After* [2010], and *Puss in Boots* [2011]) and is therefore counted as four characters even though his characterization is consistent among the films. This decision was made because the purpose of this analysis is to assess the depiction of characters as perceived by theater audiences, and any given moviegoer may see only one or any number of the films in a series.

Only theatrical versions of the films were included in the set, not director's cuts, extended cuts, etc. where available, again, because the intent was to analyze the version of the film that theater-goers would have viewed. Mid- and end-credits scenes were included in the analysis for the same reason.

TERMINOLOGY

In the chapters that follow, I use the term *English of the Dominant Culture*,[8] or *EDC*, rather than more common terms such as *standard English* because of the inherent racist, classist, and sexist biases associated with referring to a single dialect as the "standard" simply because it happens to be the dialect of the privileged class. I use the terms *stigmatized*, *marginalized*, and "*nonstandard*" dialects interchangeably to refer to any dialect considered nonprestigious by typical American speakers, particularly those dialects examined in this analysis.

A NOTE ON PRESENT TENSE *GOT*

Nearly all English language dictionaries and usage guides either consider present tense *got* to be "nonstandard" or ignore its existence completely. For example, the *American Heritage Dictionary* online says of present tense *got*:

> In colloquial use and in numerous nonstandard varieties of American English, the past tense form *got* has the meaning of the present. This arose probably by dropping the helping verb *have* from the past perfects *have got, has got. We've got to go, we've got a lot of problems* became *We got to go, we got a lot of problems.*[9]

However, my analysis of the 493-film set indicates that present tense *got* is in widespread use among *all* American English speakers, not just speakers of "nonstandard varieties." Indeed, present tense *got* is so common among speakers of all American English dialects, including EDC, that I would argue that it's inaccurate to continue to refer to it as "nonstandard." Even EDC speakers who use no other "nonstandard" grammar frequently use present tense *got*; it appears in both formal and colloquial contexts, in both scripted and unscripted dialogue. Therefore, for the purposes of this analysis, because it's not a reliable indicator of "nonstandardness" or stigmatization in a speaker's speech, it was not counted as a stigmatized feature.

THE MYTH OF "BA ENGLISH"

In June 2014, NPR's Robert Siegel interv wed author Ammon Shea about his new book, *Bad English*. Shea argues hat linguists already know, that English is a living, growing language, and at usages that were once considered incorrect or inappropriate—such as u g *lunch* as a verb or *dilapidated* to describe a structure not made of stone— e today an unremarkable part of the standard language. Further, Shea says, is process is ongoing, and many of today's neologisms, slang words, anc grammatical "errors" will form tomorrow's standard English.[10]

NPR received hundreds of responses to s interview from listeners (some of whom obviously either missed or were interested in Shea's point) eager to share their personal linguistic pet peev . Among them: using *nauseous* for *nauseated*, *between you and I* instead o *etween you and me*, *less* instead of *fewer*, and *try and do* instead of *try to* .[11] These responses demonstrate what anyone who is active in public life on social media already knows: the English-speaking populace has a lot o pinions about speaking English. Many people—particularly educated peop —believe they know what is and is not proper English, what constitutes corr t grammar and usage, and so on. They believe that there's a single correct v sion of the language—the "standard"—and that everything else is incorrec or, as conservative commentator C. Mason Weaver posited, "slang."[12] "No tandard" dialects such as Black English, Chicano English, Appalachian E glish, etc. are "bad English" or "bad grammar," used by people who are her incapable of speaking properly or uninterested in doing so. Only "st dard" English is appropriate for academia, the business world, and public l .

Are they correct? Are speakers of these tigmatized dialects incapable of serious intellectual conversation, or perha simply opting out of it? If not, then where do these beliefs come from? Ho did a single dialect of English—the English of Dan Rather and the *Eveni News*, of Frasier Crane, of, in other words, upper-class White men—com o be considered the only correct way to speak by English speakers across t country?

English is a diverse language, due part to centuries of invasion of and by England. With diversity often comes p udice, and dialect prejudice has a long history. It seems humans have alw s had a tendency to look down upon those who speak differently from the —at least as far back as we have records. In his *Fight for English*, linguis David Crystal writes of a "text assigned to the monk Robert of Gloucest [which] makes it clear that, as early as the end of the thirteenth century, re is a clear difference between the language used by upper and lower c ses. . . . 'Unless a man knows

French he is thought little of[.] And low-born men keep to English, and to their own speech still.'"[13]

Indeed, as far back as 63 AD, an ancient Roman grammarian complained about what he saw as the decline of his language: "Spoken Latin has picked up a passel of words considered too casual for written Latin, and the grammar people use when speaking has broken down. The masses barely use anything but the nominative and the accusative . . . it's gotten to the point that the student of Latin is writing in what is to them an artificial language, and it is an effort for him to recite in it decently."[14] Perhaps it's ironic that this new dialect of Latin was actually the beginning of what was to become French—the knowledge of which Robert of Gloucester considered a necessity of high-born men.

These linguistic prejudices are also connected to—and reflective of—prejudices about the speakers themselves. When we admire a group of people, we consider their speech to be proper, educated, correct. When we disdain a group of people, we find their speech to be lazy, ungrammatical, inarticulate. Writing again of these prejudices, Crystal cites

> George Puttenham, who published *The Arte of Poesie* in 1589. . . . He is advising poets on the kind of language they should use if they want to be successful. And he is in no doubt. A poet's language should be "natural, pure, and the most usual of all his country." So where is this to be found? "in the kings Court, or in the good townes and Cities within the land, [rather than] in the marches and frontiers, or in port townes, where straungers haunt for traffike sake, or yet in Vniuersities where Scholers vse much peeuish affectation of words out of the primitiue languages, or finally, in any vplandish village or corner of a Realme, where is no resort but of poore rusticall or vnciuill people." The ideal norm is evidently aristocratic usage. . . . And even within the "good towns and cities," the poet needs to be careful to find the right class of person: "neither shall he follow the speach of a craftes man or carter, or other of the inferiour sort, though he be inhabitant or bred in the best town and Citie in this Realme, for such persons do abuse good speaches by strange accents or illshapen soundes, and false ortographie. But he shall follow generally the better brought vp sort, such as the Greekes call *charientes*, men ciuill and graciously behauioured and bred."[15]

Puttenham associates "inferior" people with inferior speech—"strange accents," "illshapen sounds"—and civil people of good breeding with "natural, pure" language. The immigrant, the foreigner, the frontiersman, the rustic, the poor man, the blue collar craftsman: these types of people "abuse good speech"; and as we shall see in later chapters, these specific prejudices toward the speech of marginalized communities continue today.

In the mid-1800s, U.S. public school reforms, spearheaded by Massachusetts secretary of education Horace Mann, began codifying these dialect prejudices into law. States passed laws to fund free p lic schools and educate teachers and made attendance compulsory through least elementary school, and this rapidly expanding public school system quired an expanded curriculum. Language arts, which were formerly rest ted to simple reading, spelling, and elocution lessons, began to incorporate ammar, vocabulary, and diction. Unsurprisingly, the educated, upper-class ite males who staffed the newly formed school boards and normal schools eacher colleges) used their own dialect as the standard for these new curr la. Over the next century and a half, the public schools were extremely eff tive in teaching the idea that this "standard" English—the English of the Do inant Culture, or EDC—was not only the way well-educated people spoke, was in fact the *only correct* way to speak. Any usage, any grammatical for any pronunciation that differed from EDC was not simply different, not s ply a marker of region or social class, but *wrong*, and anyone who persiste n speaking that way was at best lazy and at worst intellectually inferior or norant.

This belief is so pervasive—hammered ome by generations of teachers who believe it to be accurate and passed own by generations of students to their children and grandchildren—tha t bears repeating that it is, in fact, false.

There is nothing inherently correct or inc rect, nothing inherently superior or inferior, about EDC or any other Englis dialect.

Let's use contrastive analysis to examin an example.

Speakers of EDC and many other dialec of English, in describing a male individual of impressive stature, would *He is tall*. Speakers of Black English and some forms of Southern U.S. glish would say *He tall*. The latter form is known as *zero copula*: the *be*-ve —the copula—is unnecessary in present tense. (Many other modern langua , such as most Slavic languages, also don't use a *be*-verb in present tense. he meaning of the sentences is identical.

There is nothing inherently correct or erior about either construction, despite what any grammar textbook mig say. It is *pure chance* that our upper-class White forefathers said the fo er and not the latter, and that is why the former is now considered the sta rd. If these forefathers had spoken a zero copula dialect instead, we woul ow consider *He tall* to be correct and *He is tall* to be the aberration. And if w re more inclined to label *He tall* "lazy" rather than "efficient," that gives u nsight into our beliefs about the character of Black and Southern people w speak this way. We'll examine many more specific examples of this in la chapters.

Each dialect of English has its own rule The ways in which a stigmatized dialect differs from EDC are not errors or errations; study upon study has shown that these dialects are systematic a that their speakers follow grammatical rules as consistently as do speak of EDC. To say that speakers of Black English, Southern U.S. English, and other stigmatized dialects are breaking the rules of EDC, or are attempting to speak EDC correctly and failing, is as illogical as to say that French speakers are breaking the rules of English or attempting to speak English correctly and failing. It's nonsensical to try to apply the grammar rules of one language to another; it is similarly nonsensical to apply the grammar rules of one *dialect* to another. That one set of rules became the standard and other sets became stigmatized is pure chance, not a result of anything inherently better or worse about any set. And our beliefs about the laziness or ignorance of these dialects is, in fact, a reflection of our beliefs about the people who speak them.

REPRESENTATIONS OF STIGMATIZED DIALECTS OVER TIME

Stereotypical depictions of "nonstandard" English speakers are, of course, not limited to film; such representations have existed in writing for centuries before the medium of film was invented. In "The Treatment of Dialect in Appalachian Literature," Michael Ellis defines these "literary dialects" as "an attempt by a writer to portray a regional, social, or ethnic language variety" and reminds us that "[t]hese authors are writing for audiences of nonspecialists, are not linguists themselves, and are often not attempting to produce a realistic or authentic spoken language"[16]—as we'll see, these factors hold true for film depictions of stigmatized dialects as well. Indeed, Qiuana Lopez and Mary Bucholtz, in their article "'How my hair look?' Linguistic Authenticity and Racialized Gender and Sexuality on *The Wire*," refer to authenticity as "a jointly produced semiotic effect" and argue that "authenticity is the result of authenticating practices that are enacted by users of language . . . *and* ratified by those who observe these practices [emphasis added]."[17] That is, authenticity is not a fundamental property which can be somehow objectively measured—rather, it is cooperatively constructed by both writers/speakers and readers/listeners. A number of scholars of literature and linguistics have examined these literary portrayals with a range of goals: to assess their value as linguistic evidence; to expose the ways in which writers from the dominant culture use them advertently or inadvertently to perpetuate stereotypes about their speakers; and to analyze their use by writers of color and speakers of those same marginalized dialects.

Richard W. Bailey, for instance, examines the problems with centuries-old representations of Black speech by White writers. In *Speaking American: A History of English in the United States*, he writes of free and enslaved African Americans who spoke both English and west African languages "with a great variety of inflections and accents, but racism among the literate reduced their speaking to a series of stereotypes in the w[illegible]en record which, though to some extent revealing, do little to illuminate the [illegible]tails." He cites as an example a 1776 play called *The Fall of British Tyran[illegible]* which represents Black English via a handful of simplistic grammar and [illegible]nunciation features, such as the use of *me* as the first person subject and [illegible]bstituting an *r* /ɹ/[18] sound for an *l* /l/ sound in certain words. The ubiquit[illegible]f such stereotypical representations, he writes, "reflects an idea about [illegible]eech but not necessarily speech itself";[19] in other words, these literary dia[illegible]cts—like the film portrayals we will examine in this book—reveal more [illegible]out their writers' and audiences' beliefs about speakers of Black English [illegible]n they do about Black English itself. This depiction also illustrates a proc[illegible] known as iconization, in which only a few well-known or iconic features a[illegible] used (often with varying degrees of accuracy) to signify a particular dialect. [illegible]is, too, occurs frequently in film depictions, providing viewers with inauth[illegible]ic and simplistic representations of these often quite complex and nuanced [illegible]alects.

Historian Lawrence W. Levine, in his 1[illegible]7 book *Black Culture and Black Consciousness: Afro-American Folk Thou[illegible]t from Slavery to Freedom*, used historical transcriptions by White writer[illegible]f interviews and conversations with Black people to examine formerly en[illegible]aved people's personal reactions to emancipation from shortly before the C[illegible]il War through the 1940s. In an introductory "Note on Black Dialect," he [illegible]cknowledges the problems with White representations of Black English:

> The language employed in these quotations, [illegible]course, is not invariably the language actually spoken by black Americans [illegible] representations of that language recorded by observers and folklorists, the g[illegible]at majority of whom were white and a substantial proportion of whom were [illegible]thern. The language I have been forced to rely upon is a mélange of accur[illegible] and fantasy, of sensitivity and stereotype, of empathy and racism. The dis[illegible]tions, where they exist, were not always conscious; people often hear what t[illegible] expect to hear, what stereotype and predisposition have prepared them to h[illegible] Thus the variety and subtlety of Negro speech was frequently reduced to wha[illegible]e auditor thought Negroes spoke like. Even when the pronunciation of a giv[illegible] word was precisely the same as that of the collectors, their desire to indicate [illegible]e exotic qualities of black speech led them to utilize such misleading and supe[illegible]ous spellings as *wen* for "when," *fo'ks* or *fokes* for "folks," *w'ite* or *wite* for "[illegible]hite," *wuz* for "was," *bizness* for "business," *neer* for "near," *wurst* for "wors[illegible] *frum* for "from," *reel* for "real," *cullered* for "colored," *cundemn* for "con[illegible]nn," *fast'n* for "fasten," and so on and on.[20]

The practice of using a nonstandard s[illegible]lling even when the pronunciation is similar or identical to the "standar[illegible] is called *eye dialect*. The White writers that Levine describes approached [illegible]ir tasks having already decided consciously or subconsciously that Black speech was “exotic,” was Other, and their biases show up in the bizarre orthographies of their transcriptions.

Many more examples of these orthographies appear in *Slave Narratives: A Folk History of Slavery in the United States from Interviews with Former Slaves*, a collection of over 2,000 interviews with formerly enslaved Americans conducted by the Federal Writers’ Project as part of the Work Projects Administration from 1936 to 1938. “A Note on the Language of the Narratives” on the Library of Congress website, where the narratives are published in their entirety, provides an excerpt of project editor John Lomax’s instructions to transcribers: “[W]ords that definitely have a notably different pronunciation from the usual should be recorded as heard,”[21] “the usual” presumably referring to White or “standard” dialects of English. The Library of Congress’s “Note” points out that “by the 1930s, when the interviews took place, white representations of black speech already had an ugly history of entrenched stereotype dating back at least to the early nineteenth century. What most interviewers assumed to be ‘the usual’ patterns of their informants’ speech was unavoidably influenced by preconceptions and stereotypes.”[22] The administrative files of the narratives do include a brief list of “Negro Dialect Suggestions” for transcribers that admonishes against the kinds of exoticizations that Levine describes but simultaneously reveals the administrators’ preconceptions about the interviewees’ speech:

> Do not write:
>
> Ah for I
> Poe for po’ (poor)
> . . .
> Wuz for was
> Wha for whar (where)
> Moster for marster or massa
> Gwainter for gwineter (going to)
> . . .
> Ifn for iffen (if)
> . . .
> Uz or uv or o’ for of
> Poar for poor or po’
> . . .
> Tho’t for thought[23]

and so on. The writer of these instructions anticipated the interviewers’ temptation to use the kinds of eye dialect described by Levine—*wuz* for “was,” *uv* for “of,” *tho’t* for “thought,” etc.—but also presumes that the Black interviewees will use stereotypical pronun ations such as "whar," "massa," and "gwineter."

The narratives themselves also demonst te a highly stereotypical orthography in their transcriptions that is likely s Levine writes, a "mélange of accuracy and fantasy." For instance, inter ewer Mrs. Bernice Bowden, in her conversation with Israel Jackson, age 7 of Pine Bluff, Arkansas, records him as saying

> Miss, de white folks has done so bad here d I don't know what dey's gwine a do. . . . Miss, I don't 'cept none of 'em. I w ıldn't want to go on and tell you how dey has treated me. Dey ain't no use to k 'cause I ain't gwine to tell you. The people is more wicked and more wuss a l ever'thing. I don't think nothin' of 'em. . . . Miss, I would starve till I was a tiff as a peckerwood peckin' at a hole 'fore I'd sign anything on my deed.[24]

In addition to the stereotypical represe ıtions of Black speech in spellings such as "gwine" and "dey," Mrs. I wden uses exoticized spellings for pronunciations that would have been ıared by both Black and White Arkansans—"nothin'," "'cause," and "'em

In "Out of the Mouths of Slaves: The x-Slave Project and the 'Negro Question,'" a chapter in her 2016 book o the WPA slave narratives *Long Past Slavery: Representing Race in the F eral Writers' Project*, Catherine A. Stewart called the interviewers' orthogra ıy "a type of literary minstrelsy" and describes how White project administ tors and editors curated the narratives based on how well the interviewers ranscriptions of Black language fit the White public's preconceived notio s about Black people's speech, creating a vicious cycle in which those pr onceptions were then reinforced by the narratives' publication.[25] Stewart des ibes how the administrators' initial acknowledgment that Black English is ot a single homogenous dialect, but that it varies among speakers and fro region to region, devolved over a period of months into an insistence that e transcriptions be standardized into a "Negro dialect" already familiar to hite readers from popular literature such as that of Joel Chandler Harris creator of the Black storyteller character Uncle Remus.

The orthography of this "Negro dialec " Stewart writes, "was a visual defamiliarization of black speech, and a iterary means of racial 'othering.' . . . State directors quickly became a are that the authenticity of their slave narratives would be judged by these s ndards and that submissions that deviated from Lomax's guidelines would e found wanting by the federal office."[27] The literary representations of the lack interviewees' language that were finally published were not, therefore good faith attempts to represent Black English accurately, but were rather lited specifically for uniformity and to conform to White audiences' expectations and need to see Black speech as foreign, as something Other than English. These transcriptions, and the narratives themselves, the Library of Congress "Note" reminds us, are "the products of a particular time and particular places in the long and troubled mediation of African-American culture by other Americans."[28] This point is prescient for the research that follows in this book, which explores modern mainstream Hollywood depictions of speakers of stigmatized dialects which are, overwhelmingly, mediated by White creators[29] and as such, are often no more an accurate representation of reality than the language of the *Slave Narratives* transcribed by White people nearly a century ago.

Other scholars have critiqued the representation of Black English in works of fiction by White writers such as Twain, Faulkner, and the aforementioned Joel Chandler Harris. Jeffrey Hadler traces the development of what might be called a "standard nonstandard"—the WPA's "Negro dialect," what Hadler himself calls "Remus orthography" in his 1998 article of that name—showing that it was first popularized after the Civil War by White supremacists "as a response to African-American social and political participation and inclusion in the public record." Its use has since become "pervasive and largely unquestioned," even in scholarly work and the media.[30] (We find an illustrative example created by a fan of the 2019 *The Lion King* on IMDb, the Internet Movie Database, which functions partially as a wiki. The film's official page allows registered but anonymous users to add their own quotes from the movie, and one line, spoken by a bush baby and voiced by Chance Bennett—better known as Chance the Rapper—is rendered on the page as "What 'bout food? Have you thought 'bout feeding that thing?"[31], a use of Remus orthography. In reality, in the film the character quite clearly says, "What *about* food? Have you thought *about* feeding that thing?" Indeed, as Levine says, "[P]eople often hear what they expect to hear, what stereotype and predisposition have prepared them to hear.")

2018's *Sorry to Bother You*, written and directed by Boots Riley, is the rare film that addresses the discrepant treatment of stigmatized and "standard" dialects directly, as H. Samy Alim points out in his analysis of it, "Sorry to Bother You: Deepening the Political Project of Raciolinguistics." The protagonist of *Sorry to Bother You*, Cassius (LaKeith Stanfield), is a struggling Black telemarketer who suddenly realizes success and wealth beyond his dreams when he learns to use his "White voice" on his phone calls. The film's anticapitalist critique draws explicit connections between the identity elements of language, race, gender, and class, and shows that, as Alim puts it, "the Black user of the white voice wins limited material success but suffers severe cultural and linguistic deprecation" in the sacrifice of his native Black dialect.[32] Alim also discusses the film's deconstructionist approach to language, highlighting the point that language, like race, is constructed, usually at the direction of White people. im claims that “white folks can and often do *invent* the language practice of People of Color in ways that align with the stereotypes that they hold out them.”[33] In other words, we hear what we expect to hear based on the econceived ideas we hold about the speaker in question.

In a unique study on portrayals of accent and dialects in television, Marko Dragojevic, Dana Mastro, Howard Giles and Alexander Sink analyzed the speech of 1,252 characters on primet ie shows across nine networks. They categorized them as speakers of “S ndard American,” “Nonstandard American . . . including all regional and hnic accents native to the US,” “Foreign Anglo . . . including all nor American, Anglo accents” and “Foreign-Other . . . including all other nc Anglo, foreign accents.”[34] They found, unsurprisingly, that “Standard Am ican” speakers greatly outnumbered all other speakers on these shows d were more likely to be main characters, and that both “Standard Americ n” and “Foreign Anglo” speakers were depicted as significantly more intelli nt, attractive, and even slimmer than “Nonstandard American” speakers a speakers of non-Anglo foreign languages.[35] “[M]edia may be the first, a sometimes ONLY, exposure to a particular accent, for many viewers, pa cularly young children,”[36] they write, meaning that these negative portray s might have real-world impacts on viewers’ attitudes about these speakers.

The television series *The Wire*, which a ed on HBO from 2002 to 2008, provides another opportunity for the explc tion of authenticity in the representation of Black language by a White c ator, in this case, David Simon. Lopez and Bucholtz note that the series wa idely acclaimed for its supposed authenticity as decided by its predominantl upper-class White audience, yet it still manages to reinforce Black linguis stereotypes. “In particular,” the authors write, “in creating its characters t show wholeheartedly embraces the widespread language ideology of Afric American English as inherently cool, tough, and masculine (cf. Bucholtz 2 1b, Morgan 1999); in fact, every character who uses African American Eng sh is either male or represented as hard or masculinized in some way.”[37] is is yet another example of our conflation of the perceived characteristics f the speakers of a dialect with the perceived characteristics of the dialec tself—we believe that authentic Blackness is hypermasculine; therefore th use of Black English by exclusively masculine characters *is* authentic tc he White audience. We’ll return to this discussion in the following chapter.

Black English is not the only stigmatized ialect that has been reconstructed by EDC speakers to conform to their preco eived notions about it; Southern U.S. dialects spoken by rural and blue c ar White people have received similar treatment from writers which have, turn, been similarly critiqued by scholars. In “The Treatment of Dialect in A palachian Literature” by Michael

Ellis, part of the 2013 anthology *Talking Appalachian: Voice, Identity, and Community*, the author surveys the representation of Appalachian English over the last 175 years, from George Washington Harris's 1845 sketch "The Knob Dance—A Tennessee Frolic"—replete with eye dialect, such as *sum* for "some"—to modern literature produced by Appalachian writers using literary dialect to represent their native dialects, such as Lee Smith's 1988 novel *Fair and Tender Ladies*. Ellis, like the scholars mentioned above, acknowledges the stigma associated with Appalachian speech and provides examples of Appalachian writers' self-aware commentary on this stigma, as in Affrilachian poet Crystal Wilkinson's short story "Holler," in which the Black narrator speaks with a Black police officer: "Almost immediately I see the law man's face and shoulders get set a certain way as he listens to the way I talk with all the Mission Creek in me spilling out into the room. And it's then, when he acts like each word I speak is throwing shit on him, that I know it doesn't matter what else I say so I stop talking all together."[38] As Ellis points out, though the narrator and the officer are both Black, the narrator's rural dialect Others her in the mind of the officer.

Cynthia Goldin Bernstein, in her 2000 article "Misrepresenting the American South," discusses features stereotypically associated with Southern speech and their misuse in both fiction and scholarly work. Non-Southern writers, she claims, latch onto specific pronunciations, grammatical features, and word usages that are indeed used by Southern speakers, but then overrepresent them and use them inaccurately in their depictions of Southern speech; in other words, iconization. A familiar example is *yall*, the second person plural pronoun in most Southern dialects of English. In the exaggerated representations of Southern speech written by non-Southern writers, *yall* is often used to address a single person (the accuracy of which is still debated among linguists), and *all* is sometimes attached to other pronouns, as in *he all* or *we all*, a feature which does not actually occur in these dialects.[39]

Bernstein further points out the stigma associated with Southern dialects, noting that in fiction, including in film, "the absence of these dialect features gives a character a cultured air, [and] their presence has the opposite effect."[40] "When a positive image is desired, the Southern dialect features may be underrepresented. Bernstein and Torrey's (2000) study of [the film] *Steel Magnolias* shows that *yall* is underrepresented in that film: native Southerners would use *yall* far more often than the characters in the film do."[41] Here, as in the examples above, we see literary dialect represents not an accurate picture of a language but rather the attitude toward its speakers that exists in the minds of the writers.

Even linguists—who at least in theory aim to be as objective as possible in their study of human language—have been caught in inaccurate depictions of Southern speech: Bernstein claims that collecting data on regional dialects, "field-workers were specifically inst cted to prefer a sample of older, less-educated, more-rural, less-well-trave l informants. Although dialect geographers have generally differentiated long regional and social categories within the South, summaries of featu from atlas samples necessarily leave the impression that 'Southern dialect s less cultured than the speech of the general population."[42] Selective sampl g in linguistic data collection—as in any other science—will produce in curate results, though Bernstein acknowledges that other linguists (includ g herself) are conducting better research and producing results that work a inst these negative stereotypes.[43]

Roberta T. Herrin explored the depictic of Appalachian English in children's stories in her 1991 article "'Shal We Teach 'Em or Learn 'Em?' Attitudes Toward Language in Appalacl n Children's Literature." Like Bernstein, she concludes that writers are ot concerned with accuracy in their presentation of Appalachian literary lect, but rather latch onto a few specific features of the dialect which they en overuse, in this case, Herrin writes, "the common ones which purists d schoolmarms have sought to stamp out for decades with no success."[4 The stories do accurately depict societal attitudes toward both Appalachian nglish and "standard" English,[45] she says, treating Appalachian English as i proper and "bad grammar"[46] and EDC as inherently superior and correct. d though children's characters who aspire to speak "correctly" are mock at home for talking "proper,"[47] the stories take it as self-evident that mast of the standard is necessary for social and economic mobility,[48] a belief w ch abounds in American culture today. The stories reveal these attitudes w out deconstructing them; Herrin writes, "It is true that many of these book address the emotional effects of assimilation and isolation; that in itself is f great value to the child reader who has endured ridicule from within and om without his own culture. But what is absent from all these books is any u lerstanding of the language these children actually speak."[49] In this respect s we shall see in a later chapter, modern film depictions of Appalachi English and other stigmatized Southern dialects have actually taken a st backward—they concern themselves neither with accurate representation f the language *nor* with empathy toward its speakers.

The scholarly research on the represent on of Spanish-accented English and various Spanish-influenced dialects o English (SIE) including Chicano English in literature authored by nonnat e speakers of these dialects is shockingly bare, but what studies exist sh that the treatment of SAE, SIE, and their speakers in literature and media i trikingly similar to that of Black English and Southern U.S. English and ir speakers. As Joyce Penfield and Jacob Ornstein-Galicia point out in t ir 1985 book *Chicano English: An Ethnic Contact Dialect*, "The goal of e writer/actor appears to be to represent Chicano speech in the way it is viewed as typical according to the stereotypic notions about the character depicted. . . . [S]tereotypic depictions of Chicano speech by Anglos may have been totally resulting from a desired effect, probably to present the 'exotic,' or perhaps also to meet the expectations of an Anglo audience."[50] The accuracy of the language is less important than whether the depiction of the language conforms to the stereotypical expectations of primarily White audiences. This precisely mirrors Stewart's claims about the transcriptions of Black English that were eventually published in the WPA slave narratives.

Penfield and Ornstein-Galicia further note that "stereotypic representations of dialects in literature tend to select a few markers of a particular variety and use them consistently without real attention to the details of the variety in question."[51] This, too, echoes Bernstein's discussion of non-Southern writers' attempts to represent Southern speech through iconization. For example, non-Chicano writers often use *ee* in place of *i* or *y* to represent pronunciation in words such as "*kees* for 'kiss'; *Billee* for 'Billy'; *keed* for 'kid'; *heem* for 'him'; *thees* for 'this'; and *leetle* for 'little'"—according to Penfield and Ornstein-Galicia, this is the most common phonological transcription used to represent Chicano English, yet real Chicano English speakers, particularly new English learners, are more likely to substitute a short *i* /ɪ/ sound in place of a long *e* /i/, "the opposite of what is represented by Anglo authors."[52]

In her 2019 article "Lupe Vélez and Her Spicy Visual 'Accent' in English-Language Print Media," Sara Veronica Hinojos uses an intersectional methodology which combines feminist, race, and class theory to analyze media's written representation of the speech of popular Mexican film actor Lupe Vélez, star of the 1939–1943 Hollywood film series *Mexican Spitfire*. Hinojos' analysis provides further evidence that mainstream attitudes toward a stigmatized dialect are in fact proxy for mainstream attitudes toward that dialect's speakers. Hinojos writes, "The actor's voice represented visually in print demonstrates how Hollywood during the late 1920s to 1940s encased the bodies of Mexican women for mainstream production, consumption, and circulation as exotic, humorous, and easily mocked beings."[53] Later we'll discuss the ways in which SAE and SIE are still treated as inherently funny in the eyes of White audiences today.

Hinojos examined printed interviews with Vélez that appeared in *Motion Picture Magazine*, which mentioned the actor at least 468 times between 1928 and 1941.[54] Although there is little consistency in the orthographic representation of her dialect, Hinojos identified patterns that fit those discussed by Penfield and Ornstein-Galicia, such as the substitution of *ee* for a short *i* /ɪ/ sound as in "'Meestar,' 'hees,' 'eef,' 'beeg,' 'eet,' . . . and 'heem.'"[55] The interviews also use eye dialect, purposely misspelling words in which Vélez's pronunciation was actually similar to a "standard" English speaker's to further foreignize and exoticize her lang ge, as in *dam* for "damn."[56] And, as in Bernstein's identification of reduce Southern features where writers wish to portray Southern characters as pos ve or cultured, Vélez's speech is "standardized" when interviewers want he o be taken more seriously, as in this example from a 1933 interview: "Hol vood—and the rest of the world for that matter—is a funny place. If you d 't follow the accepted standards of living, no matter how stupid they may b you're declared eccentric, crazy, trying to 'put on.' It never occurs to an ie that you may choose to live your own life, and set your own standar of living."[57] As Hinojos points out, "Vélez can be taken seriously when comical visible 'accent' is not present. The tone of the direct quote chan when not mocked."[58] Again, in the eyes of White writers and White audie es, only EDC is appropriate for serious discourse. In the coming chapters, ve'll see that this belief appears again and again in dialect representation o screen.

Hinojos further argues that—as Stew t, Bernstein, and Penfield and Ornstein-Galicia also claim—accurate re esentation of the dialect is less important to White writers than that the lect *appears* authentic to White readers, thus its orthography is edited to readers' stereotypical expectations of SAE and its speakers. "Vélez's so id came to represent an 'authentic' Latina," she writes. "The representati of Lupe Vélez's visual 'accent' adds an important layer to audiences' un rstanding of the construction of Latinidad in mainstream media and popul culture. The visual 'accent' continues to flatten the differences among an between Latina/os,"[59] just as the meshing of the many regional varieties of ick English into a single homogenous "Negro dialect" in the WPA slave ratives flattened the differences among Black people throughout the Ame an South in service of a Black stereotype that already existed in the mind of White readers.

Studies of the depiction of gendered dial ts in literature and film are more sparse than even those of SAE and SIE, p iaps in part because the study of gendered dialects in general is somewhat n er to the field of sociolinguistics than the study of race-and class-based dial s. Much research has been done on the differences in language used to *de ibe* male and female characters in writing, but far less on the differences language used by the male and female characters themselves. Complicat matters further, some speech patterns typically associated with women, h as creaky voice (better known to lay audiences as "vocal fry"), are diffi lt to represent in text. Thus the quantity of literature on the subject is sma

One study from Alexandra Schofield and o Mehr, "Gender-Distinguishing Features in Film Dialogue," published in 2016 *Proceedings of the Fifth Workshop on Computational Linguistics Literature*, examines 617 film scripts for patterns of gendered difference n the speech of men and women and seeks to determine whether these patterns are reflective of gendered differences in real speech as described by scholars such as Deborah Tannen and Robin Lakoff. Schofield and Mehr look only at word usage frequency—not grammar or other speech patterns—but they find statistically significant patterns of differences between men's and women's scripted lines: men are more likely to curse, while women are more likely to say "please"; women use more "adverbial emphatics like 'so,' and 'really.'" These patterns, the authors say, "conform to classic hypothesis [*sic*] about gendered language in the real world."[60]

Similar recent research by Carmen Fought and Karen Eisenhauer examines the speech of Disney Princesses, first simply comparing the number of words spoken by male and female characters in the Disney Princess canon, then more closely analyzing male and female usage of specific discourse items such as directives and compliments. They found, interestingly, that in earlier films such as *Cinderella* (1950) and *Sleeping Beauty* (1959), women outpace men in total words spoken, whereas the reverse is true in more modern films, sometimes drastically so. In *Beauty and the Beast* (1991), for example, men speak 3,573 words to women's 1,481. Less surprising is Fought's and Eisenhauer's observation that female characters are much more likely to use indirectness and "mitigation strategies" in their speech: where men give commands, women make requests and pleas, softening them with hedges such as *just* and *a little* and politeness markers such as *please* and *thank you.*[61]

Richard W. Bailey's *Speaking American*, uniquely, describes Hollywood's treatment and popularization of a specific gendered dialect, Valley Girl. Coined by Frank Zappa in his 1982 song of that name, which featured Zappa's teenaged daughter Moon Unit speaking over the music, the term now refers to a dialect associated almost exclusively with young women and typically with Southern California. The 1983 film *Valley Girl*, Bailey writes, appealed to teenage girls and glamorized the dialect, "ma[king] it seem attractive to speak in the most up-to-date of these ways."[62] Finding a profitable market among high school aged girls, the television and film industries have continued to produce media targeted at them, including the 1995 film *Clueless* and the 1997 to 2003 TV show *Buffy the Vampire Slayer*, which not only use their audience's dialects unironically, but in the case of *Buffy*, Bailey says, add to and expand upon them. According to Bailey, "One of the writers, Jane Espenson, had studied metaphor in the graduate linguistics program at the University of California at Berkeley," and contributed new slang that the show then popularized, such as *angsty* and *hotness*.[63]

Today the depiction of gendered dialects and speech patterns in film depends largely on to whom the film is marketed; teenage girls, of course, are more likely to see their own dialects treated as legitimate, while adult and male audiences are encouraged to treat them with scorn. We will examine in depth the unique ways in which this scorn directed at the young women to whom these dialects are most frequently ributed in a later chapter. We'll also examine additional literature on stigm zed dialects and speech patterns that apply directly to specific segments of alysis in this book.

NOTES

1. Rosina Lippi-Green, *English with an Acce Language, Ideology, and Discrimination in the United States* (New York: Routle , 2012), 109.

2. Lippi-Green, *English with an Accent*, 122.

3. Stacy L. Smith, Marc Choueiti, and Kathe e Pierper, *Inclusion or Invisibility? Comprehensive Annenberg Report on Diversit Entertainment*. Institute for Diversity and Empowerment at Annenberg (IDEA) (C Annenberg School for Journalism and Communication, 2016), 7.

4. Nikolas Coupland, "The Mediated Perforn ce of Vernaculars," *Journal of English Linguistics* 37, no. 3 (2009): 297, https://d rg/10.1177/0075424209341188.

5. "Where Does Box Office Mojo by IMDbI Get Its Data?," IMDb, 2021, https://help.imdb.com/article/imdbpro/industry-rese h/box-office-mojo-by-imdbpro-faq/GCWTV4MQKGWRAUAP?ref_=mojo_cso_ #data.

6. "How Are Grosses Adjusted For Ticket Pr Inflation?," IMDbPro, 2021, https://help.imdb.com/article/imdbpro/industry-rese h/box-office-mojo-by-imdbpro-faq/GCWTV4MQKGWRAUAP?ref_=mojo_cso_ #inflation.

7. The rest of this book contains major spoi s for many of the films on this list. Readers have been warned.

8. A glossary of the linguistics terms used this book can be found at www.lindseyclouse.com.

9. *American Heritage Dictionary*, online ed 021, s.v. "get," https://ahdictionary.com/word/search.html?q=get.

10. Ammon Shea, interview by Robert Sieg *All Things Considered*, NPR, June 3, 2014, https://www.npr.org/transcripts/31857 07.

11. "Letters: Reactions To 'Bad English,'" *Things Considered*, NPR, June 4, 2014, https://www.npr.org/2014/06/04/318888 /letters-reactions-to-bad-english.

12. C. Mason Weaver, "Funding Ebonics Is a New Idea, It's Just a Bad One," The National Center for Public Policy Researc April 1, 1997, https://nationalcenter.org/project21/1997/04/01/funding-ebonics-isn -new-idea-its-just-a-bad-one/.

13. David Crystal, *The Fight for English* (O rd: Oxford University Press, 2006), 7.

14. Hubert Monteilhet, *Neropolis: Roman de Temps Néroniens* (Paris: Éditions du Juillard, 1984).

15. Crystal, *The Fight for English*, 43–44.

16. Michael Ellis, "The Treatment of Dialec n Appalachian Literature," in *Talking Appalachian: Voice, Identity, and Commun* , eds. Amy D. Clark and Nancy M. Hayward (Lexington: University of Kentucky ss, 2013), 165.

17. Qiuana Lopez and Mary Bucholtz, "'How my hair look?' Linguistic Authenticity and Racialized Gender and Sexuality on *The Wire*," *Journal of Language and Sexuality* 6, no. 1 (2017): 4, https://doi.org/10.1075/jls.6.1.01lop.

18. The characters contained between the forward slashes come from the International Phonetic Alphabet, an alphabet used by linguists worldwide to create a one-to-one correspondence between language sounds and their symbols.

19. Richard W. Bailey, *Speaking American: A History of English in the United States* (New York: Oxford University Press, 2012), 91–92.

20. Lawrence W. Levine, *Black Culture and Black Consciousness: Afro-American Folk Thought from Slavery to Freedom* (New York: Oxford University Press, 1977), loc. 110. Kindle.

21. John Lomax, quoted in "A Note on the Language of the Narratives," Library of Congress, accessed October 5, 2020, https://loc.gov/collections/slave-narratives-from-the-federal-writers-project-1936-to-1938/articles-and-essays/note-on-the-language-of-the-narratives/.

22. Lomax, quoted in "A Note on the Language."

23. United States Federal Writers' Project, Work Projects Administration, *Slave Narratives: A Folk History of Slavery in the United States from Interviews with Former Slaves* (Washington, DC: Library of Congress, 1941), xvii-xviii, https://hdl.loc.gov/loc.mss/mesn.001.

24. United States, Federal Writers' Project, Work Projects Administration, "Volume II Arkansas Narratives Part 4." *Slave Narratives: A Folk History of Slavery in the United States from Interviews with Former Slaves* (Washington, DC: Library of Congress, 1941), 6–7. https://hdl.loc.gov/loc.mss/mesn.024.

25. Catherine A. Stewart, *Long Past Slavery: Representing Race in the Federal Writers' Project* (Chapel Hill: University of North Carolina Press, 2016), 65.

26. Stewart, *Long Past Slavery*, 80.

27. Stewart, *Long Past Slavery*, 85.

28. "A Note on the Language of the Narratives," Library of Congress, accessed October 5, 2020, https://loc.gov/collections/slave-narratives-from-the-federal-writers-project-1936-to-1938/articles-and-essays/note-on-the-language-of-the-narratives/.

29. Smith, Choueiti, and Pierper, *Inclusion or Invisibility?*, 10.

30. Jeffrey Hadler, "Remus Orthography: The History of the Representation of the African-American Voice," *Journal of Folklore Research* 35, no. 2 (1998): 118.

31. "The Lion King (2019) Quotes," IMDb, 2020, https://imdb.com/title/tt6105098/quotes/?tab=qt&ref_=tt_trv_qu.

32. H. Samy Alim, "Sorry to Bother You: Deepening the Political Project of Raciolinguistics," in *Raciolinguistics: How Language Shapes Our Ideas About Race*, ed. H. Samy Alim, John R. Rickford, and Arnetha F. Ball (New York: Oxford University Press, 2020), 353.

33. Alim, "Sorry to Bother You," 357.

34. Marko Dragojevic et al., "Silencing Nonstandard Speakers: A Content Analysis of Accent Portrayals on American Primetime Television," *Language in Society* 45, no. 1 (2016): 74. https://doi.org/10.1017/S0047404515000743.

35. Dragojevic et al., "Silencing Nonstandard Speakers," 74–76.

36. Dragojevic et al., "Silencing Nonstandar peakers," 77.

37. Lopez and Bucholtz, "'How my hair loo ," 6.

38. Crystal Wilkinson, "Holler," *Slice Magaz* , no. 6 (2010), quoted in Ellis, "The Treatment of Dialect," 177.

39. Cynthia Goldin Bernstein, "Misreprese ng the American South," *American Speech* 75, no. 4 (2000): 339.

40. Bernstein, "Misrepresenting the Americ South," 340.

41. Bernstein, "Misrepresenting the Americ South," 342.

42. Bernstein, "Misrepresenting the Americ South," 341.

43. Bernstein, "Misrepresenting the Americ South," 341.

44. Roberta T. Herrin, "'Shall We Teach ' or Learn 'Em?' Attitudes Toward Language in Appalachian Children's Literature *Journal of the Appalachian Studies Association* 3 (1991): 192, https://jstor.org/stab 41445612.

45. Herrin, "'Shall We Teach 'Em or Learn n?'," 192.

46. Herrin, "'Shall We Teach 'Em or Learn n?'," 196.

47. Herrin, "'Shall We Teach 'Em or Learn n?'," 193.

48. Herrin, "'Shall We Teach 'Em or Learn n?'," 195.

49. Herrin, "'Shall We Teach 'Em or Learn n?'," 197.

50. Joyce Penfield and Jacob Ornstein-Gali , *Chicano English: An Ethnic Contact Dialect* (Amsterdam: John Benjamins Pub hing, 1985), 74–5.

51. Penfield and Ornstein-Galicia, *Chicano glish*, 75.

52. Penfield and Ornstein-Galicia, *Chicano glish*, 82.

53. Sara Veronica Hinojos, "Lupe Vélez ar Her Spicy Visual 'Accent' in English-Language Print Media," *Latino Studies* 17, . 3 (2019): 340, https://doi:10.1057/s41276-019-00194-y.

54. Hinojos, "Lupe Vélez," 343.

55. Hinojos, "Lupe Vélez," 354.

56. Hinojos, "Lupe Vélez," 353.

57. Lupe Vélez (1933), quoted in Hinojos, " pe Vélez," 357.

58. Hinojos, "Lupe Vélez," 357.

59. Hinojos, "Lupe Vélez," 358–9.

60. Alexandra Schofield and Leo Mehr, "G ler-Distinguishing Features in Film Dialogue," *Proceedings of the Fifth Worksh on Computational Linguistics for Literature*, San Diego, June 2016. (Stroudsber Association for Computational Linguistics, 2020), 5, https://doi:10.18653/v1/W1 2.

61. Karen Eisenhauer, "Field Report: The P cess Problem," interview by Carrie Neill, Dscout, accessed March 26, 2022, https: cout.com/people-nerds/field-report-the-princess-problem.

62. Bailey, *Speaking American*, 173.

63. Bailey, *Speaking American*, 174.

Chapter 2

"She Pretty—and She Talk Good Too"

Black English and Its Speakers

The 2000 film *Me, Myself, and Irene* stars Jim Carrey as mild-mannered Rhode Island state trooper Charlie, who at the beginning of the film marries a beautiful young woman who is president of the Providence chapter of Mensa. She immediately begins a years-long affair with the Boston Mensa chapter head (Tony Cox), a Black man who is also a tenured professor of molecular genetics at Brown University. Over the course of this affair, she gives birth to three obviously Black sons, Lee Harvey, Jamaal, and Shonté Jr. (Mongo Brownlee, Anthony Anderson, and Jerod Mixon, respectively), all of whom Charlie claims as his own. Eventually she abandons the family to run off with her lover, leaving Charlie to raise the boys alone. The kids grow up watching Black comedians such as Richard Pryor and Chris Rock every night on television, and as adults, they become super geniuses who speak profanity-laden Black English, as in the following scene in which Shonté Jr. struggles with his quantum physics homework:

> SHONTÉ JR.: Damn, I can't figure out the atomic mass of this motherfuckin' deuteron.
>
> JAMAAL: Shit! Man, that shit's simple! Look it. Tell me. Tell me. What's a deuteron made up of?
>
> SHONTÉ JR.: It's a proton and a neutron.
>
> JAMAAL: Then what's this motherfuckin' electron doin' right there!
>
> SHONTÉ JR.: I don't know.
>
> JAMAAL: Well get it outta there then!

SHONTÉ JR.: Okay, so you sayin' I add up t atomic masses of the proton and the neutron right?

JAMAAL: Mhm.

SHONTÉ JR.: I sees that, but what do I do ith the goddamn electron? Can I bring it over here?

JAMAAL: Enrico Fermi'd roll over in his n therfuckin' grave if he heard that stupid shit. I mean he'd just turn over ass u n your face. He wouldn't give a fuck.

LEE HARVEY: Man, Jamaal, man, just cut y man some slack, dog.

JAMAAL: Look here, I'm just trying to help im save face, alright? I mean you know he keep asking questions like that, mo rfuckers gonna think he's stupid.

SHONTÉ JR.: I ain't stupid.

CHARLIE: Mornin' fellas.

LEE HARVEY: Oh, hey, Dad.

JAMAAL: Hey, Pops, how you doin', man?

CHARLIE: What's all the commotion down ere?

JAMAAL: Ah, you know, just school shit a shit.

CHARLIE: How's my little guy doin'?

JAMAAL: Strugglin'!

SHONTÉ JR.: This quantum physics is con sin'! If I don't buckle down, I'm gonna get myself another B+!

CHARLIE: Ooh! That'd be whack!

LEE HARVEY: He so fuckin' dumb, he thir calculus is a goddamn emperor!

SHONTÉ JR.: Yeah, well you think polypep le's a motherfuckin' toothpaste!

CHARLIE: I'm gettin' outta here! I don't w t to have to bust a cap!

Throughout the film, the three contin to discuss complex scientific, political, and sociological topics, always sing strong Black English pronunciation and grammar and constant pro nity. At first glance, this might come across as a positive representation f Black English speakers; they are, after all, having intelligent conversati s using Black English. But this is, in fact, the joke: for the presumed W ite audience, *it's funny to hear Black English speakers having intelligen onversations in Black English.* Extensive research shows that Americans—especially but not exclusively White Americans—consider Black Englis o be improper, "bad" grammar, and the provenance only of the uneducated and the ignorant. The contrast between Jamaal, Lee Harvey, and Shonté Jr.'s language (not only their Black English pronunciation and grammar but also their nonstop profanity) and their topics of conversation *is* the source of humor, and the audience must be privy to the prevailing beliefs about Black English to get the joke. As we shall see, the data from our film set show that American audiences and filmmakers consider Black English to be many things—ignorant, criminal, threatening—but above all else, to be funny.

WHAT IS BLACK ENGLISH?

Black English is a collection of dialects which are spoken primarily (though not exclusively) by Black Americans all over the United States and which—like all dialects—vary from region to region and among different age groups, genders, and social classes, encompassing a range of phonological, grammatical, and lexical features. Since Geneva Smitherman's pivotal 1977 text *Talkin and Testifyin: The Language of Black America*, it has been one of the most widely studied American dialect groups. It is also commonly referred to as African American Vernacular English (AAVE), Black Vernacular English (BVE), and African American Language (AAL), and it's worth taking a moment to discuss my choice to use the term *Black English* in this book.

First, polls show that today, Black Americans have a slight preference for the term *Black* over the term *African American*,[1] and with the rise of movements such as Black Lives Matter that embrace the former, one can make the case that *Black* is the more modern, progressive, and inclusive term. Some would argue that when discussing this dialect group, *African American* is the more accurate descriptor because the language arose among enslaved people indigenous to Africa, but today one need not identify as Black or be of African descent to use Black English (indeed, four of the Black English-speaking humans in our film set are not Black).

Regarding the term *vernacular*, the first definition provided for this word by *The American Heritage Dictionary* online is "The everyday language spoken by a people as distinguished from the literary language."[2] Part of the purpose of this book is to argue that stigmatized dialect groups such as Black English, Southern U.S. English, etc. *should not be* "distinguished from the literary language," and that to treat some dialects as "literary" and others as not literary is to reinforce the linguistic segregation that is already in practice in our schools, courtrooms, and board rooms, which we will discuss in more detail later.

Finally, some argue for the use of *African American Language* or *Black Language* as the most modern and appropriate term, one that best acknowledges the dialect's validity as a la guage.[3] But while Black English is, indeed, a language, for the purposes our analysis and this book, it is foremost *a variety of English*. It is mu ally intelligible with other dia-lects of English and it is widely used in merican cinema targeted to an English-speaking audience. Therefore goi forward I'll exclusively use the term *Black English*.

As noted above, this term encompasses vide range of dialects and speak-ers who use a range of features; thus "Blac English-speaking character" is a difficult category to define. This is further mplicated by the fact that actors are often called upon to perform a dialect hich they do not speak natively and may or may not be able to produc accurately. Additionally, Black English-speaking characters often use Bla English inconsistently through-out a film. Sometimes this is due to intent nal code-switching (adjusting or switching one's dialect depending on the ntext in which one is speaking), and sometimes the reasons for the incons ency are unclear. Consequently in this analysis we must ask questions like 'If a Black character uses only a single instance of 'nonstandard' grammar, Black English vocabulary, and moderate Black English pronunciation, s uld they be classed as a Black English speaker?" In service of answering estions like these, let's examine both the phonological and grammatical fea res of Black English dialects.

Black English includes a broad range of ialects, and within those dialects are a broad range of phonologies. Some B k English dialects, for instance, are Southern-shifted (this term will be di ssed in more detail in the next chapter), while others are not; some are rh —meaning speakers pronounce the *r* sound in words like *hard* and *mother* while others are nonrhotic.

However, Smitherman and others have d ined a few features that are char-acteristic of many Black English dialects a will be recognized by American listeners as such. (A number of studies hav shown that listeners can identify the race or ethnicity of a stigmatized sp ker by sound alone, sometimes from an utterance as brief as one second i length.[4]) These include initial *th* /ð/[5] rendered as *d* /d/ (e.g., pronouncing *t* *e* as *dere* /dɛr/), *going* rendered as *gone* /gɔn/ or /gɔŋ/, and elision of wo -final consonants (for instance, *jus* /dʒʌs/ for *just* or *shif* /ʃɪf/ for *shift*) in umber of contexts. For the pur-poses of simplification, going forward I'll fer to this specific combination of features as "Black English pronunciati " and any speaker that uses this combination with or without other Black nglish features as "using Black English pronunciation." "Black English gr mmar" will be defined as any of the grammar features that appear in Table below; these are the most com-mon—though not the only—stigmatized f tures used by Black speakers in our data. (Note that *ain't* is not included in e list because, while it is not as common among EDC speakers as present nse *got*, it is widespread among American English speakers of many dial ts and racial backgrounds, and

Table 2.1. Stigmatized Grammar Features Used by Black English Speakers

Feature	*Number of Users*	*Sample User*	*Film*	*Usage*
zero copula	274	Moto Moto (will.i.am)	*Madagascar: Escape 2 Africa* (2008)	"You huge . . . You as quick as you are hefty . . . It won't be hard because you so plumpy."
negative concord	156	Detective Latoya (Erika Alexander)	*Get Out* (2017)	"Don't ever say I don't do nothin' for you."
uninflected third person singular verb	73	Patty (Leslie Jones)	*Ghostbusters* (2016)	"He think this is his studio. . . . Patty come with benefits."
zero auxiliary *do*	65	Mirror Man (T.J. Cross)	*Gone in 60 Seconds* (2000)	"How you know that?"
third person singular *don't*	63	Donkey (Eddie Murphy)	*Shrek 2* (2004)	"This don't feel right."
singular *you is* or *you was*	53	Ripcord (Marlon Wayans)	*G.I. Joe: The Rise of Cobra* (2009)	"I thought you said you was the best at this."
article *a* followed by a vowel	51	Max (Jamie Foxx)	*Collateral* (2004)	"It'll be like a island on wheels."
plural *is* or *was*	47	Dr. John Dolittle (Eddie Murphy)	*Dr. Dolittle 2* (2001)	"You never even wondered what your sharp claws was for, have you?"
adjectival *them*	47	Julius Campbell (Wood Harris)	*Remember the Titans* (2000)	"Did I tell you all them White boys weren't gonna play for no brother?"
zero auxiliary *has, have,* or *had*	42	Agent J (Will Smith)	*Men in Black 3* (2012)	"We been doin' smart stuff, we been followin' clues, doin' real police work."
suffixed *-ass*	40	Dean 'MF' Jones (Jamie Foxx)	*Horrible Bosses* (2011)	"I can't walk around in this neighborhood with that Disney-ass name."
uninflected possessive noun or pronoun	38	Minny Jackson (Octavia Spencer)	*The Help* (2011)	"Don't hit on they children. White folks like to do they own spankin.'"

Feature	Number of Users	Sample User	Film	Usage
zero *of* following prepositional *out*	29	Buddy Love (Eddie Murphy)	*Nu … Professor … The … mps* (… 00)	"I'm gonna get that knot out your back."
habitual *be*	26	Jay (Romany Malco)	*Th … 0-Year- … d Virgin* (… 05)	"She just thought that I wouldn't be a good father in light of the fact that I be cheatin' on her all the time."
emphatic *done*	26	Brenda Meeks (Regina Hall)	*Sc … Movie 3* (… 03)	"Another little White girl done fell down a well."
auxiliary *ain't* plus infinitive	21	Charlene Morton (Queen Latifah)	*Br … ing Down … House* (… 03)	"I ain't do the crime."

Source: Lindsey Clouse

Black characters do not use it significantly … ore than other demographics.) A "Black English speaker" will be defined a… ny speaker who uses unambiguous Black English pronunciation at any po… in their film or uses some combination of the stigmatized grammar feat… s listed in the table along with either Black English pronunciation or "sta… ard" pronunciation. This distinction is made to differentiate Black English … eakers from other marginalized speakers; there's a great deal of overlap … tween Black English grammar features and "nonstandard" grammar feat… s in many White Southern U.S. English dialects, and many Black English … eakers also use Southern-shifted vowels, but White Southern speakers typi… lly don't use the Black English pronunciation features discussed above.

BLACK ENGLISH SPEAKE… IN THE FILM SET

Using the definition described above, … ve can identify at least 468 Black English-speaking characters in our … taset, including 57 protagonists in 43 films, 270 secondary characters, an… 41 minor and background characters.[6] These characters appear in 187 fil… , or 37.9% of total films; 107 of these films include only a single Black En… ish speaker. Sixty-three of these characters use only Black English pronunc… ion, while the remaining 405 use one or more stigmatized grammatical feat… s—this differs from speakers of Southern U.S. English and Spanish-accen… English, the majority of whom use the grammar of the dominant culture. … f the 468 total characters, 56 are nonhumans and four are humans who are, as best I can determine, not Black. The grammar features that occur most frequently appear in Table 2.1. Some of these features, such as habitual *be*, are unique to Black English, while others are common in other marginalized dialects both in the film data and in reality. In addition to the grammar features listed in the table, the pronunciation of the verb *ask* as *aks* /æks/—possibly the most stigmatized feature of Black English pronunciation[7]—is used by 12 characters.

IS BLACK ENGLISH INHERENTLY FUNNY?

As noted in the introduction to this chapter, the most common quality shared among these characters is humor: 167 Black English-speaking characters—35.7% of the total—are comedic, meaning that their primary role, like Lee Harvey, Jamaal, and Shonté Jr., is to provide levity, to make jokes, or to be the object of derision. This includes 30 of the 57 protagonists, or 52.6%. Filmmakers clearly believe that White Americans (the presumed default audience for most mainstream films) find Black English and its speakers inherently funny. This assumption is often further emphasized by exaggerated, over-the-top performances by Black English-speaking characters who swear or yell far more than their non-Black English-speaking counterparts—a furtherance of the racist trope that Black people are especially loud[8] and a characterization that aligns with the stereotype of the Angry Black Man or Woman.

The character of Snowball (Kevin Hart) in *The Secret Life of Pets* (2016) and *The Secret Life of Pets 2* (2019) is an instructive example. Snowball is a small, fluffy white rabbit intent on building an army of discarded pets to kill humans and overthrow their society; he even attempts to kill pets that he discovers are not antihuman. He is one of the smallest, most physically vulnerable animals in the two films, yet he is consistently also the loudest and most boisterous. The contrast between this tiny, cute *white* creature and Kevin Hart's exaggerated performance and obviously Black speech (he uses strong Black pronunciation and fairly consistent Black grammar including zero copula, negative concord, and uninflected third person singular verbs) is part of the joke inherent to the character. If Snowball had been voiced by an actor who used EDC, the contrast between his behavior and his appearance might still be comedic, but the casting of an actor who speaks Black English adds another layer of comedy to Snowball's characterization. Snowball is not only violent and filled with rage; he is, in effect, an Angry Black Man in the body of a tiny white bunny.

Black voices are also frequently a source of humor in films that are otherwise not strictly comedies, and the humor often lies less in the character's lines than in the fact that they are speaking those lines in Black English. In other words, the same lines spoken in ED would not be read as funny; it is the use of Black English itself that is the jo . For example, the *Transformers* franchise never shies away from using ra -based humor and racial stereotypes for comedy, as in the characters of idflap (voiced by Reno Wilson) and Skids (voiced by Tom Kenny, a White tor) in *Transformers: Revenge of the Fallen* (2009). Mudflap and Skids are utobots—giant alien robot good guys—but unlike most of the other Auto its who are serious and heroic, Mudflap and Skids are bumbling, foolish and illiterate, bicker constantly, and, like other comedic characters discus d later in this chapter, seem to equate talking a lot with being funny. Sk has a gold tooth. In the scene that comprises most of their dialogue, the argue with human character Leo (Ramon Rodriguez) about how best to av the authorities that are chasing them, using their high-pitched voices and s ng Black English pronunciation:

> SKIDS: Yo, Leo!
>
> LEO: This thing's gonna give me a heart att k, I swear.
>
> MUDFLAP: That's 'cause you is a wuss.
>
> LEO: You guys forced me into that car, righ So . . .
>
> MUDFLAP: Ooh, I think he's scared.
>
> SKIDS: Hey, Mudflap, what are we gonna with this shrimp taco?
>
> MUDFLAP: Let me just pop a cap in his a throw him in the trunk and then nobody gonna know nothing, know what I n an?
>
> SKIDS: Not in my trunk.
>
> LEO: Yo, bumper cars? I'm hearing you, o y? I'm right here and I can hear you! No one's popping any caps in any asse okay? I've had a hell of a day!
>
> MUDFLAP: Boo hoo hoo hoo hoo.
>
> SKIDS: Why don't you get a haircut with y bitch ass?
>
> MUDFLAP: Go whine to your boyfriend!

Transformers (2007) features a similar ch acter in Jazz (Darius McCrary), also an Autobot, who appears only briefly nd who uses Black English pronunciation and dated, cliché Black slang his few lines; when introduced to the main human characters, he greets em with, "What's crackin' little bitches? This looks like a cool place to kic t." The image of superadvanced, building-size alien robots using stereotypi l Black English *is* the joke, and Jazz receives no characterization beyond t . And in this film he is the only Transformer who uses anything other than C or "standard" British English and, notably, he is also the only Autobc who dies. The message in this franchise is that Black English speakers are not characters but caricatures, on screen for a few brief minutes to entertain White audiences, then disposed of.

Code-Switching for Comedy

Because Black English itself is presumed to be funny, Black actors in numerous films code-switch between EDC and Black English for comedic effect. Will Smith, a master code-switcher, appears in several films in which he uses both Black English and EDC, choosing the former when he wants to be funny. The 2018 live-action remake of *Aladdin*, like the original 1992 film, includes a comedic character in the Genie, this time played by Smith. The Genie code-switches throughout the film, using the grammar of the dominant culture for serious moments and more prominent Black pronunciation and Black grammar—including zero copula, negative concord, and singular *you was*—for jokes. As relationship expert Hitch in the 2005 film of the same name, Smith uses primarily EDC, but, again, switches to Black English pronunciation and grammar for an occasional joke or snarky comment. And as Agent J in the *Men in Black* franchise, Smith uses Black English to make jokes and to rant at ignorant or noncompliant New Yorkers who interfere with his work monitoring alien visitors to Earth. For instance, after a giant alien worm attacks a subway train, J berates the jaded passengers who ignored his instructions to move to a different car as he attempted to stop the attack: "Had this been an actual emergency y'all woulda been eaten . . . How a man gonna come bashin' through the back of a subway when—That's the problem with all y'all New Yorkers . . . now I come in, I as' [ask] you nice, move to the next car, y'all just sit there like—." The rant is a moment of levity that relieves the tension after an action sequence, and, as usual, Smith switches to Black English for the humor.

Smith, of course, is not the only Black actor who follows this pattern. In *G.I. Joe: The Rise of Cobra* (2009), co-protagonist Ripcord (Marlon Wayans) functions as the comic relief, using EDC for most of his lines but switching to Black English pronunciation and very occasional Black English grammar when he behaves particularly buffoonishly, while the *Fast and Furious* franchise uses Black English to distinguish between the Black characters who make occasional jokes and those who consistently provide comic relief. In fact, two characters in this expansive and popular franchise deserve closer scrutiny.

Chris "Ludacris" Bridges' character Tej appears in four films in the franchise, over the course of which his characterization changes significantly and, notably, as the character becomes smarter, more skilled, and more serious, his Black English disappears and is replaced by EDC. The character makes his first appearance in 2003's *2 Fast 2 Furious* in which he is merely the emcee of a series of illegal street races. In this lm he uses a number of Black English grammar features including zero opula, uninflected third person singular verbs, zero auxiliary *do*, third per n singular *don't*, adjectival *them*, and uninflected possessives. In *Fast Five* (11), Tej has been retconned into a demolitions expert and a safe cracker, d while he still employs Black English pronunciation, the only Black En sh grammatical feature he uses in this film is zero copula, and a consider y higher percentage of his lines use the grammar of the dominant culture. his pattern continues in *Fast & Furious 6* (2013), in which he uses zero c ula, uninflected possessives, and suffixed *-ass*, but still, the significant ma ity of his lines use EDC grammar. By *Furious 7* (2015) Tej has also be me a hacker and his language is almost totally "standard," using only occ onal Black pronunciation and a single instance each of zero copula and a ectival *them*. The implication is that because Black English is not only "ba grammar" but is also inherently funny, smart, serious Black characters don use it.

Tyrese Gibson also makes his first ap arance in *2 Fast 2 Furious* as Roman, a street racer and childhood frie l of co-protagonist Brian (Paul Walker). (Brian is one of only a few non lack characters who uses Black English earnestly, as opposed to mockingl employing zero copula and zero auxiliary *do* occasionally in his conversat s with Roman.) Roman himself uses Black English pronunciation and man Black English grammar features, including zero copula, negative concord, ninflected third person singular verbs, uninflected possessives, auxiliary *a t* followed by an infinitive, zero auxiliary *do*, third person singular *don't*, si ple past tense *seen*, singular *you is*, plural *is* and *was*, adjectival *them*, and iffixed-*ass*. Roman has recently been released from prison and reluctantly ins Brian to take down a major drug dealer via street racing; his character alternately serious and comedic. He also returns in *Fast Five*, and like Tej, s character has undergone some revision. He's now described by another c racter as "a fast talker, someone who can bullshit their way out of anything, nd is not only a fast talker in the idiomatic sense; he literally talks fast and, some scenes, almost constantly, cracking jokes, flirting with female cha ters, and taunting antagonists. However, unlike Tej, Roman continues t use Black English consistently, employing almost exactly the same comb ation of grammatical features in *Fast Five* that he uses in *2 Fast 2 Furious* He also continues serving as the comic relief and using a number of Black nglish grammar features in *Fast & Furious 6*, and *Furious 7*, and *The F of the Furious* (2017). In this franchise as in other popular, big-budget ns, Black English is for humorous characters and funny moments while DC is for smart characters and serious moments.

The Stereotype of Loud Black People

Like Roman, other Black English-speaking characters in other films seem to rely on the notion that simply using Black English and talking a lot is a recipe for comedy gold: if a few lines of Black English are a little bit funny, then a character who speaks Black English and talks nonstop must be *really* funny. These characterizations, too, are a means of furthering the stereotype of Black people as especially loud, as taking up more than their share of the air in the room. The character of Donkey (Eddie Murphy), who appears in four films in the *Shrek* franchise (2001, 2004, 2007, 2010) fits this pattern. Donkey is loud and talkative to the point of absurdity, rambling nonstop about a range of trivial nonsense despite his companions' frequent pleas for him to stop talking. He uses numerous stigmatized grammar features throughout the four films, including the most iconic Black English features of zero copula and habitual *be*. In fact, Donkey's incessant talking, his silly and stereotypically high-pitched voice, and his usage of Black English serve as the primary sources of the character's humor far more than anything the character actually *says*; again, Black voices and the English they speak are, to White audiences, inherently funny.

In addition to Eddie Murphy's Donkey, other comedic performances by Black English speakers in the film set seem to rely on the character simply speaking as much as possible for humor. These include most of the Klump family (all played by Eddie Murphy) in *Nutty Professor II: The Klumps* (2000), who ramble, talk to themselves, and talk over each other almost nonstop throughout the film. The one Klump in the film who defies this pattern, protagonist Sherman (also played by Eddie Murphy), is a chemistry professor and is clearly depicted as more intelligent than the rest of his family and, significantly, he does not use Black English grammar until a failed experiment causes him to gradually lose his intelligence, another instance of a film using Black English to distinguish between smart and dumb characters. We'll discuss Sherman and his role as a Black professional in more detail in a later section. *Shark Tale* (2004) features Oscar (Will Smith), a small fish who talks fast and constantly uses numerous Black English grammar features, and Carter (Chris Tucker) of *Rush Hour 2* (2001) and *Rush Hour 3* (2007) also talks almost nonstop while on screen, in addition to speaking loudly and behaving buffoonishly. These characterizations all rely on the trope that Black English itself is funny, therefore the people who speak it are funny, and the more they speak, the funnier they are.

In *Big Momma's House* (2000), Martin Lawrence manages to capture two tropes at once when his character, Malcolm Turner, goes undercover posing as a large, elderly Black woman in hopes of catching an escaped felon with ties to her family. While in costume as Hattie Mae Pierce—or Big Momma, as many people call her—Malcolm, like m ıy other Black comic characters, talks almost nonstop and literally embod s the stereotypical Sassy Black Woman caricature, berating the men arour her and even physically assaulting a self-defense instructor. When the real attie's boyfriend, Ben, arrives at the house to woo her, Malcolm scolds him nd sends him away:

> MALCOLM: Who the hell do you think yo re? Comin' up here, tryin' to put your nasty-ass lips on me. I am not street b y. I will not be treated like street poontang! Ben, if you wanna get with me— ıean, you will never get with me! Understand? And even if I was interested, ıich I definitely am not, you be goin' about it the wrong way.
>
> BEN: How am I supposed to go about it?
>
> MALCOLM: You don't come up in a w an's house and lead with your shaboink-boink! Women don't respond to th
>
> BEN: I should've bought you somethin'. Li a corsage.
>
> MALCOLM: This ain't no damn prom.

The comedy in this scene relies not o on the absurdity of the situation—Ben somehow believes that Martin ıwrence in a fat suit and wig is his girlfriend Hattie—but also on Lawren s use of Black English and fast, high-pitched, almost cartoonish delivery. otably, again, the more serious characters in the film—Hattie's niece She y (Nia Long), Sherry's criminal boyfriend Lester (Terrance Howard), and e family's preacher—use Black English grammar little or not at all becaus as it bears repeating, EDC is for serious characters in serious situations, wh Black English is for comedy.

The Scarcity of Serious Black English peaking Protagonists

Because White audiences believe Black E lish to be inherently funny, it is very rarely used by serious characters in rious situations, especially protagonists. As noted above, 57 Black Eng h-speaking protagonists appear in 43 films, meaning 8.7% of the 493 f ıs in our film set have at least one Black-English–protagonist. In my 2 9 paper "Django Unbleached: Language, Power, and Authenticity in M ıinstream Film," I argued that Django (Jamie Foxx) of 2012's *Django nchained* was the only serious Black English-speaking hero in mainstrean ıction films.[9] Having now examined 492 other high-budget, high-grossing ıainstream films, I can confirm that this was not an overstatement. Thou ı a pair of other serious action films feature Black protagonists who ver occasionally use Black English features to be funny or sassy—Deke Kaye L Cool J) and Sgt. Dan "Hondo" Harrelson (Samuel L. Jackson) in 2003's *.W.A.T.* and Del Spooner (Will

Smith) in 2004's *I, Robot*—Django remains the only action hero who uses Black English grammar and pronunciation consistently throughout his film, both in funny moments and in serious ones.

Other serious protagonists who use Black English with a high degree of consistency include a crime boss, three domestic servants, four musicians (albeit successful ones), and a football coach, plus Django, a freed slave—no doctors, scientists, professors, teachers, lawyers, or writers. Those very few serious protagonists in more prestigious fields—engineer Mary Jackson (Janelle Monáe) and mathematician Katherine Johnson (Taraji P. Henson) of *Hidden Figures* (2016)—use only occasional Black English features, and they never use Black English while at work. Even *The Pursuit of Happyness*'s (2006) Chris Gardner (Will Smith), who spends most of the film working in an unpaid internship as a stockbroker, uses Black English pronunciation but very little Black English grammar—just two instances, one of which involves him joking with a client. The message to Black English speakers is that if you insist on using your native dialect in all parts of your life—not simply to be funny or sassy—you cannot aspire to an educated, white collar life. This message bears out in reality, as we shall see below.

Even films written and directed by Black creators do not escape the stereotype that Black English is inherently comedic and nonserious. Jordan Peele's 2017 horror film *Get Out* stars Daniel Kaluuya as Chris, a young Black photographer who is meeting his White girlfriend's wealthy parents for the first time. Chris is not particularly funny and, as we might expect, he uses little Black English—stigmatized grammar appears in only six of his many lines throughout the film. On the other hand, his best friend, T.S.A. agent Rod (Lil Rel Howery), provides the film's comic relief, cracking jokes in nearly every scene in which he appears, including in otherwise serious contexts. He also uses far more Black English features than Chris despite having less screen time, including ten uses of zero copula, six uses of uninflected possessive nouns and pronouns, two uses of uninflected third person singular verbs, two uses of article *a* followed by a vowel, two uses of negative concord, and one use each of plural *was*, zero auxiliary *have*, and *aks*. The pattern of relegating Black English to the realm of the comedic performance implies that the Black hero simply cannot be taken seriously if he uses Black English consistently.

This is almost certainly why Black English speakers are poorly represented among superheroes. Superhero movies are today's most lucrative genre, representing 63 films in our film set, including five of the top ten grossing films, and billions of dollars in sales annually. Yet only six Black English-speaking superheroes appear in our data, and most of them use Black English only occasionally or even rarely, including *X-Men Origins: Wolverine*'s (2009) John Wraith (will.i.am), a secondary character with less than five minutes of screen time and Frozone of *The Inc* *ibles* films, a more significant secondary character, but one who uses o a single Black English feature (zero copula) in only one of the two film *The Incredibles 2*, 2018). Miles Morales (Shameik Moore) of *Spider-Ma* *Into the Spider-Verse* (2018) is the only unambiguously positive represen ion of a Black English-speaking superhero protagonist in our film set; but p aps unsurprisingly, he uses very little Black English. Miles, a high school dent, is bilingual, speaking both Spanish and English at home and with frie s—we'll talk more about this in Chapter 4. He is also biracial, but his Black lice officer father uses no Black English grammar and only moderate Blac nglish pronunciation, and Miles himself also uses almost no Black Englis ronunciation and employs zero copula only twice—this is the extent of hi lack English use.

We do see three other Black superher in the film set who use Black English more regularly, and we'll examin em in the next section.

IS BLACK ENGLISH INHERE TLY THREATENING?

In the introductory chapter, we discussed t ways in which our beliefs about stigmatized dialects are actually proxy fo ur beliefs about the people who speak them: if, for example, we consider W te blue collar Southern grammar to be ignorant, it's because we consider ite blue collar Southern *people* to be ignorant. Similarly, one of the few ys in which film characters are permitted to use Black English other tha or humor is when they want to be threatening—and Black English is inh ntly threatening because White audiences think Black people, especially ck men, are threatening.[10] Some Black characters use mostly EDC in their lms and code-switch into Black English when they want to sound threat ing, while others use primarily Black English and are characterized as th tening or dangerous throughout their films.

The three remaining Black English-spe ng superheroes—Hancock (Will Smith) of 2008's *Hancock* and Deadshot so Will Smith) and Killer Croc (Adewale Akinnuoye-Agbaje) of 2016's *S* *ide Squad*—all provide illustrative examples.

Unlike most other superhero films, *Ha* *ck* is not part of a franchise or an extended cinematic universe; it is the original story that exists independently of other film universes. Hancoc imself has Superman-like powers—flight, super strength, super speed— t he is not widely considered a hero in his city. When we first meet him, 's passed out drunk on a public bench, dirty and unshaven; pedestrians pas y him without acknowledgment (except for the woman whose rear end he es to grab). He has a reputation for causing willful and wanton destruction when he can be bothered to fight crime, and many people consider him a public nuisance. After he saves good-hearted public relations expert Ray (Jason Bateman) from being hit by a train, Ray convinces Hancock to try to change his image, arguing that he should be beloved, not hated, by the citizens of his city. Hancock agrees and undergoes a series of behavior changes, including serving prison time for the property damage he is guilty of, wearing a tight-fitting superhero uniform, and praising legitimate law enforcement officers for their efforts. Interestingly, as Hancock's character changes, so, too, does his language—namely, his Black English grammar features disappear as he becomes an upstanding citizen.

In the first half of the film, prior to a hostage situation which marks the turning point in Hancock's character, he uses the following Black English grammar:

zero auxiliary *do* (two uses)
zero auxiliary *have* (one use)
article *a* followed by a vowel (two uses)
suffixed *-ass* (one use)
zero copula (four uses)
negative concord (one use)

He also uses *ain't* twice, for a total of 13 "nonstandard" grammar usages. After the hostage situation, he uses auxiliary *ain't* plus an infinitive and negative concord in a single sentence ("You ain't do nothin'"), plus one additional use of *ain't*, for a total of a mere two lines of "nonstandard" grammar. In other words, Hancock uses stigmatized grammar more than four times more frequently when he is behaving like a drunken, misogynistic criminal and menace to society than when he is behaving like a traditional superhero.

Suicide Squad's Deadshot and Killer Croc also fit into the categories of both criminal and superhero. Both are incarcerated at the start of the film, Deadshot—an expert marksman—for murder in his job as hitman for hire, and Croc—a super strong sort of human-crocodile hybrid—for unspecified crimes, though another character later remarks that he "eats people." The two are unwillingly recruited by government agent Amanda Waller (Viola Davis) for covert missions and, by the end of the film, having served their purpose, are back in prison. Deadshot, one of the film's protagonists, uses numerous Black English features throughout the film including pronunciation and grammar, while Croc uses strong Southern Black English pronunciation but only two stigmatized features—a personal dative and *ain't*. However, because he has only eight brief lines, these usages represent a major portion of his speech. Unlike Hancock, Deadshot and Croc's use of Black English is consistent throughout their film, but so too are their statuses as criminals—they begin the film in prison, and they end th ilm back in prison, in the exact same cells in which we first meet them. W le Hancock gets to evolve out of both his menacing personality and his stig tized dialect, Deadshot and Croc are stuck with both.

Because Black English is so often cha terized by films as threatening, it's frequently associated with criminalit and is even used to segregate Black villains from heroes. We noted abo that Miles Morales of *Into the Spider-Verse* very rarely uses Black Engli , but his Uncle Aaron, a.k.a. the Prowler (Mahershala Ali), one of the film' villains, uses considerably more, especially relative to his screen time. W e Miles uses only zero copula, Aaron uses zero copula, plural *is*, zero au iary *do*, zero auxiliary *have*, and negative concord, as well as moderate B k English pronunciation. After he discovers that his nephew is one of the veral Spider-People making life difficult for his boss the Kingpin, he neg ts to kill Miles when given the opportunity, and the Kingpin shoots him the back as retribution. He dies in Miles's arms, and in this emotional sce he uses no Black English grammar—now that his character has been rede ned, he uses EDC.

Black Panther (2018) is another rare s erhero film that features both a Black hero and a Black villain, and whil in many ways the two are mirror images of each other, their speech di rentiates them. Erik Killmonger (Michael B. Jordan), a U.S. special forces perative determined to take over the world using the advanced weaponry o ctional African nation Wakanda, uses Black English grammar and pronunci on far more frequently and consistently than any other Black supervillai r hero, including auxiliary *ain't* plus an infinitive, negative concord, zero pula, plural *is*, uninflected possessive pronouns, and simple past tense *se* , as well as strong Black English pronunciation. Though the hero of the fil Wakandan King T'Challa a.k.a. Black Panther (Chadwick Boseman), is o Black, he doesn't use Black American English at all because he's a n ve of Africa. Instead, he speaks isiXhosa—a real language spoken in south n Africa—and an African dialect of English, and he uses exclusively "stan d" grammar. While many viewers find Killmonger sympathetic, the fil unambiguously portrays him as dangerous and menacing: one of his first s in the film is to shoot his own girlfriend, and he later fatally stabs a Wak dan elder who opposes him and chokes an old woman. In sum, the Black nglish speaker might be sympathetic, but he is still criminal, while the he uses the grammar recognized as prestigious by the American audience.

In part because Black English is so f uently depicted as threatening, Black English speakers are overrepresent as criminals in the film data. Of course, Black people themselves are more ely than White people to appear as criminals or gang members in media– 016 research by *Vox* found, for example, that Black actors represented ov 60% of unnamed film characters credited as "Gang member," "Gangster," or "Gangbanger," when in reality, only 35% of American gang members are Black.[11] However, Black English speakers are *even more* overrepresented as criminals and inmates than non-Black English-speaking Black characters. Seventy-four of the 468 Black English speakers in our data are depicted either as directly engaged in criminal activity during the course of the film or as incarcerated inmates—15.8% of total Black English speakers. The criminal activities depicted run the gamut and include car theft, petty theft, casino robbery, drug dealing, illegal gambling, illegal street racing, bank heists, murder, genocide, and video piracy. In some cases, the character's crimes are never made explicit; rather, they are already incarcerated when we meet them and their convictions are never discussed, as in the cast of *The Longest Yard* (2005). Twenty-three Black English-speaking characters are shown using or dealing drugs, or about 4.9%. Again, this compares to a 2009 Human Rights Watch report that found that in 2007, only about 1.7% of Black Americans were arrested for drug crimes.[12]

Not all of these fictional criminals are bad guys in their respective films; on the contrary, many are protagonists, or, like Killmonger, at least sympathetic characters. Nearly everyone in the *Fast and Furious* franchise—which includes eight films in our set and 19 Black English-speaking characters—is engaged in criminal activity at some point, yet in the world of the films, they are the heroes; so, too, the cast of *The Longest Yard* as well as that of *Chicago* (2002), which also consists primarily of inmates. But though they are heroes, they are also, unambiguously, dangerous: they murder, they steal, and, in the *Fast and Furious* franchise, they quite often cause wanton destruction of buildings and even entire city blocks, heedless of any civilian bystanders that might be in their way.

Other Black characters who are not explicitly depicted as criminals use more Black English features when they're angry or threatening others, or they use Black English features *only* when threatening others. For instance, Jamie Foxx's character in *The Amazing Spider-Man 2* (2014), electrical engineer Max Dillon a.k.a. supervillain Electro, uses EDC throughout the film with one exception: a dream sequence in which he switches to Black English pronunciation while assaulting his boss. Laurence Fishburne does something similar in two separate films in our set: in *Batman v. Superman: Dawn of Justice* (2016), his character, *Daily Planet* newspaper editor Perry White, argues with Clark Kent (Henry Cavill) over a story that Kent wants to pursue. White, like Max Dillon, uses EDC throughout the film except for this single, brief moment of anger:

KENT: If the police won't help, the press has to do the right thing.

WHITE: You don't get to decide what the ri t thing is.

KENT: When the *Planet* was founded, it sto l for something, Perry.

WHITE: And so could you if it was 1938, bu t's not 1938. WPA ain't hiring no more. Apples don't cost a nickel. Not in here ot out there. You drop this thing!

Likewise, in *John Wick: Chapter 3—Pa bellum* (2019), Fishburne's character, the Bowery King, uses EDC save fo single line at the end of the film in which he pledges vengeance against th he believes have wronged him: "They about to find out if you cut a king, u better cut him to the quick."

2019's horror film *Us* includes a simil example; Winston Duke plays Gabe Wilson, a suburban father on vaca n with his family who are terrorized by a family of evil doppelgange Wilson speaks EDC with two exceptions: a humorous line muttered to hi self when his family is annoying him ("I'm tryin' to have a vacation and m whole family lost they goddamn minds"), and his threats to the doppelgang as they stand menacingly in the dark outside his home. In this scene, he do not yet know the true threat that the doppelgangers represent; he sees only e silhouettes of a strange group of people who don't acknowledge him or ct to what he says. Unnerved by their bizarre behavior, he steps out the fro door carrying a baseball bat and warns them away: "If y'all are out here t n' to scare people. . . . A'ight, I asked you nice. Now I need y'all to get of y property. . . . Now I thought I already done told y'all to get off my prop y. . . . Now the cops are already on they way." Wilson, Max Dillon, Perry ite, and the Bowery King speak EDC by default, but when they wish to a ear tough or menacing, they use Black English to do it.

Bad Boys II's (2003), Detective Mike I wery (Will Smith), on the other hand, uses Black English throughout his f n (an action comedy), including Black pronunciation as well as multiple Bl English grammar features such as zero copula, negative concord, emphati *one*, uninflected possessive pronouns ("Somebody's on they way with yo money"), and singular *you was*. However, in a scene in which he pretend o be a recently released ex-con in order to threaten his partner's teenage ughter's boyfriend, he adds two additional features that don't appear in hi speech at any other point in the film: the word *nigga*, which he repeats m tiple times, and a question with no subject-auxiliary inversion—"Nigga, o *that is* at the door?"—a feature used by only five other characters in entire film set. In other words, Mike's usual Black speech gets even Blac when he wants to intimidate.

In *21 Jump Street* (2012), Ice Cube's cha cter, Captain Dickson, addresses these stereotypes about Black men direct hen two new White officers are introduced to his unit:

> Get your motherfucking ass up when I'm talking! You will be going undercover as high school students. You are here simply because you look young. You some Justin Bieber, Miley Cyrus-looking motherfuckers. I know what you're thinking. "Angry Black Captain. It ain't nothing but a stupid stereotype." Well, guess what, motherfuckers. I'm Black. And I worked my ass off to be the captain! And sometimes I get angry. So suck a dick! What I'm trying to show you is, embrace your stereotypes.

Dickson uses few Black English features in this monologue, but throughout his two films (both of which are comedies) he uses many Black English grammar and pronunciation features regularly. And although Dickson says that he "sometimes" gets angry, whenever we see him in either film, he is *always* angry, always berating and swearing at the inept protagonists. The filmmakers, perhaps, believe that by inserting this metacommentary to acknowledge the stereotype, they are then free to exploit it, but the film never actually *critiques* the stereotype; rather, it simply depicts an angry, threatening Black man who acknowledges that he is angry and uses Black English to do it.

IS BLACK ENGLISH IGNORANT?

As we discussed in the introduction to this book, one of the most pervasive beliefs that people hold about stigmatized dialects is that they are "bad" English—that they represent ignorance, a lack of education, and even stupidity. As a result, Black-English–speaking individuals working in professional fields and prestigious jobs are severely underrepresented in our data, and, significantly, those who do show up use Black English features in their speech far less frequently on average than other Black English speakers in the film set. They comprise only 17 total characters, several of whom use only a single instance of Black English grammar, including newspaper editor Perry White and electrical engineer Max Dillon, discussed above, as well as a genetics professor, an astronaut, a medical doctor, a lawyer, a Congresswoman, and a physical therapist. None of these characters are protagonists. Other professional characters who use few stigmatized features include the professor of molecular genetics from *Me, Myself, and Irene*, a spaceship captain, a wealthy entrepreneur, an engineer, a mathematician, an American envoy, and a scientist. Only two of these—Mary Jackson and Katherine Johnson of 2016's *Hidden Figures*—are protagonists in their films.

The one exception we see of a professional protagonist who uses significant Black English is Dr. John Dolittle (Eddie Murphy) of 2001's *Dr. Dolittle 2*. Dolittle is a veterinarian in a family comedy, and while most of his lines use EDC, he also uses numerous Black nglish features, including zero copula, negative concord, uninflected thirc)erson singular verbs, and plural *was*. Most of these usages, however, occ r when Dolittle is either angry, annoyed, or making a joke, consistent with e other patterns we've discussed in which Black characters use Engl 1 for humor or to express anger or threatening behavior.

Other films go out of their way to chara erize Black English speakers as ignorant, especially in relation to the non-I ick English-speaking characters. We mentioned the Klump family of *Nutty ofessor II: The Klumps* above—all but protagonist Sherman use Black En sh consistently and are depicted as not only ignorant but uncouth to the p nt of farce—the movie is filled with belches, fart jokes, and other gross- t humor. Sherman, on the other hand, is a chemistry professor and super enius, and while he uses strong Southern Black English pronunciation thi ighout the film, his grammar is almost always that of the dominant cultu . However, after an experiment gone wrong causes him to gradually lose hi ntelligence, his grammar slowly becomes more "nonstandard." The first evi nce of this appears during a class in which a student asks him a question tha stumps him, and he responds, "I ain't got a clue"—his first use of *ain't* in t film. He also forgets the meaning of uncommon words such as *ethical* an *uandary*. As the film progresses and Sherman gets dumber, his language ge Blacker, incorporating plural *is*, third person singular *don't*, emphatic *don* suffixed *-ass*, article *a* followed by a vowel, negative concord, and a reg arized past tense verb, *blowed*. Other characters notice this change and nment on it: one young family member remarks that Sherman is beginnir to sound like his less intelligent brother Ernie, while antagonist Buddy Lo (also Eddie Murphy) comments on Sherman's use of *ain't*: "'No I ain't, no in't.' That's interesting. Starting to sound kinda ignorant." Buddy points ou xplicitly what the audience also likely believes—that "nonstandard" gram r is a sign of ignorance. By the end of this process, just before Sherman's dy devolves into primordial goo, he is barely able to speak intelligibly at al 'Me no smart. Never. No more." The implication is clear: language exists o a hierarchy with EDC at the top and gibberish at the bottom, and Black En sh somewhere in between.

2009's *The Blind Side* also comments d ctly on the perceived ignorance of "nonstandard" usage, and its character itions prop up the other stereotypes we've discussed. The film is based o ie true story of Michael Oher, an impoverished Black teenager without stab housing who was adopted by a wealthy White family and went on to beco a successful college and professional football player. Quinton Aaron plays Michael, but he's not the protagonist; the story is told from the perspective c the wealthy White mother Leigh Anne Tuohy (Sandra Bullock), and the foc is not on Michael's experiences but on Leigh Anne's—her White guilt wh she realizes how privileged her life is relative to Michael's; her sudden discovery that her wealthy White friends are rather racist; her efforts to track down Michael's drug-addicted mother before she decides to adopt Michael legally. It is the epitome of the White savior tale, in which the deserving but helpless Black character can only be rescued from his impoverished life by the generosity and benevolence of the White characters. They even teach him how to play football.

We'll return to our discussion of Leigh Anne and her Southern-speaking friends and neighbors in Chapter 3, but here let's examine the Black English speakers in the film. They include Michael's biological mother, Denise (Adriane Lenox), a drug dealer in Michael's neighborhood named Alton (Irone Singleton), a pair of minor characters with only a few moments of screen time each, and Michael himself.

Denise is a failed parent, having been arrested for drug possession many times. She has at least twelve children and, according to the social worker that Leigh Anne consults, probably doesn't even remember how many children she actually has, and she doesn't know who Michael's father is. In her only scene, a conversation with Leigh Anne about Michael, she uses Black English pronunciation, zero copula, negative concord, uninflected third person singular verbs, and singular third person *don't*. Leigh Anne has sought her out not to ask for her blessing to adopt Michael (Michael is a ward of the state, so Leigh Anne has no need to ask her permission), but to obtain his birth certificate to make the process easier. In fact, Leigh Anne doesn't ask Denise's opinion about Michael's adoption at all, let alone his adoption by a White family.

Alton, who lives near Denise and is her drug supplier, is usually seen hanging out on the front steps of his apartment complex. When Michael and Leigh Anne arrive to pick up Michael's clothes, Michael instructs Leigh Anne not to leave the car, implying that Alton and his friends are dangerous. Alton eyes Leigh Anne as she waits in the car, commenting crudely on her appearance—his characterization is overtly menacing. In a later scene he makes another misogynistic comment about Leigh Anne and her teenage daughter, prompting Michael to threaten him physically; Alton then raises his shirt to reveal a gun tucked into his pants. Like Denise, he uses Black English pronunciation and numerous grammar features including zero copula, negative concord, uninflected third person singular verbs, emphatic *done*, and suffixed *-ass*, among others. And like so many Black English speakers in film, Alton and Denise are ignorant, poor, and criminal, and, in Alton's case, violent and dangerous as well.

Michael himself is depicted as quiet and reserved, particularly in the first half of the film; until he becomes more comfortable with his adopted family, he barely speaks. He's not too bright—he doesn't read well—but he is hard-working and willing to do anything a White person in authority tells him to do for his own good. He is physically imposing but passive, unwilling to hit another player on the football field until Leigh Anne frames blocking and tackling as "protecting his family." His threatening of Alton is his only use of violence off the field, and this, too, is framed by the film as protecting his family. He uses occasional Black English pronunciation and very few Black English grammar features, even relative to his small number of lines: a single instance of third person singular *don't* ("Is that why Mr. Tuohy don't have to go to work?"), a single instance of zero auxiliary *do* ("What you know about this?"), and a single instance of zero *of* following *out* ("Don't get out the car").

Significantly, Leigh Anne sees Michael as *worthy* of rescuing from his impoverished circumstances, while she leaves his mother Denise to waste away in her tiny, filthy apartment littered with empty liquor bottles. It is true that Denise is an adult while Michael is a minor, but rather than using her vast resources (her family owns more than 80 Taco Bells) to help lift Michael *and* his family out of poverty and addiction, Leigh Anne instead whisks Michael away, leaving behind the dirty, dangerous, drug-ridden neighborhood where he was born for the open, affluent White suburbs. In the transition from his poor Black life to his wealthy new White life, Michael's language at one point becomes a subject of Leigh Anne's scrutiny. Leigh Anne herself uses Southern-shifted U.S. English—which we'll define in the next chapter—along with completely "standard" grammar. Michael, too, uses mostly "standard" grammar, but when Leigh Anne offers to buy him new clothes, he protests, "I got clothes," and she immediately corrects him: "I *have* clothes." As we discussed in the introduction, present tense *got*, though it is widely used by speakers of all demographics, is still marked as "nonstandard" in usage guides; in this scene, it is proxy for all the failures of Michael's childhood—particularly his poor education, which was compounded by his unstable home. The message of *The Blind Side* is clear: "nonstandard" English is the provenance of poverty, violence, drugs, and homelessness; EDC is the pathway out to a life of affluence and ease, and Leigh Anne is determined to set Michael on that path.

In addition to criminals, inmates, and a very few professionals, the remaining Black English speakers in our film set comprise a range of job titles and characterizations, but they are overwhelmingly working class: 30 police officers, detectives, and security guards (6.4%); 15 members of the military (3.2%); a plethora of domestic and blue collar workers including janitors, hospital orderlies, maids, cooks, butlers, chauffeurs, stable hands, retail employees, and factory workers; a pair of nursing home attendants; ten enslaved individuals appearing in films that take place before the Civil War; and just a handful of people working in secondary education, including two high school teachers, one principal, and two high school football coaches.

The evidence is unambiguous: if you are a Black English-speaking actor in Hollywood, you are far more likely to be asked to play a criminal than a white collar worker, and about two and a half times more likely to play a slave than a teacher. These films reinforce the beliefs that audiences already hold: that Black English is ignorant, and so are its speakers.

SASSY BLACK ENGLISH-SPEAKINGSPEAKING WOMEN

Perhaps unsurprisingly given the patterns we've discussed so far, Black women are drastically underrepresented on screen. The 2016 USC Annenberg study on diversity in media found that only about 4% of speaking or named characters across film, television, and streaming shows were Black women;[13] and our film set contains 15 Black female protagonists out of a total of approximately 777 protagonists, representing about 1.9%. (This includes three appearances of Gloria the hippo [Jada Pinkett Smith] in the *Madagascar* franchise as well as one of Ellie the woolly mammoth [Queen Latifah] in the *Ice Age* franchise, who are not actually human and arguably shouldn't be counted as Black women.)

Female Black English speakers are even more poorly represented, comprising only 11 of our Black English-speaking protagonists (19.3%) and only 107 of total Black English speakers (22.9%). Like Black English-speaking men, Black English-speaking female characters are largely comedic, and though they are slightly less likely to be depicted as inmates or criminals, they are just as often relegated to other stereotypical roles: domestic servants (the cast of *The Help* [2011] alone comprises ten Black English-speaking maids, or 9.3% of total Black English-speaking female characters), antebellum slaves, nagging wives and mothers, and, of course, Sassy Black Women.

The Sassy Black Woman media trope—a subset of the stereotype of Black people being louder and more talkative than their White counterparts—has been analyzed at length by other writers, but it's important for our purposes to note the consistency with which these characters use Black English. The Sassy Black Woman is, with very few exceptions, a Black English speaker, and she straddles a line between two stereotypical characteristics of Black English speakers: she is both funny and threatening. While her exaggerated characterization, like that of other Black characters, is often treated as inherently funny by the films in which she appears, her treatment of male characters is threatening to their masculinity and, sometimes, even to the safety of others. In *Wild Hogs* (2007), co-protagonist Bobby (Martin Lawrence) works a thankless job as a cleaner and lives with his unappreciative wife (Tichina Arnold) and mother-in-law (Bebe Drake), Black English-speaking women who harass and berate him in every scene which they appear, sparking his motivation to embark on a cross-country otorcycle trip with his friends. Similarly, Frozone (Samuel L. Jackson) c The Incredibles (2004) and *The Incredibles 2* (2018) lives with his wife H ey (Kimberly Adair Clark), who is never seen on screen and exists only as loud, angry Black female voice that harangues Frozone from off-screen w never he is forced to rush off to save the city. Consider this exchange from e *Incredibles*, which takes place after a giant robot armed with lasers passe heir apartment window:

> FROZONE: Where is my super suit?
>
> [. . .]
>
> HONEY: *Why* do you need to know?
>
> FROZONE: I need it!
>
> HONEY: Uh uh. Don't you think about run ' off to do no derring-do. We've been planning this dinner for two months!
>
> FROZONE: The public is in danger!
>
> HONEY: My *evening's* in danger!
>
> FROZONE: You tell me where that suit is, oman! We are talking about the greater good!
>
> HONEY: Greater good?! I am your *wife*! I the greatest *good* you are ever gonna get!

Sassy Black nagging wife Honey is unwil g to sacrifice an evening out so that her husband can save the city from de uction.

S.W.A.T. (2003) and *I, Robot* (2004) al include two parallel scenes of angry Black women appearing on scree solely to harass Black men. In *S.W.A.T.*, two protagonist police officers s nt several blocks chasing a fleeing suspect before capturing him, only t e verbally assaulted by a loud, angry Black woman (Octavia Spencer) sw ing her apartment steps: "Don't ya'll got nothin' better to do than be[14] hau ' another Black man off to jail? Just perpetuatin' the cycle, ain't ya?" An in *I, Robot* protagonist cop Del Spooner (Will Smith) spies a running rob carrying a purse, assumes it has robbed someone, and chases it across the y. He finally tackles it just as it delivers the purse to its owner, a loud, f Black woman (Sharon Wilkins) who sent the robot to fetch her asthma m cation. She berates Spooner for his efforts: "You are a asshole. . . . You lu y I can't breathe or I'd walk all up and down your ass." In both films, the n (the point-of-view characters) passively absorb the women's chastisem t, their heroic acts unacknowledged and unappreciated.

Perhaps the most on-the-nose example of a sassy Black female character and the torment she inflicts on those around her appears in *Scary Movie* (2000), a parody of slasher films such as *Scream* (1996). In one scene, high school student and Black English speaker Brenda (Regina Hall) attends a movie with her boyfriend during which she talks and shrieks loudly at the screen and even answers her cell phone and proceeds to have a noisy conversation.[15] We see the White moviegoers sighing and rolling their eyes, and when several ask her to quiet down, she responds belligerently: "I think I paid my money like everybody else up in here." Just as the film's masked killer is about to stab her, the White patrons around her pull large knives from their pockets and do it for him, and the entire theater cheers as she dies. Although the film is satire, like *21 Jump Street* it participates in the perpetuation of a Black stereotype without actually critiquing it; Brenda's obnoxious behavior in the theater is presented through the lens of the White gaze, and the real presumed White audience is assumed to empathize with the put-out White audience of the film who celebrate Brenda's murder.

Even animal characters are not exempt from the Sassy Black Woman stereotype. *Dinosaur* (2000) includes two elderly female characters, a brachiosaurus, Baylene, voiced by a White English woman (Joan Plowright), and a styracosaurus, Eema, voiced by a Black woman (Della Reese) who uses Black pronunciation and occasional Black English grammar. Both have difficulty keeping up with the herd's movement and are at risk of falling victim to the predators that trail them, but while Baylene is polite and proper to the younger, smaller dinosaurs, Eema advocates simply kicking them out of the way. *Over the Hedge* (2006) similarly includes a female skunk, Stella (Wanda Sykes), who uses Black English and threatens to "gas" another character "so hard your grandchildren'll stink!"

The important point here is that these stereotypes are bound up not just in Blackness itself, but in Black language specifically. The most stereotypical Black characters on our movie screens—the criminal, the drug dealer, the buffoon, the sassy Black girlfriend—are Black English speakers, while the smart, serious, professional, and heroic Black characters are, with very few exceptions, EDC speakers.

CAN YOU BE BLACK AND GAY?

Like Black women, LGBTQ+ characters are hugely underrepresented in film generally—the 2016 USC Annenberg study found that just 2% of speaking or named characters in media were coded as lesbian, gay, or bisexual, and less than 1% were transgender.[16] As we'll see in this chapter and others, this pattern holds true for queer speakers of marginalized dialects. Only six unambiguously queer Black English speakers appear in our film set, representing only 1.3% of Black English-speaking characters, and while their portrayals range from reasonably positive to highly problematic, none of them are fully fleshed out characters. Instead, their sexuality is the object of ridicule or they exist only to further the character development of the protagonists.

2000's *Scary Movie* appeared in our discussion of Sassy Black Women, and it appears again here with the character of Ray (Shawn Wayans), a Black English-speaking high school athlete whose sexuality is the butt of jokes throughout the film as Ray constantly engages in suspiciously gay behavior while denying being gay. He dresses his girlfriend, Brenda, in his football uniform and calls her "Brendan" in bed, comments pointedly on the appearance of other men, and makes Freudian slips such as this one:

> CINDY (Anna Faris): Ray, if you see Bobby will you tell him that I love him?
>
> RAY: Okay, if I see Bobby, I'll tell him I love him.

Many of the characters in this parodic horror film are murdered, but Ray's death is particularly gruesome; while at the movie theater with Brenda, he goes to the restroom, where he spots a glory hole in the side of the stall; when he puts his head up to it, he is impaled through the ear by a large White penis—his sexuality is almost literally weaponized against him. Like many Black English-speaking characters whose Black English *is* the joke, in *Scary Movie*, the fact that a Black male athlete—the stereotypical image of Black masculinity—is gay is presumed to be inherently funny.

2008's *Tropic Thunder* also includes a young, Black English-speaking closeted gay character in hip hop artist Alpa Chino (Brandon T. Jackson), who has built his image on the stereotype of the misogynistic and sexually promiscuous young Black man. He markets an energy drink called Booty Sweat, and we're first introduced to him in a commercial for the drink in which he raps about how much he loves "the pussy" while two women gyrate around him. However, midway through the film, he unintentionally admits to being in love with someone named Lance, and when the White male actors with whom he is shooting a film react with surprise, he denies it vehemently, using stronger Black English pronunciation as he does so: "Look, I'm Alpa Chino, okay? I love the pussy! A'ight?" Although his co-stars try to reassure him ("Man, everyone's gay once in a while! This is Hollywood!"), he continues to exclaim that he's not gay and attempts to redirect the conversation. Alpa's Black identity is closely tied up with another rigid definition of Black masculinity which includes Black stereotypes such as heterosexual promiscuity; because admitting that he is gay would threaten this identity, he cannot do so even if his co-stars are accepting. Like *Scary Movie*'s Ray, the fact of Alpa Chino's sexuality itself—the fact that this lecherous young Black man who raps about "pussy" is gay—is the joke.

2005's *The Longest Yard* features the only Black English speaker who could arguably be said to be coded as transgender, and again, the combination of the character's race, sexuality, gender identity, and appearance are meant to be the source of humor. Ms. Tucker (Tracy Morgan) is one of a group of inmates called "the girls" and "ladies" who are referred to alternately using feminine pronouns and masculine pronouns in an obvious caricature of incarcerated men who enter into gay relationships in prison. "The girls" cut their clothes in feminine styles, flirt openly with the male inmates (who sometimes reciprocate), and otherwise engage in exaggerated, stereotypically feminine behavior. During the football game between the inmates and the prison guards that is the film's climax, they're dressed in sparkly red cheerleader uniforms and they perform practice routines on the sidelines. The sight of a Black man in a sequined bra and short skirt, holding pom-poms and doing backflips, flirting with male football players is presumed to be inherently humorous, and Ms. Tucker receives no character development beyond this caricature.

2015's *Pitch Perfect 2* includes the only Black English-speaking lesbian in the film set in the character of Cynthia Rose (Ester Dean), a member of the all-female acapella group that is the center of the story. Like the other queer characters, she receives no character development beyond her race and sexuality, which are occasionally mined for jokes. For instance, when the group goes on a camping retreat and finds themselves squeezed together into a too-small tent, the camera pans across Cynthia's smiling face and she remarks, "I hope the sun never comes up." When another character asks sharply, "Are you touchin' my goodies?," Cynthia responds straight-faced, "Yes." While the inclusion of an out lesbian—especially a Black lesbian, and especially one that doesn't exist solely to titillate male characters—is incredibly rare in the film set, this depiction is little more than tokenism.

Other gay Black English speakers serve mainly to further the stories of their straight White protagonists. For example, Paul (Craig Chandler) is a Black English speaker and steel stamp mill co-worker of protagonist Rabbit (Eminem) in 2002's *8 Mile*. Paul appears in only two scenes and has just a handful of lines, and during a lunch-time rap battle among the workers he becomes the target of homophobic remarks by a character credited as Male Lunch Truck Rapper (Xzibit):

> Speakin' a dressers, take a look at Paul the fruit cake.
> When you travel you probably pack panties in your suitcase
> made out of lace from Victoria's Secret.
> If ten men came in a cup you'd probably drink it.

Rabbit intervenes and sticks up for Pa only to retort with more homophobic slurs aimed this time at Lunch Tru Rapper:

> Okay, folks, enough with the gay es,
> especially from a gay, broke bitch ourself, eh low?
> His style's doo-doo.
> You've worked here longer than and I get paid more than you do.
> Dawg, take a seat.
> What's this guy standing in line f He ain't got money to eat!
> Check this out, yo yo.
> This guy cashed his whole check d bought one Ho Ho.
> Fucking homo, little maggot, you n't hack it.
> Paul's gay—you're a faggot.
> [. . .]
> Hey, why you fuckin' with the ga uy, G?
> When really you're the one who's ot the HIV.
> Man, I'm done with this clown. H s soft.
> Fuck it, I'll let homegirl finish yo ff.

The crowd reacts uproariously to this tu of events, but the picture painted here is one of obvious hostility toward op ly gay men, whether or not the slurs are aimed at them directly. Paul's rol n the film is to accept the abuse from Lunch Truck Rapper so that Rabbit n come to his defense and play the good guy, earning him status in the s of a presumably sympathetic White audience.

The final Black English-speaking gay aracter in our discussion serves the opposite purpose: to show his film's tagonists and the audience how out of touch they are. Juario (Justin Hires) high school student, appears in *21 Jump Street*, and the film's protagonist Schmidt (Jonah Hill) and Jenko (Channing Tatum), are police officers wh ave gone undercover at Juario's school in hopes of tracking down the de r of a new synthetic drug. On their first day of school, Jenko tries to gai popularity by bullying a "nerd," only to discover that the social behavior e learned in high school have become outdated:

> JENKO: Look at him. He's trying. He's ac lly trying. What a nerd. Look at the nerd. Look at the nerd. Look at him. Lo at the nerd.
>
> JUARIO: Who you calling a nerd, man?
>
> JENKO: I'm sorry, what? [punches Juario v ently in the face]
>
> SCHMIDT: Shit, dude.

ERIC (Dave Franco): Are you okay, man? [to Jenko] Hey, what the hell? Are you serious?

JENKO: Well, turn that gay-ass music off.

JUARIO: You punched me because I'm gay?

JENKO: What? No. Oh, come on!

SCHMIDT: That's not cool, man.

ERIC: That is really insensitive.

JENKO: I didn't punch him because he's gay. I punched him, and then he happened to turn out to be gay afterwards.

JUARIO: I was gay when you punched me!

SCHMIDT: In a weird way, it might have been homophobic *not* to punch you just because you were gay.

JENKO: Right.

Juario is a small secondary character who, like the other Black English-speaking gay characters, receives no other development beyond this scene. While his sexuality is not depicted negatively, and in fact homophobic behavior is explicitly condemned in the film, neither is he a fully realized character; rather, he is a tool used by the film's creators to establish that Jenko—once one of the cool, popular kids—is out of place in this twenty-first century school environment.

As we acknowledged in our discussion of Black English-speaking female characters, this underrepresented demographic exists at the intersection of several underrepresented groups. Indeed, among the 777 protagonists in our 493-film set, there are *no* openly LGBTQ+ protagonists; the nearest approximation is the light queer-coding of Captain Marvel, a.k.a. Carol Danvers, which, according to the film's writers, is in the eye of the beholder.[17] We shall see in later chapters that queer and queer-coded characters are also poorly represented among other marginalized speakers.

MOCKERY

Mockery refers to the parodic performance of a language or dialect by a non-native speaker. Jane H. Hill popularized adjectival *mock* in her seminal discussion of Mock Spanish, part of her 1998 paper "Language, Race, and White Public Space." Mock Spanish and Hill's work on it will be discussed in greater detail in Chapter 4, but in brief, Hill found that Mock Spanish performances relied on racist stereotypes a l beliefs about Spanish-speaking people,[18] and as we shall see, this claim h ds true for other types of mockery, including Mock Black English, Mock outhern, and Mock White Girl. Importantly, not all uses of Black Englis y non-Black people are mockery—as we noted above, not all Black pe le speak Black English, and not all Black English speakers are Black. Whi people and other people of color who grow up in environments where Bla English is widely spoken and who associate with Black English speaker ill learn to speak Black English natively, and this is not mockery. Rather, ckery occurs when a non-native Black English speaker appropriates Bla English features. This appropriation may or may not attempt to repro e Black English accurately, but whether it makes this attempt or not, it us ly fails, instead relying on iconized features to produce a parodic, hyper- al version which some scholars call *linguistic minstrelsy*. This type of mins lsy also often incorporates other signifiers of Blackness, such as clothing a body language.[19]

Non-Black English speakers use Mock ck English in films for a variety of reasons—to taunt or deride Black peopl o gain cachet with Black people or appropriate Black people's perceived c ness for themselves, for humor, or some combination of these reasons, a their performances range from fairly accurate uses of Black English pron ciation and grammar to parodic nonsense. Let's examine some of the exan es found in the film set.

In the 2005 comedy *The 40-Year-Old gin*, White title character Andy (Steve Carell) works at a big box electron store, and when his coworkers learn of his virgin status, they insist on ta ng him to a speed-dating event. While there, Black English speaker Jay (omany Malco) writes a number of misogynistic comments about the fem participants on his dating card, which his girlfriend, Jill (Erica Vittina Phil s), later finds. To save face with her, Jay accuses Andy of writing the comm ts, and Jill confronts Andy at his workplace. Andy plays along, awkwardly ng parodic Black English grammar and slang and taking the ruse a bit fa r than Jay may have intended:

> ANDY: Who the fuck are you to put me on ial? I've never even met you. So why don't you back the shit off, all right? A stop with the inquisition.
>
> JILL: That's how you talk?
>
> ANDY: You know what, I don't have to a wer to you. You ain't my bitch. Know what I saying? So, shit, man. Fuck it.
>
> JILL: [to Jay] You shouldn't even be hangin out with this pervert.
>
> JAY: I don't hang out with him. I work with n and that's it. I tried to introduce him to a few nice people. He made a fool himself. I don't mess with him, baby. That's not me.

ANDY: You should keep your ho on a leash.

JAY: I can't let you be talking to my woman like that, dog. Know what I'm sayin'?

ANDY: Bitch is running wild, man.

While Andy uses Mock Black English to taunt Jill (who is, herself, Black but not a Black English speaker), the combination of his language and his awkwardness are meant to be funny to the presumed White audience. If, as we established earlier, Black English is inherently funny, then watching a socially awkward middle-aged White man use Black English must be *really* funny. This scene is also an illustration of the important distinction between linguistic stereotypes and racial stereotypes: it is not the Black people who are behaving rudely and ignorantly here; it is the Black English speaker doing so.

A similar (but longer and more difficult to watch) example appears in 2013's *Anchorman 2: The Legend Continues*. After White protagonist Ron Burgundy (Will Ferrell) begins dating his Black boss Linda (Meagan Good), she brings him home for dinner with her well-to-do family. Neither Linda nor the rest of her family speak Black English; in fact, their speech is not just "standard," but usually quite formal. However, in an attempt to win their favor, Ron delivers an extended monologue in painfully caricatured Black English pronunciation, grammar, and slang, laden with Black stereotypes, and it's worth examining in its entirety. Italics indicate an exaggerated high pitch:

LINDA'S MOTHER (Darlene French): How long have you and Linda been dating?

LINDA: Mother.

RON: No, it's all right. It's a logical question. Ours is a new love, but it burns very brightly. And it gets hot and sweaty and stanky. There's some stank on that love.

MOTHER: What . . . What are you talking about?

RON: Let's put it this way. I be bustin' nuts like a squirrel.

LINDA'S FATHER (L. Warren Young): Uh, now, we don't have conversations like that over dinner.

LINDA: [whispering] What are you doing?

RON: I'm addressing the white elephant in the room. I'm breaking down the barriers of race by assimilation, and that's all I'm doing.

LINDA: Well, you're coming off like a jerk.

RON: I think it's going well.

FATHER: If you haven't noticed, we don't c verse like that.

RON: Okay, okay. Look at big Papa down l e. He's saying to himself, "Shit! Look at this honky. Sittin' at my table, eati *my food*. In *my house*? *Touching my daughter*?" I have. I have touched your d ghter. We have done things, Papa. You ain't gone like. You ain't gonna like it n ne!

MOTHER: Oh, my goodness!

RON: I mean, I'm just a guy from Terre Ha , Indiana with a big ol' dick and a fat wallet and a spleef the size of a baby n. Just looking for someone who wants to smoke it. Let's get some smoke go in this place, right?

LINDA'S BROTHER (E. Roger Mitchell): T s ain't no Super Fly. What is your problem, man?

MOTHER: Linda, I don't understand what y are doing with him.

RON: Oh, you know what I'm comin' at y with, you big Black mother of Linda. Mix it up in a pot! Makin' it spicy!

MOTHER: Oh my Lord!

RON: In the back, cooking up chitlins. Big titties. Big ol' titties.

MOTHER: Excuse me?

BROTHER: That's my mama, man.

RON: Wave your hands in the air. Wave you ands in the air like you just don't care.

LINDA: Please, don't do this.

RON: Now, which one of you pipe-hittin itches can pass me the mashed potatoes?

[everyone gasps]

In a single brief exchange, Ron manag to reference large penises and breasts, marijuana, chitlins, and crack pi s, and ties them all not just to Black people but to Black English. The up r-class Black family, again, uses the grammar and pronunciation of the do nant culture. From the perspective of an audience member, the point is n lost that it is not only the White man making a fool of himself—it is the *Bl k English speaker* making a fool of himself. Many White audience member night walk away from this scene reinforced in their belief that Black Englis s inherently funny and that only ignorant people speak it.

Will Ferrell makes another appearance i his discussion in the character of Allen Gamble of 2010's *The Other Guys*, a inept police officer who, prior to the events of the film, unwittingly became pimp in college. In the scene we see rendered in flashback, Allen begins wearing gold teeth and progressively more outlandish clothes as the group of girls whose "dating schedule" he is "organizing" grows larger, and though he still does not understand himself to be a pimp, he begins going by the name Gator. Later in the film, while having a stressful dinner with his wife, he flashes back to his college days and begins ranting in Mock Black English: "Gator don't play no shit. You feel me? Gator never been about that. Never been about playin' no shit." A few moments later when his wife tells him that she's pregnant, he responds, "Whose baby is that? Who's the man who did that to you? Gator's bitches better be usin' jimmies!" The association specifically of Black English with the stereotypical role of the pimp closely mirrors the dinner conversation in *Anchorman 2*; the implication is that pimps must speak Black English whether or not they are actually Black. Yet again, the supposed humor derives from the incongruity between this unassuming, bookish White man and the threatening language of a Black pimp.

Appropriating Black English for Social Cachet

At least as frequently, White people use Mock Black English to, as H. Samy Alim puts it, "purchase the cool that comes from associating with Black people, Black culture, and Black art without appreciating any of it on its own terms."[20] A fascinating example of this principle, this idea that Blackness is cool, and that White people can appropriate it for themselves with the use of Mock Black English, occurs—believe it or not—in 2002's live-action *Scooby Doo*. In the film, demons are kidnapping and possessing the bodies of young adults, but apparently need coaching in the art of acting like a normal human twenty-something in order to blend in and carry out their plot. Our gang of young detectives stumble upon a training video that teaches the demons how to do this with a skit narrated by a pleasant, EDC-speaking White lady (Holly Ann Brisley). In the skit, two young men—one White, one possibly Latino—bump into each other at a party, one causing the other to spill his drink:

NARRATOR: Remember, today's young people have a language all their own.

GUY #1: (Robert Díaz): Sorry, bro.

GUY #2: (Remi Broadway): No big whoop, dog. Yo, did you catch that new vid on the box?

GUY #1: True dat. I'm up to snizuff on all popular trends.

GUY #2: Word!

The young men use EDC pronunciation, a at no point in the training video or in the film itself does anyone mention tl this language is actually stereo- typical Black slang. In fact, there are no ack people in the video or even in the scene: everyone attending the party the background of the video is White. Viewers will understand the conv sation to be a parody, but what they might not notice is that embedded wit the humor of seeing non-Black young people speak this way is also an umption that "cool kids" know how to "talk Black." If they did not at lea subconsciously understand that Black English slang was associated with odernity and social cachet, the joke would not land.

Later in the film, blonde, White co- tagonist Fred (Freddie Prinze, Jr.) is kidnapped by the demons, and whi they occupy his body they use Mock Black English like that heard in tl video: "Yo yo, the bi-atch was like '*whaaat?*' and I was like, 'Later on!' . [to Shaggy] What up, dog? [to Scooby] And uh, dog? . . . Man, we got ts like it was the lizz nizz [last night?] on Earth, you know what I'm say , G?" Unlike the young men in the training video, Fred attempts some M k Black English pronunciation and also uses a more high-pitched tone th his usual one. After his friends succeed in ousting the demon and returni Fred's soul to his body, he con- tinues faking his Mock Black English perf nance so as not to raise the other demons' suspicions: "Yo yo yo yo, home gs! Y'all forgot the next part of the dance! Where we do the electric slide ou know!" Fred's fakery is not noticeably different from his demon poss or's earnest use of Mock Black English, but when awkward, nerdy Velma inda Cardellini) is also forced to fake a possession, her performance is less atural: "Yo, yo . . . you . . . yo." Blackness and Black speech are cool, and cause Fred is already cool, he is better able to perform Blackness, while Ve a fails at it.

Charlie of *Me, Myself, and Irene* also ses stereotypical Black English slang when joking with his Black sons, a n demonstrating his own famil- iarity with Black culture to "purchase the ool" with both his sons and the audience: "That'd be wack! . . . I don't w t to have to bust a cap. . . . I'm not leaving 'til the morning, but you know e rules: no bitches after eleven." And we find a different take but the san underlying principle in 2006's *Borat: Cultural Learnings of America for lake Benefit Glorious Nation of Kazakhstan*, a partially unscripted satiri documentary starring English actor Sacha Baron Cohen as Borat, a Ka khstani visitor to the U.S. who bumbles around various environments inf ting himself upon unsuspecting people in an attempt to elicit a humorous action from them. In one scene, Borat and his driver, Azamat (Ken Davitia are driving around a city late at night, lost. When they spot a group of six ung Black men hanging out on a street corner, they decide to stop to ask f directions. Of course, the White audience is primed to think that this is a ba idea by decades of media selling the notion that dark city streets and Black men are a dangerous combination. However, the young men are friendly to Borat, humoring him when he asks them to teach him how to dress and talk like they do. We don't actually get to see these language lessons, though; instead, the film hard cuts to Borat and Azamat stopping at a high-end hotel where Borat tries out his new dialect on the staff: "What's up with it, vanilla face. Me and my homie Azamat just parked our slab outside. We're looking for somewhere to post up our Black asses for the night. So bang bang skid skid, nigger. We're just a couple of pimps, no hoes." He is immediately thrown out of the hotel.

It's not difficult to dissect the editing choices made here. The film cuts away quickly from Borat's interaction with the young men—real Black English speakers, as evidenced by their apparently unscripted dialogue—because they almost certainly didn't teach him anything close to the Mock Black English that he uses in the hotel. Cohen likely pre-prepared the script of Mock Black English so as to sound as absurd as possible and elicit the most entertaining reaction possible from the unlucky hotel staff forced to deal with him. The humor is predicated on both the hotel staff's reaction and, again, the incongruity of hearing Mock Black English spoken by a White man with a supposed Kazakh accent, and it perpetuates the idea that Black English doesn't belong in sophisticated society. The character of Borat still gains the social cachet of associating with and apparently winning over the young Black men; he simply doesn't understand that their language (or his satirical representation of their language) isn't welcome in starchy White spaces.

2003's *Bringing Down the House* includes perhaps the most blatant examples of White characters using Mock Black English to appropriate Black social capital and, at least in the world of the film, succeeding.

At the beginning of the film we're introduced to wealthy White lawyer Peter Sanderson (Steve Martin), who is corresponding online with a woman he believes to be a petite, blonde, White lawyer named Charlene (Queen Latifah). We soon learn that Charlene is actually a tall Black woman who has recently escaped from prison and is mining Peter for answers to her legal questions so that she can clear her name. She installs herself in Peter's house, blackmailing him with threats to humiliate him in front of his racist White neighbors if he doesn't help her.

Charlene speaks Black English and uses supposedly modern (for 2003) Black slang, and Peter derides her for this constantly throughout the film, telling her to go back to school and "get at least a passing familiarity with the English language." After he learns that she has educated herself extensively on the legal aspects of her case, he chides her, "You know something, you're smart. If you would just deign to speak English, with what you learned on the internet and in prison, you could be a paralegal tomorrow." He also uses Mock Black English to ridicule both her Blackness and her speech: when he learns that she's hiding from the law, he a s her derisively, "What did you do, smoke some homies on a drive-by?," a d during a conversation between Peter, Charlene, and Peter's White colleag Howie (Eugene Levy) in which Charlene cites case law relevant to her sit tion, he condescendingly insists, "You obviously have pockets of intelligen . Why do you walk and talk and act the way you do?" Charlene responds:

> CHARLENE: It ain't actin'! This is who I ar I mean you think I can't talk like you? [using "standard" pronunciation]: Oh P er, I absolutely love what you've done with the place! It's so sterile, so bland. wonderful!
>
> PETER: See, you can do it!
>
> CHARLENE: Well, you can kiss my natur Black ass because I don't need your approval!
>
> HOWIE: [sincerely] She don't need your ap oval!
>
> PETER: You don't think I compromise the y I act? You think I like walking around like an uptight honky? Yes, I know y r lingo!

The joke, of course, is that Peter do not actually know Charlene's "lingo"—at no point does she call him o anyone else a "honky." At this point in the film, Peter has not yet earned s social cachet—his mockery of Charlene's language distances him from he and, by proxy, from the coolness of Black culture.

Peter's co-worker Howie uses Mock Bl k English with a different motivation: to win Charlene's approval. He be omes enamored with her at first sight, describing her as a "cocoa godde ," and this fetishistic attraction somehow gives him a proximity to Black ess that Peter does not possess: Howie's use of Mock Black English is ac ally successful in winning over Charlene. Later in the film, he asks Peter deliver a message to Charlene: "Please tell her the cool points are out window and she's got me all twisted up in the game." We, the presumed White audience, are not meant to understand this message; we are meant on to understand that it consists of supposed Black English slang and that it's nny to hear a middle-aged White man say it. However, when Peter passes a ng Howie's words to Charlene, she is touched, responding, "Really? That the nicest thing anybody's ever said to me." Later, she goes on a date with owie where he tells her directly, "You got me straight trippin,' Boo," and s e is visibly flattered. Charlene's validation of Howie's use of Black Englis indicates that he *has* earned the proximity to Blackness that Peter, up to th point, only imagines he has. At the end of the film, we see Charlene braid g Howie's hair in a traditionally Black style, a symbolic initiation into Blac ness.

Peter has to work harder to earn his "cool points," but as he spends more time with Charlene and begins to enjoy her company, he starts to acquire the proximity to Blackness that Howie had from the beginning, and even succeeds in using Black English in a way that, while still sounding rather absurd to the audience, wins over the Black people in the film. In a scene near the end, Peter devises a plan to sneak into a night club to find Charlene's ex-boyfriend, Widow (Steve Harris), who framed Charlene for the crime of which she was convicted, intending to coerce him into a confession which Peter will covertly record. However, knowing he can't get into the club in his usual business attire, he buys a blue basketball jersey, a red long-sleeved t-shirt, baggy jeans, a beanie, a gold chain, and a boombox on a strap off of a passing young Black man. He then enters the club performing an absurd caricature of a hip Black man, affecting a high-pitched voice and Mock Black English pronunciation, grammar, and vocabulary, and rather than attempting to avoid calling attention to himself, he makes off-hand comments to nearly everyone he passes: "Say yo, what's the dealio? Mm, who's your daddy? Back that booty up and put it on the glass. Anybody here dig what I'm sayin'? . . . Say any of you homies holdin' any of that Jimmy High? 'Cause I'm all about crunchin' some a that boo fanny tonight. . . . What's up with you? You been drinkin' some of that haterade?" Initially the other club patrons regard him with suspicion, but they soon begin warming up to him, and eventually a young woman asks him if he can dance. He responds, "Do I got honky spray painted on my forehead? Course I can, I'm tryin' to peep a bowwow"—meaning that he is looking for someone—but the woman's friends coerce him into dancing with her despite his continued protests ("I can't, I got bidness"). He dances for several minutes, first with two women, then with a number of male break dancers who perform complex moves around him while Peter essentially jogs in place, swinging his arms widely and occasionally attempting a handstand. He finally manages to speak with Widow, who immediately sees through his ruse, and yet Peter is able to get Widow to confess to his crime on tape.

At the end of the film, Peter is rewarded by once again winning back the affection of his ex-wife, using Howie's line on her, "The cool points are out the window, and I'm all twisted up in the game." And despite his pathetic attempts to imitate Black English, mannerisms, and dancing, Charlene also bestows a compliment on him, claiming that he is no longer White; now he is "off-White." Of these types of minstrelsy performances, Bucholtz and Lopez note that "in flirting with black language and culture both literally and figuratively, the characters experience a temporary blackness that variously gives them insight into sex, dancing, social justice, and the importance of family."[21] Peter achieves all of these through his Mock Black English performance—Charlene coaches him to be more sexually aggressive; the night club patrons are impressed by his absurd, flailing dance moves; he agrees to help Charlene clear her name in her criminal case; and h ins back the love of his ex-wife and the admiration of his children.

This film is perhaps the most explicit in framing Blackness as cool, hip, and trendy, and Whiteness as stuffy, ight, and old-fashioned. To reiterate H. Samy Alim's point, White peopl "can't distinguish between 'the real' and 'the wack.' They just want to p chase the cool that comes with associating with Black people."[22] The pres ned White audience understands that Peter's performance is a caricature— is designed to be absurd for our entertainment—but they also believe that oximity to Blackness is a form of social capital for White people, and thi confirmed when Peter uses the "cool points" line apparently correctly an wins back his wife. "By engaging in Black linguistic practice," Peter, lik he White partygoers in *Sorry to Bother You* of which Alim writes, is "elev d from 'corny' to 'cool,'"[23] ultimately winning over not only Charlene anc is ex-wife, but also the audience. But, as Qiuana Lopez points out, Peter ma ains his White privilege because he is "able to utilize the dialect without be affected by the stigmatizations that usually go along with using it"[24]—he i ble to return to his White family, his high-income profession, and his White fe.

Perhaps the most problematic use of M k Black English in the film set doesn't fit neatly into the patterns of Mock lack English we've examined so far, but it's worth taking a close look at. It o urs in 2008's *Tropic Thunder*, in which White American actor Robert Down , Jr. plays White Australian actor Kirk Lazarus, a method actor known for i nersing himself so fully into his roles that he does not break character at a point during filming. In *Tropic Thunder*, Lazarus and several other actors re shooting a film called *Tropic Thunder*, which takes place in a Vietname jungle that is home to a heroin cartel. Lazarus has undergone a "pigmenta n procedure" to darken his skin and wears a black wig to play a Black c racter, Sergeant Lincoln Osiris, and he uses an unnaturally deep, gravell voice and Mock Black English throughout the film. Of course, in reality, is is simply Robert Downey, Jr. in blackface. Downey, Jr./Lazarus attem Black pronunciation and uses several Black English grammar features lbeit inconsistently) throughout the film, including singular *you was* ("You as fartin' in bathtubs and laughing your ass off!"), zero copula ("Actin' ke you some one-man GPS!"), and negative concord ("Ain't nobody doin nothing to no one or nobody!"), as well as references to Black cultural ste otypes ("I bet I could collard up some of them greens"). The actual Black ctor involved with the shooting of the in-universe fictional film, hip hop tar Alpa Chino, understandably bristles at this, mocking both Lazarus's B ck English performance and his Australian identity, which, in turn, provok Lazarus. At last, near the end of the production of the fictional *Tropic Thun* r, Lazarus tears off his black wig and removes his brown contact lenses to reveal his natural blonde hair and blue eyes and re-embraces his true identity and native dialect.

There is a lot to unpack here. Notably, at no point during the film does anyone other than Alpa Chino object to Lazarus's use of blackface or his Mock Black English performance. On the contrary, the introductory footage of Lazarus frames his choice to play a Black man as bold and courageous in the world of the film. This is also metacommentary on Downey, Jr.'s choice to wear blackface and perform blackvoice, a decision that White audiences might also consider courageous, and that gives him the coveted proximity to Blackness and coolness that White people crave. The Black character that Lazarus plays is a stereotype, but the film's actual Black character, Alpa Chino, is also a stereotype—and the film doesn't distinguish between Lazarus's inauthentic portrayal of supposed Blackness and Alpa Chino's apparently real portrayal of Blackness beyond Alpa's criticisms of Lazarus. And the White audience, who "can't distinguish between 'the real' and 'the wack,'"[25] is invited to laugh at both. Lopez points out that this "use of metaparody . . . functions to disavow racism even while it reproduces it."[26] Downey, Jr.'s character parodies blackface while Downey, Jr. himself actually participates in it, undermining any real critique the film might be aiming for. Lopez believes that "Alpa's reaction to Lazarus-as-Osiris informs the audience that they should disapprove of his performance as well,"[27] but I would argue that the presumed White audience is less likely to identify with the already rather parodic character of Alpa than with the other White characters who laud Lazarus's performance. Quite simply, regardless of any deconstruction of Black stereotypes that the film might be half-heartedly attempting, the White audience is invited to be comfortable with and to laugh at 90 minutes of a famous White actor in blackface.

CONSEQUENCES

Peter's early comments about Charlene's language highlight the common beliefs about Black English that persist today: that it is "bad" English, or perhaps not even English at all. In *English with an Accent*, Lippi-Green cites example after example of both White and Black listeners demonstrating their contempt for Black English, such as a male audience member on the *Oprah Winfrey Show* in 1987 who argued, "There is no such thing as Black English. The concept of Black English is a myth. It is basically speaking English and violating the correct rules of grammar."[28] In the wake of a mid-1990s controversy that drew nationwide attention when the Oakland, California, public school board attempted to define "Ebonics" as a unique language and institute policies that treated Ebonics spea rs as English language learners, commentators of every stripe spoke out ag nst the consideration of Ebonics as anything other than a failed attempt t speak EDC, including political science graduate student and second-year w student Theresa Wilson, who wrote in the *Iowa State Daily*, "I cringed in in when I first heard of Ebonics, also crudely called 'black English.' . . . I n not a linguistic anthropologist, but my heart tells me that Ebonics is not language. Ebonics is not black English. It is bad English."[29] And in 2010, hen the U.S. Drug Enforcement Agency released a call for translators in o r a hundred languages including "Ebonics," *Washington Post* columnist Jo than Capehart scoffed, "Where to begin? First, of all, it ain't even a real nguage. A dialect? Sure. But a language like Spanish, Vietnamese or Ko n, which the Atlanta office also needs help with? Seriously? Then that w ld make me and other African Americans you know bilingual. After all, can lop off words and run them together with the best of them."[30] Black E lish, far from being a "real language," is simply "lop[ping] off words an un[ning] them together."

Persistent media portrayals that confir these inaccurate beliefs in the minds of White audiences have real impa on actual Black English speakers. Lippi-Green notes, "It's important to emember that for most Anglos, the primary and sometimes sole experie e of African Americans comes through mass media, where Black men a d women in power suits sound Anglo or very close to it";[31] whereas, as w ave seen, Black people who use Black English are more likely to be portra d as comedic or in stereotypical ways. In his 1997 study "Effects of Ster typical Television Portrayals of African-Americans on Person Perception," homas E. Ford found that White viewers were more likely to rate a hypoth cal Black suspect as guilty of an assault after watching stereotypical depict ns of Black people in a comedy skit. Ford hypothesizes that humor plays a le here, because it "increases our tolerance or acceptance of discrimination gainst out-groups." Disparaging humor toward Black people creates an o ortunity for White people, who might outwardly claim to be antiracist, to ngage in a more socially acceptable form of prejudiced behavior.[32] As w have seen, in mainstream film Black English is highly likely to be portray l as inherently funny and used in comedic contexts. Ford further notes that W ite people who would not "commit overt or blatant acts of discriminatio " will, instead, "discriminate in subtle, indirect ways that can easily be rati alized as socially acceptable . . . In accordance with this argument, researc has shown that discrimination is most likely to occur when nonracial justi ations for discriminatory behavior are available."[33] A supposedly "nonr ial justification for discriminatory behavior" can certainly include a su ect's perceived refusal to speak "good" or "correct" English. Indeed, A a Henderson found that Black English speakers were rated lower than "st dard" English speakers and even disfluent French-accented English speakers by hiring managers in metrics such as intelligence and which jobs they were qualified for,[34] demonstrating that linguistic discrimination is real and has tangible effects on people's lives. In their 2004 study "Reactions to African-American Vernacular English: Do More Phonological Features Matter?," Rodriguez, Cargile, and Rich demonstrated that listeners can distinguish between strong and moderate "AAVE accents" and tend to rate Black English speakers with "strong accents," i.e., more Black English phonological features, as less intelligent, less educated, lower class, less friendly, and less likable than those with fewer or no Black English phonological features.[35] The pervasive belief, reinforced as we have seen by Hollywood, that Black English is inherently funny or ignorant keeps Black English speakers out of serious, professional public spaces in real life. We will explore these consequences further in each of the following chapters.

In the meantime, readers might wonder why Black people do not simply learn and speak EDC in order to avoid such linguistic discrimination, but the point here is that they should not have to. Black English is not an inferior version of English; it is a complex, rule-governed dialect like EDC or any other variety of English spoken around the world. To insist that its speakers abandon it and adopt EDC so as better to assimilate in a White world is to insist that they abandon some part of their identity and to make it clear that White ways of speaking and being in the world are still widely considered more appropriate, more mainstream, more cultured than Black ways of speaking and being. As Lippi-Green writes, "The real trouble with Black English is not the verbal aspect system which distinguishes it from other varieties of U.S. English, or the rhetorical strategies which draw such a vivid contrast, it is simply this: AAVE is tangible and irrefutable evidence that there is a distinct, healthy, functioning African American culture which is not white, and which does not want to be white."[36] To demand EDC is to force Whiteness on them, and in the twenty-first century it is time to overcome such cultural bigotry.

NOTES

1. Linda Saad, "Gallup Vault: Black Americans' Preferred Racial Label," Gallup, July 13, 2020, https://news.gallup.com/vault/315566/gallup-vault-black-americans-preferred-racial-label.aspx.

2. *The American Heritage Dictionary*, online ed., s.v. "vernacular," 2021, https://ahdictionary.com/word/search.html?q=vernacular.

3. Sharese King, "From African American Vernacular English to African American Language: Rethinking the Study of Race and Language in African Americans' Speech," *Annual Review of Linguistics* 6 (2020): 286–87, https://doi.org/10.1146/annurev-linguistics-011619-030556.

4. Rosina Lippi-Green, *English with an Acc* *Language, Ideology and Discrimination in the United States* (New York: Routle , 2012), 327.

5. The characters contained between the f vard slashes come from the International Phonetic Alphabet, an alphabet use y linguists worldwide to create a one-to-one correspondence between language nds and their symbols.

6. Due to the sheer quantity of data produce om the analysis of the 493-film set, it isn't possible to list every marginalized spea in every film in this book. A comprehensive collection of the data can be found www.lindseyclouse.com.

7. Lippi-Green, *English with an Accent*, 190

8. Dana Branham, "SMU Stands By Sur Asking 'Why Are Black People So Loud?'," *The Dallas Morning News*, last dified May 18, 2018, https://www .nbcdfw.com/news/local/smu-stands-by-sur -asking-why-are-black-people-so -loud/237077/.

9. Lindsey Clouse, "Django Unbleached: Th anguages of Power and Authenticity in Mainstream Film," *Journal of Popular* *m and Television* 47, no. 4 (2019): 207, https://doi.org/10.1080/01956051.2018.15 415.

10. John Paul Wilson, Kurt Hugenberg, an Nicholas O. Rule, "Racial Bias in Judgments of Physical Size and Formidabilit From Size to Threat," *Journal of Personality and Social Psychology* 113, no. 1 017): 59, http://dx.doi.org/10.1037 /pspi0000092.

11. Zachary Crockett, "'Gang Member' and hug' Roles in Film are Disproportionately Played by Black Actors," *Vox*, Septe er 13, 2016, https://www.vox.com /2016/9/13/12889478/black-actors-typecasting.

12. "Decades of Disparity: Drug Arrests an ace in the United States," Human Rights Watch, March 2, 2009, https://ww rw.org/report/2009/03/02/decades -disparity/drug-arrests-and-race-united-states.

13. Stacy L. Smith, Marc Choueiti, and Kath ne Pierper, *Inclusion or Invisibility? Comprehensive Annenberg Report on Diversit* *Entertainment*. Institute for Diversity and Empowerment at Annenberg (IDEA) (C Annenberg School for Journalism and Communication, 2016), 7–9.

14. This line *looks* like a use of habitual *be*, o of the most iconic features of Black English grammar (and also one of the most sunderstood by non-Black English speakers), but it is actually a misuse. Habitua *e*, as its name indicates, is used to describe *habitual* actions, not one-time events. example, *He be late* does not mean *He is late* but rather *He is regularly late*. It's asonable to assume that the (likely White) screenwriters went out of their way to aracterize this woman as especially sassy and Black through her speech by using at they considered an iconic Black English feature, without understanding the feat 's true meaning.

15. The stereotype of Black people being n e talkative in movie theaters is, of course, well worn, but in this case only Brenda who has already been established as a loud and obnoxious character—is the culprit hich is why I consider her a Sassy Black Woman.

16. Smith, Choueiti, and Pierper, *Inclusion* *nvisibility?*, 11.

17. Paisley Gilmour, "Captain Marvel's Directors on Carol Danvers' Sexuality," *Cosmopolitan*, May 23, 2019, https://www.cosmopolitan.com/uk/love-sex/relationships/a27566789/captain-marvel-queer-sexuality/.

18. Jane H. Hill, "Language, Race, and White Public Space," *American Anthropologist* 100, no. 3 (1998): 680, http://www.jstor.org/stable/682046.

19. Qiuana Lopez, "Imitation or Influence: White Actors and Black Language in Film," *Proceedings of the Seventeenth Annual Symposium About Language and Society*, Austin, April 10–11, 2009, 111, https://www.academia.edu/1385768/Imitation_or_Influence_White_actors_and_Black_language_in_film.

20. H. Samy Alim, "Sorry to Bother You: Deepening the Political Project of Raciolinguistics," in *Raciolinguistics: How Language Shapes Our Ideas About Race*, eds. H. Samy Alim, John R. Rickford, and Arnetha F. Ball (New York: Oxford University Press, 2020), 353.

21. Mary Bucholtz and Qiuana Lopez, "Performing Blackness, Forming Whiteness: Linguistic Minstrelsy in Hollywood Film," *Journal of Sociolinguistics* 15, no. 5 (2011): 699, https://doi.org/10.1111/j.1467-9841.2011.00513.x.

22. Alim, "Sorry to Bother You," 353.

23. Alim, "Sorry to Bother You," 353.

24. Lopez, "Imitation or Influence," 113.

25. Alim, "Sorry to Bother You," 353.

26. Qiuana Lopez, "Minstrelsy Speaking: Metaparodic Representations of Blackface and Linguistic Minstrelsy in Hollywood Films," *Discourse, Context, and Media* 23 (2018): 19, https://doi.org/10.1016/j.dcm.2017.09.011.

27. Lopez, "Minstrelsy Speaking," 20.

28. Lippi-Green, *English with an Accent*, 199–200.

29. Theresa Wilson, "Ebonics is Actually Just Bad English," *Iowa State Daily*, January 16, 1997, https://www.iowastatedaily.com/ebonics-is-actually-just-bad-english/article_2486872c-0b88-5d6a-8c0c-e63b963b8639.html.

30. Jonathan Capehart, "DEA: the E is for 'Ebonics,'" *The Washington Post*, August 24, 2010, http://voices.washingtonpost.com/postpartisan/2010/08/dea_the_e_is_for_ebonics.html.

31. Lippi-Green, *English with an Accent*, 189–90.

32. Thomas E. Ford, "Effects of Stereotypical Television Portrayals of African-Americans on Person Perception," *Social Psychology Quarterly* 60, no. 3 (1997): 272.

33. Ford, "Effects of Stereotypical Television Portrayals," 272.

34. Anita Henderson, "Is Your Money Where Your Mouth Is?: Hiring Managers' Attitudes Toward African-American Vernacular English," PhD dissertation, University of Pennsylvania (2015), 235–6.

35. Jose I. Rodriguez, Aaron Castelan Cargile, and Marc D. Rich, "Reactions to African-American Vernacular English: Do More Phonological Features Matter?," *The Western Journal of Black Studies* 28, no. 3 (2004): 410–11, https://www.researchgate.net/publication/281526521_Reactions_to_African-American_Vernacular_English_Do_More_Phonological_Features_Matter.

36. Lippi-Green, *English with an Accent*, 209.

Chapter 3

"You Ain't from around Here, Are You?"

White Southern U.S. English

Four Christmases is a 2008 film featuring a dating couple, Brad (Vince Vaughn) and Kate (Reese Witherspoon), who spend a holiday visiting each of their divorced parents in turn. Through the first three visits, the parents' and extended families' behavior grows progressively more chaotic and embarrassing, straining Brad and Kate's relationship until, by the end of the day, they've decided to break up. However, after both Brad and Kate have introspective conversations with their fathers, they realize they want to stay together and raise a family. And this frivolous, 90-minute comedy perfectly encapsulates Hollywood's antagonistic relationship toward White speakers of Southern U.S. English.

The day begins with a visit to Brad's father Howard's (Robert Duvall) house, where they are joined by Brad's two brothers, Denver (Jon Favreau) and Dallas (Tim McGraw), as well as Denver's wife Susan (Katy Mixon) and an assortment of children. Brad's father is hostile and belligerent toward Brad: when Brad gifts him with a satellite dish and offers to pay the monthly bill, Howard exclaims, "Just because I drive a combine for a living doesn't mean I need me a fancy pants lawyer son payin' my bills for me." He laughs as Denver, Dallas, and Dallas's sons take turns violently assaulting Brad, and he refers to Brad's mother as "a common street whore." He also speaks with what most Americans would call a Southern accent, as do Susan and Dallas. Susan, who is visibly pregnant and has a nine-month-old daughter, wears a very low-cut top with a generous amount of exposed cleavage; we watch her make a dish with Spam, mayonnaise, and Doritos while she confides in Kate the rigors of childrearing.

The next visit is to the home of Kate's mother, Marilyn (Mary Steenburgen), where she, her other daughter Courtney (Kristin Chenoweth), and other female relatives including Kate's elderly grandmother (Jeanette Miller) flirt openly with Brad. Courtney in particular is depicted as promiscuous and trashy; she wears a very low-cut top, admits to having sex with an entire water polo team and smoking while pregnant, and bullies Kate. Both she and Marilyn have Southern accents.

The third visit is to Brad's mother, Paula (Sissy Spacek), who also talks openly about sex, and we learn that she's dating a much younger man, namely Brad's childhood best friend, Darryl (Patrick Van Horn). Darryl patronizes Brad, treating him like a child and offering to give him gas money for the drive; during a game of Taboo, they discuss a number of details about their sex life, making Brad quite uncomfortable. Paula, too, has a Southern accent.

Kate's final visit of the day, which she makes alone after a falling out with Brad, is to her father, Creighton (Jon Voight). Creighton is dating a woman his own age; the two of them are dressed conservatively and the visit is calm and pleasant. He empathizes with Kate, expressing understanding for why she and Brad wanted to avoid their families during the holiday, and his wisdom enables Kate to realize that she does, indeed, want to stay with Brad. Unlike the other family members, Creighton does *not* have a Southern accent. Brad, on the other hand, has returned to his father's house to apologize for his earlier behavior, and when Howard praises Brad for breaking up with Kate, Brad realizes he does not want to emulate his father, and he leaves to seek out Kate and make amends.

Four Christmases takes place in San Francisco and all four families live within driving distance of each other. Both Brad and Kate speak EDC and there's no mention of their families having relocated from other regions. In other words, there is no in-movie explanation for the Southern accents. However, through these four vignettes, *Four Christmases* makes an unambiguous statement about Southern versus non-Southern speakers: Southern-speaking women are promiscuous, inappropriately open about sex, and dress too provocatively; Southern-speaking men are violent, rude, and misogynistic. EDC speakers, conversely, are sympathetic and intelligent and understand the boundaries of social decorum and appropriate behavior. This film illustrates a pattern of Othering of Southern speakers that appears repeatedly throughout our film set, but before we explore it further, let's first examine our criteria for defining White Southern speakers.

WHAT IS A "SOUTHERN ACCENT"?

Like Black English, Southern U.S. "accents" are not a single language category but a broad collection of dialects with a range of phonological, grammatical, and lexical features, in this case united by geography. Several phonological features are shared by most Southern speakers and constitute the most recognizable characteristics of Southern dialects: 1) monophthongization of /aɪ/ sounds, such that *I* is pronounced "ah" /a/, similar to the *a* sound in *father*, but articulated in the center rather than the rear of the palate; 2) the "pin/pen merger," in which short *e* /ɛ/ sounds are conflated with short *i* /ɪ/ sounds before nasal consonants, as in the words *pin* and *pen*; and 3) what William Labov refers to as the "Southern Shift" in his 1994 book *The Principles of Linguistic Change.*[1] This term describes a series of shifts in vowel articulation in the mouth and pharynx; for instance, the diphthong /ei/ as in *made* and the vowel /i/ as in *feel* are pronounced in the rear of the mouth and lower in the pharynx of a Southern speaker, while the vowel /ɜ/ as in *head* is diphthongized, starting further forward in the mouth and ending low in the pharynx, *hay-ud* /heəd/. These shifts become more pronounced and apparent as one travels further south in the continental U.S.[2]

Because Southern U.S. English, like all living languages, is highly variable and constantly changing, it's impossible to draw a perfect and distinct boundary delineating it geographically from other forms of American English; however, by tracing patterns of vowel shifts as well as other linguistic features across the country, William Labov, Sharon Ash, and Charles Boberg of the Linguistics Laboratory at the University of Pennsylvania created an approximate "National Map of the Regional Dialects of American English." The region they categorize as "The South" encompasses Alabama, Arkansas, Florida, Georgia, Louisiana, Mississippi, North and South Carolina, Tennessee, Virginia, nearly all of Kentucky, and most of Texas and West Virginia.[3] Thus references below to populations and percentages in "The South" will consider that region to comprise those thirteen states.

In film, individual actors—particularly those who are attempting to reproduce a dialect which is not native to them—vary considerably in their consistency of pronunciation; however, those who monophthongize /aɪ/ also tend to use Southern Shift with a high degree of correlation, while the pin/pen merger appears inconsistently among these speakers. For the purpose of our analysis, then, any character who unambiguously monophthongizes /aɪ/ and uses Southern shift in the majority of their lines shall be categorized as a Southern speaker regardless of the character's actual place of origin. (Indeed, many characters who were raised in or live in the Southern U.S. do not use Southern features in their speech, and many characters with ambiguous origins or who expressly do *not* come from the Southern U.S. do use Southern features.) Grammar and lexicon also vary widely among both real Southern speakers and Southern-speaking film characters, and these shall be explored later in this chapter. Additionally, in this chapter we'll be examining only White Southern speakers; although in reality there's a great deal of overlap of the features of many Black English dialects and White Southern U.S. dialects (particularly blue collar dialects), in film, White Southern speakers and Black English speakers (Southern and otherwise) are characterized quite differently, and as we have already examined the latter in Chapter 2, this chapter will be devoted to the former.

WHITE SOUTHERN U.S. SPEAKERS IN THE FILM SET

At least 644 White Southern speakers appear in 164 films, including 26 protagonists (representing about 3.3% of total protagonists) in 24 films. These protagonists comprise seven women and [illegible] men, meaning their gender balance is close to that of protagonists in the film set broadly (182 of roughly 777 total protagonists are women). Of the remaining characters catalogued, 306 are secondary characters and 312 are minor or background characters. While not all depictions of Southern speakers are as negative as those in *Four Christmases*, a number of stereotypes and other sharply drawn patterns do appear in the film set.

First, Southern speakers are highly likely to be depicted as openly racist, bigoted, unintelligent, backward, and/or as stereotypical "rednecks." Specifically, 75 characters display openly racist or homophobic behavior—about 11.6%—and 52 characters are portrayed as stereotypically stupid, backward, or redneck—about 8.1%. Accounting for overlap between the two categories, they combine to make up [illegible]6 characters, 18% of total White Southern speakers. In fact, in 12 films, these characters are the *only* representations of Southern speakers.

Period pieces that take place in or around the civil rights movement or antebellum South are, predictably, a rich source of examples of openly racist or bigoted characters, including *Remember the Titans* (2000), *The Help* (2011), *Django Unchained* (2012), and *Lee Daniels' The Butler* (2013). But racist White Southern speakers show up in the modern era too, as in *The Blind Side* (2009), in which two genteel Southern-speaking White ladies (Rhoda Griffis and Ashley LeConte Campbell) express concern that the main character, Leigh Anne Tuohy (Sandra Bullock), has brought a Black teenage boy (Quinton Aaron) home to live in her house when she has a teenage daughter under the same roof. Both *Bad Boys II* (2003) and *Kingsman: The Secret Service* (2014) feature minor characters engaged in even more openly bigoted behavior: in *Bad Boys II*, two Southern-speaking Ku Klux Klan members are arrested by the protagonists during a raid, and in *Kingsman*, the only Southern speakers are the parishioners and a preacher (Corey Johnson) who raves about Jews, "nigger[s], and whore[s]" at a "hate group," South Glade Mission Church in Kentucky.

Avatar (2009), on the other hand, is a science fiction film that takes place in the future on the planet Pandora, whose indigenous species, the Na'vi, is an obvious allegory for indigenous Americans. Southern speaker Colonel Miles Quaritch (Stephen Lang) refers to them as "savages," "roaches," and "dumb bastards." Even in the future, it seems, White Southern speakers can't escape their racist stereotypes.

Note that characters who display bigotry but later express remorse and show a change in behavior are not counted in the numbers above; for example, several White players in *Remember the Titans* are initially hostile to their Black teammates, but after practicing and playing together for some time, their racist behavior changes.

Note also that not all racist characters are framed as antagonists; some are sympathetic and their racism is played for comedy. For instance, *Anchorman 2: The Legend Continues* (2013) features Champ Kind (David Koechner), a major secondary character and part of the protagonist's television news team, who, prior to the events of the film, was fired from a job for making disparaging comments about Filipinos. At the start of the film he runs a restaurant that doesn't admit Catholics or Jews, and he believes that "the census is a way for the UN to make your children gay." *Identity Thief* (2013) similarly includes a secondary character named Big Chuck (Eric Stonestreet), a large, lonely man whom co-protagonist Diana (Melissa McCarthy) meets and seduces in a bar, then returns with to her motel room for an extended scene of kinky sex. We later learn that he's a Realtor who refuses to sell to "homosexuals," "foreigners," and "Blacks." White audiences might outwardly condemn this bigoted behavior, but the filmmakers are counting on the fact that it won't prevent them from rooting for these sympathetic characters.

In addition to the many examples of open racism and bigotry displayed by Southern speakers, we also see a number of Southern-speaking characters who are depicted as unintelligent, easily fooled, or backward. These are nearly always comedic. For instance, in *Monsters, Inc.* (2001), the monsters under our beds inhabit their own universe and believe human children to be deadly toxic. After Boo (Mary Gibbs), a tiny, sweet-faced human toddler, makes her way into the monster universe, chaos breaks out when she is spotted running loose in an upscale monster restaurant, and the residents of the monster world panic. After the incident, a television news broadcast features two Southern-speaking monsters who describe the event in hyperbolic terms evocative of alien abduction stories: "Well, a kid flew right over me and blasted a car with its laser vision," and "I tried to run from it but it picked me up with its mind powers and shook me like a dog!" These characters aren't human and these events take place in a parallel universe, not the United States, yet the filmmakers still chose to represent these creatures as Southern so as to emphasize their stupidity. *Talladega Nights: The Ballad of Ricky Bobby* (2006) stars Will Ferrell as North Carolinian NASCAR driver Ricky Bobby and John C. Reilly as his best friend and competitor, Cal Naughton, Jr., and most of the comedic scenes are built around the idea that Ricky Bobby, Cal, and their friends are quite dumb. For example, after a crash, Ricky Bobby, believing he is on fire (he is not), tears off his clothing and runs around the track in his underwear screaming, "Help me, Jesus! Help me, Jewish God! Help me, Allah! Help me, Tom Cruise!"

An interesting stereotype that we do *not* find among White Southern speakers—particularly compared to their representation alongside Black English and Spanish-influenced English speakers—is that of drug use. While 4.9% of Black English speakers and 10.4% of Spanish and Spanish-influenced English speakers are shown using or dealing drugs, only *two* Southern speakers are shown doing so—*Talladega Nights*' Reese Bobby (Gary Cole) and *Inglourious Basterds*' (2009) Aldo Raine (Brad Pitt). This is despite the fact that numerous studies show that White Americans use illicit drugs at the same rate as or more than Black and Latinx people.[4] Instead, Southern speakers are more likely to be characterized as drunkards, such as Johnny Cash (Joaquin Phoenix) in 2005's *Walk the Line*, Rooster Cogburn (Jeff Bridges) in 2010's *True Grit*, Jackson Maine (Bradley Cooper) in 2018's *A Star is Born*, and Rick Dalton (Leonardo DiCaprio) in 2019's *Once Upon a Time in . . . Hollywood.* This is likely due to the stereotypical association of Southerners with bootleg liquor (Basterd Aldo Raine even mentions off-hand that his family were bootleggers) and the "redneck" association with beer guzzling discussed in the next section. Even so, Southern speakers are depicted drunk only a handful of times in the film set, far less often than Black English speakers or Spanish-influenced English speakers are depicted using or selling drugs.

STIGMATIZED GRAMMAR

Southern Shift is the most iconic Southern linguistic feature, but "nonstandard" grammar also characterizes many Southern dialects both in reality and in film. Most of the White Southern speakers in the dataset—470 out of 644—exclusively use the grammar of the dominant culture. However, a sizeable number—174, or 27%—use one or more stigmatized grammar features. The most common stigmatized features that appear in the film set's dialogue are shown in Table 3.1.

Readers may notice that stigmatized Southern grammar features overlap *completely* with stigmatized Black English features (though they're used at different rates by the two groups). This is not surprising, since the two dialect groups share a long history—enslaved Africans forcibly brought to the U.S.

Table 3.1. Stigmatized Grammar Features Used by Southern Speakers

Feature	*Number of Users*	*Sample User*	*Film*	*Usage*
ain't	108	Rick Dalton (Leonardo DiCaprio)	*Once Upon a Time in . . . Hollywood* (2019)	"If comin' face to face with the failure that is your career ain't worth cryin' about, I don't know what is."
negative concord	50	Celia Rae Foote (Jessica Chastain)	*The Help* (2011)	"I know you didn't fall in no tub, Minny."
adjectival *them*	35	Yondu (Michael Rooker)	*Guardians of the Galaxy Vol. 2* (2017)	"We'll take them batteries."
plural *is* and/or *was*	24	Johnny Cash (Joaquin Phoenix)	*Walk the Line* (2005)	"We was at the fair."
singular third person *don't*	22	Mrs. Jolly (Elizabeth Marvel)	*Lincoln* (2012)	"Mr. Jolly's emphysema don't care for cigars."
zero copula	21	Calvin Candie (Leonard DiCaprio)	*Django Unchained* (2012)	"You in trouble now, son."
personal datives	15	Captain Knauer (William Fichtner)	*The Longest Yard* (2005)	"We got us a fine little football team."
simple past tense *done*	13	Sarge (R. Lee Ermey)	*Toy Story 3* (2010)	"We done our duty."
emphatic *done*	11	Sandy (Carolyn Lawrence)	*The SpongeBob Movie: Sponge Out of Water* (2015)	"I done figured it out!"
simple past tense *seen*	10	Maggie Fitzgerald (Hilary Swank)	*Million Dollar Baby* (2004)	"I seen the world."

Source: Lindsey Clouse

learned English first from blue collar White overseers (not wealthy plantation owners), who themselves spoke stigmatized dialects descended from "nonstandard" English, Irish, and Scottish dialects and languages, including Scots, Irish, Cornish, and Manx.

Note also that although *ain't* was not counted among the stigmatized features of Black English, it is being considered here because it is by far the most common "nonstandard" feature used by Southern speakers. In fact, *40* Southern speakers use *ain't* alone among stigmatized features, whereas only three Black English speakers do so. Thu we can consider *ain't* to be an iconic part of stigmatized Southern speech ut not of Black English.

When we compare the Southern-speaki characters who use stigmatized grammar against those who don't, a clear ttern emerges: the *vast* majority of characters who use it are explicitly depic d as rural, blue collar, poor, ignorant, backward, bigoted, or some combinat n. These are the ignorant, goofy NASCAR drivers of *Talladega Nights* and eir friends; the Confederate soldiers of the rural mountain town of *Cold ountain* (2003); the residents of the tiny towns of Pigeon Creek in *Sweet H e Alabama* (2002) and Radiator Springs in the *Cars* franchise; the poor, all-town protagonist of *Million Dollar Baby* (2004) and her lazy, greedy f ily; the rough, rural Westerners of *True Grit* (2010) and *Rango* (2011); and e numerous slave owners, overseers, and other antebellum White racists *Django Unchained* (2012).

Not all of these portrayals are strictly n ative—there are likeable people in Pigeon Creek, Cold Mountain, and Ra itor Springs—but the persistent association of "nonstandard" grammar wit overty, ignorance, and a lack of sophistication sends a clear message, a v similar message to the one we saw in Chapter 2: smart, serious, worldly, althy, and successful people use "standard" grammar.

The Southern Redneck

One of the ugliest and most harmful stere pes that we see associated with "nonstandard" Southern speech is that of th edneck. The *American Heritage Dictionary* online classifies *redneck* as ffensive slang" and defines it broadly: "Used as a disparaging term for a mber of the white rural laboring class, especially in the southern United S es"; the secondary definition is "A person regarded as having a provincia conservative, often bigoted attitude."[5] In "A Short History of Redneck: Th Fashioning of a Southern White Masculine Identity," author Patrick Huber rees, noting that

> For approximately the last one hundred yea the pejorative term *redneck* has chiefly slurred a rural, poor white man of th American South and particularly one who holds conservative, racist, or reacti ry views.[6] . . . Today the redneck is generally depicted in novels, films, and t vision shows as a greasy-haired, tobacco-chewing, poor southern white man th a sixth-grade education and a beer gut. He lives in a double-wide trailer w his homely, obese wife—who is probably also a first cousin—and their broo of grubby, sallow-faced children and a couple of scrawny coon dogs. . . . He oys guzzling six-packs, listening to country music, and hanging out with his uddies in pool halls and honky-tonks, that is, when he's not fishing, poachin leer, cruising in his pickup truck, going to stock car races, beating his wife, attending Klan rallies. And, of course, the redneck supposedly hates black Jews, hippies, union organizers,

> aristocratic southern whites, Yankees, and, for good measure, "foreigners" in general.[7]

In other words, the stereotype of the redneck appears at the intersection of race (White), class (poor), gender (male), geography (the rural South), and beliefs (small-minded, conservative, and racist), and in media we recognize him by the tropes that surround his appearance and behavior. Other characteristics that Huber notes are associated with rednecks are "drunkenness and sexual excess—often including bestiality, incest, and other aberrant sexual practices."[8]

The most villainous residents of Cold Mountain are rednecks—the evil Teague (Ray Winstone) and his posse, who hunt and torture Civil War "deserters" for sport. Another character in the film, Junior (Giovanni Ribisi), lives in a remote cabin with his wife and her two sisters, who encourage two male visitors to get blackout drunk on their moonshine, then have sex with them in full view of their many children (aberrant sexual practices indeed). A host of overseers, slave catchers, and other poor Whites in *Django Unchained* and *Lee Daniels' The Butler* (2013) also meet Huber's definition. Johnny Cash's abusive father (Robert Patrick) is a redneck in *Walk the Line*, and Maggie's mother (Margo Martindale) in *Million Dollar Baby* is a redneck wife—"homely, obese," and living in a cramped, cluttered trailer with a "brood" of children and grandchildren. When Maggie (Hilary Swank) gifts her with a house, she complains that now the state will take away her welfare. All of these characters use stigmatized grammar features in addition to their Southern shift.

Another example of the redneck stereotype in film bears closer examination and discussion: the character of Mater (Larry the Cable Guy), who appears in three films in our set, *Cars* (2006), *Cars 2* (2011), and *Cars 3* (2017). These animated films feature anthropomorphic cars in a universe apparently devoid of humans and revolve primarily around the exploits of famous racecar Lightning McQueen (Owen Wilson). Mater (short for Tow Mater) appears early in the first film and quickly befriends McQueen. In the rather convoluted plot of the second film, Mater is a co-protagonist who becomes embroiled in the exploits of an international spy organization, but in the final film he returns to his former role as McQueen's sidekick.

Mater is a tow truck completely covered in rust; he sports large, mismatched buck teeth and uses a strongly Southern-shifted blue collar dialect. He's also unintelligent and ignorant of other cultures: in their first scene together, McQueen has been arrested for damaging the roads in Mater's small hometown, Radiator Springs, and easily tricks Mater into setting him free (until the sheriff intervenes). In *Cars 2*, Mater arrives to watch kabuki theater in Japan in stereotypical kabuki makeup and carrying a parasol, greeting

McQueen in Mock Japanese: "Domo arig o." At a sumo match, he sports both a black topknot and a four-tiered bee elmet (containing oil rather than beer), and at the first round of McQueen's ajor international race, he causes a scene when he mistakes wasabi for pista o ice cream. Although a modern children's film is unlikely to depict open cism on screen, we might interpret this cultural ignorance—a major plot oint that causes a temporary rift between Mater and the more worldly Mc en—as its proxy.

As noted above, working class roots a also central to the redneck stereotype, and Mater's creators interpret t quite literally: he is an actual tow truck who does the work of a tow tru driver, rescuing other cars who have become stranded in and around Radi r Springs. His voice actor, Larry the Cable Guy (born Daniel Lawrence W ney), is a Nebraska native who became known for his work with the Blu Collar Comedy Tour[9] helmed by Jeff Foxworthy who is, himself, best know for his redneck-themed jokes.

Significantly, Mater also uses quite a l of stigmatized (a.k.a. "nonstandard") grammar, even relative to other re eck characters. Across his three films, we see multiple uses of the followi features found in Southern and other marginalized American dialects:

- ain't ("I ain't perfect.")
- plural *is* and *was* ("Tractors is so dumb.
- negative concord ("Don't tell nobody.")
- emphatic *done* ("This here fancy new r d that Lightning McQueen done just made.")
- simple past tense *done* ("That jet lag re done a number on you.")
- adjectival *them* ("Mind if I borrow a fe bucks for one of them drinks?")
- nominative *them* ("Them's all original p ts.")
- simple past tense *seen* ("I seen these tw fellers.")
- zero copula ("You leakin' oil again.")
- personal datives ("I got me a date tomo w.")
- simple past tense *run* ("Like them Gren ns and Pacers we run into at the party and the race and the airport.")
- regularized past tense forms ("he know " "guns drawed")

He also uses at least one form that appe s to be simply wrong—i.e., not standard in any real Southern dialect—a m dal verb paired with an irregular simple past tense: "I use to crash into her t so I could spoke to her."

Elaine Wonhee Chun argues in "List ing to The Southern Redneck: Pathways Of Contextualization On YouTu " that there is a linguistic component to the redneck stereotype, and in h analysis of over 500 user comments on a *YouTube* video featuring sev l South Carolinians discussing racism in the South, she demonstrates that significant number of comments that disparage the interviewees as racist also call attention to their pronunciation and grammar via exaggerated orthography and eye dialect. She draws a direct line between the commenters' perceptions of the Southerners' racist beliefs and their perceptions of the Southerners' language, which "was heard by many as naturalized icons (Irvine and Gal 2000) of the stereotypical backwardness of the redneck's intellect and morality."[10] Irvine and Gal argued that "[l]inguistic features that index social groups or activities appear to be iconic representations of them, as if a linguistic feature somehow depicted or displayed a social group's inherent nature or essence";[11] in other words, if we associate Southern linguistic features with Southern people, and we associate racism, ignorance, or lack of education with Southern people, then Southern linguistic features also become associated with those characteristics in listeners' minds.

Does "Bad" Grammar Make You a Bad Person?

As we saw above, Southern-speaking film characters are likely to be portrayed as having stereotypical characteristics such as racism, bigotry, lack of intelligence, or as being a redneck—nearly a fifth of Southern speakers fall into one or more of these categories. However, both Huber and Chun also point to "*moral* [emphasis added] and linguistic backwardness" as stereotypical redneck qualities,[12] and our data indeed show that the 174 Southern-speaking characters who use stigmatized grammar are more likely to be framed by their films as morally corrupt even *apart* from racism or other regressive beliefs.

Among the 470 Southern speakers who do *not* use stigmatized grammar, 67 are framed by their films as unambiguously immoral, about 14.3%. To be categorized as "unambiguously immoral," characters must not simply be rude or confrontational, but must engage in serious unethical behaviors, such as murder, rape, theft, adultery, fraud, etc. This does not include characters who are redeemed, show remorse, and change their behavior throughout the course of the story; it also doesn't include characters whom the audience might view as immoral but who are not framed this way by the film, such as *Anchorman 2*'s Champ Kind. Among the 174 Southern-speaking characters who do use stigmatized grammar, 43 are framed as immoral, about 24.7%, meaning stigmatized grammar users are 1.7 times more likely to be characterized as immoral than "standard" grammar users. Presented another way, 39.6% of immoral characters use stigmatized grammar, while only 24.4% of moral and neutral characters use stigmatized grammar.

Those characters categorized as immoral include some overlap with characters categorized as openly racist, but most of the 43 do *not* display racist or homophobic behavior; in fact, users of stigmatized grammar are only slightly more likely to be depicted as openly bigoted than nonusers: 13.2%

versus 11.1%. Rather, their immorality is separate and apart from the racist Southern or redneck stereotype. This may indicate that in addition to the *specific* types of "moral backwardness" that Chun and Huber identify within the redneck stereotype (bigotry, domestic violence, drunkenness, incest, etc.), Southern users of stigmatized grammar are simply more likely to be viewed as *bad people*.

Protagonists

As noted, characters who use stigmatized grammar are a minority among Southern speakers; however, 15 out of 26 protagonists use stigmatized grammar—58%. Let's examine two possible explanations for this discrepancy.

The simplest explanation is that protagonists have more lines and more screen time than other characters, which presents more opportunity to use a "nonstandard" feature. Secondary characters also use stigmatized grammar at a significantly higher rate than minor and background characters, indicating that more lines and screen time lead to more stigmatized usages.

An additional explanation is the manner in which Southern speakers are characterized. Among those who use stigmatized grammar, their Southern, rural, and/or blue collar roots are usually central to their identities, whereas this is rarely the case among those who use strictly the dominant culture's grammar. In fact, some Southern-speaking protagonists who use only "standard" grammar are never explicitly identified as being from the South—they simply happen to be played by Southern actors—such as Ben (Matthew McConaughey) in *How to Lose a Guy in 10 Days* (2003) and Helen Parr/Elastigirl (Holly Hunter) in *The Incredibles* (2004) and *The Incredibles 2* (2018). In other instances, the "standard" grammar-using protagonists' Southern heritage is incidental to, rather than central to, their characterization; examples include Clarice Starling (Julianne Moore) in *Hannibal* (2001), John Nash (Russell Crowe) in *A Beautiful Mind* (2001), Johnny Blaze (Nicolas Cage) in *Ghost Rider* (2007), and Benoit Blanc (Daniel Craig) in *Knives Out* (2019). And in one instance, the protagonist is expressly *not* from the South: Jackson Maine (Bradley Cooper) of *A Star Is Born* (2018) grew up in Arizona; his Southern shift (which he uses inconsistently throughout the film) appears to be an affectation that he assumed to aid his musical career.

Conversely, protagonists who use stigmatized grammar are usually characterized as explicitly Southern and closely connected to their rural Southern roots. *Walk the Line* features extended sequences of Johnny Cash's (Joaquin Phoenix) childhood in rural Arkansas; similarly, *Pearl Harbor* (2001) shows several scenes of the protagonists', Danny (Josh Hartnett) and Rafe (Ben Affleck), childhood on a rural Southern farm, and *Talladega Nights* begins with Ricky Bobby's birth and several scenes from his childhood in North

Carolina. *American Sniper* (2014) likewise begins with scenes from Chris Kyle's (Bradley Cooper) Texas childhood. *The Aviator* (2004) begins with a brief but significant scene of Howard Hughes' (Leonardo DiCaprio) childhood in Texas, which is implied to be the root of the obsessive compulsive behaviors that plague him as an adult, and *The Curious Case of Benjamin Button* (2008) follows the protagonist (Brad Pitt) through his entire life, which begins and ends in New Orleans. Aldo Raine of *Inglourious Basterds* mentions his ties to the Smoky Mountains several times, and the plot of *Sweet Home Alabama* revolves around Melanie's (Reese Witherspoon) return to her small Southern hometown where she reconnects with family, friends, and her estranged husband and rediscovers her Southern roots. Note that *all* of these characters are explicitly depicted as having grown up poor or blue collar—as the redneck stereotype is inextricable from its roots in classism, so too is the depiction of the "nonstandard" Southern speaker.

Exceptions to this pattern are Hawk Hawkins (Tommy Lee Jones) of *Space Cowboys* (2000), Cooper (Matthew McConaughey) of *Interstellar* (2014), and Rick Dalton (Leonardo DiCaprio) of *Once Upon a Time in . . . Hollywood* (2019). These characters each use Southern shift and multiple stigmatized grammatical features, but, like those protagonists who use only the dominant culture's grammar, their Southernness is incidental to their character. *Cars 2*'s Mater is also never explicitly said to be from the South, but as we discussed above, his characterization as a stereotypical redneck is unmistakable.

Segregating Southern Speakers

Although "nonstandard" grammar is fairly common among White Southern-speaking protagonists, the significant majority of Southern-speaking characters in professions associated with a high level of education or intellectualism use exclusively "standard" grammar. In fact, among the seven Southern-speaking doctors, six lawyers, three teachers, three nurses, one scientist, one university professor, and one veterinarian in the film set, *none* uses stigmatized grammar features at any point in their film. Similarly, the nine Southern-speaking superheroes in the set[13] all use nonstigmatized grammar with the exception of a single "ain't" from secondary character Caretaker (Sam Elliott) in *Ghost Rider* (2007), who is not revealed to be a superhero until late in the film. As we saw with Black English, the use of stigmatized Southern grammar by serious professional or heroic characters in serious films is exceedingly rare.

Filmmakers also use grammar to draw distinctions between Southern-speaking characters within a single film. For example, *Cold Mountain* (2003) contrasts the educated and comparatively wealthy protagonist Ada Monroe

(Nicole Kidman) with the blue collar prot[illegible]onist Inman (Jude Law) and the uneducated significant secondary characte[illegible]uby Thewes (Renee Zellweger). The film begins at the start of the Civil [illegible]r; Ada and her father have just moved to the remote town of Cold Mou[illegible]in, North Carolina, from urban Charlotte so her father can serve as a mi[illegible]er there. Monroe is highly educated but unskilled in farm labor and oth[illegible] forms of survival, and after her father dies suddenly, she requires the help[illegible]f hired woman Ruby Thewes to run her farm and make it through the win[illegible]. As she teaches Ada to survive, Ruby quizzes her on the names of trees an[illegible]he types of edible wild herbs in the forest; Ada retorts that she can speak L[illegible]n and read French and can name the rivers on a map of Europe. Ruby uses [illegible]merous stigmatized grammatical features, while Ada uses exclusively “sta[illegible]ard” grammar. Ada is delicate, genteel, and soft spoken; Ruby is rough, f[illegible]ward, and talkative. In her introductory scene, she nonchalantly pops the [illegible]ad off of an ornery rooster with her hands and informs Ada that they will [illegible]eating at the same table and that she will not be emptying Ada’s “night jar.”

Cold Mountain native Inman is a lab[illegible]r and, though he’s blue collar, he reads and writes adeptly, indicating th[illegible]he is educated (the uneducated Thewes reads slowly and haltingly). Like [illegible]la, he is quiet and reserved, but his letters to her from the battlefield are in[illegible]spective and, at times, eloquent. His grammar is closer to Ada’s than Ruby[illegible]he uses exactly one stigmatized feature in one sentence: “[It] don’t matt[illegible]if they’re real or only things I made up.” He falls in love with the refine[illegible]da, while a poor musician from Georgia who lives in a cave (Jack White) [illegible]ls for Ruby.

Notably, Ruby is not unintelligent—she [illegible]an expert in farming, navigating the difficult mountain terrain, and surviv[illegible] in harsh climates. Her highly stigmatized variety of Southern speech [illegible]esn’t always indicate stupidity in film characters, but it is *never* associat[illegible] with intellectualism. The most intellectual Southern-speaking characters[illegible]those depicted as highly educated, white collar, sophisticated—use o[illegible] the grammar of the dominant culture: John Nash, *Star Trek*’s (2009, 2[illegible]3, and 2016) Leonard McCoy (Karl Urban), *Catch Me If You Can*’s (20[illegible]) Roger Strong (Martin Sheen), and so on. And those Southern speakers in[illegible]restigious white collar jobs who do use stigmatized features—Hawk Hawk[illegible]s of *Space Cowboys* and Cooper of *Interstellar*—are explicitly characteriz[illegible] as less educated or intelligent than the characters around them. Hawk H[illegible]wkins does become an astronaut over the course of *Space Cowboys*, but hi[illegible]rimary career is as an Air Force Colonel, and he makes a point of contras[illegible]g his ignorance with the NASA engineers’ intellectualism: he doesn’t tr[illegible] the space shuttle’s computer (though an engineer assures him that it [illegible]s never failed), and during his physical he proclaims, “What is a pancre[illegible] anyhow? I mean, I don’t know what the damn thing does for you, besides [illegible]ve you cancer.” Indeed, the film is even titled *Space Cowboys*, emphasizing the protagonists' rough and rural traits over their education and intelligence.

Interstellar's Cooper is an engineer and also becomes an astronaut, and he's clearly intelligent, but he is also the audience's proxy: the other major characters (all scientists with PhDs) spend significant time explaining to him and, by extension, us the complex scientific principles around which the film revolves—wormholes, black holes, time dilation, multidimensional travel, even population dynamics. His Southern pronunciation and two brief uses of "nonstandard" grammar ("She didn't do nothin'" and "It ain't workin'"—a very small fragment of his many lines in this 169-minute film) distinguish him from the EDC-speaking scientists and mathematicians who surround him.

True Grit also uses grammar to distinguish between Southern-speaking characters. While the primary point-of-view character, Mattie Ross (Hailee Steinfeld), does not use Southern shift, most of the other White characters do, including co-protagonist and Arkansas resident Deputy U.S. Marshal Rooster Cogburn. Cogburn is a crude and gruff drunk who lives in a tiny and cramped single room and doesn't hesitate to use extralegal violence to accomplish his ends; his counterpart in the search for murderous outlaw Tom Chaney (Josh Brolin) is Texas Ranger LaBoeuf (Matt Damon), who is strait-laced, by the book, and, frequently, smug. Though his character is not necessarily presented as more admirable to the audience's eyes than Rooster (he is by turns dismissive and abusive to Mattie until she earns his respect via her grit), he's unquestionably more educated and refined, as evidenced by this exchange:

> LABOEUF: As I understand it, Chaney, or Chelmsford, as he called himself in Texas, shot the senator's dog. When the senator remonstrated, Chelmsford shot him as well. You could argue that the shooting of the dog was merely an instance of *malum prohibitum*, but the shooting of a senator is indubitably an instance of *malum in se*.
>
> COGBURN: Malla-men what?
>
> MATTIE: *Malum in se*. The distinction is between an act that is wrong in itself, and an act that is wrong only according to our laws and mores. It is Latin.
>
> COGBURN: I am struck that LaBoeuf is shot, trampled, and nearly severs his tongue, and not only does not cease to talk, but spills the banks of English!

True Grit's outlaws are also distinguished by their speech and grammar. Though Ned Pepper (Barry Pepper) and Tom Chaney travel together as part of a gang, they're framed quite differently in terms of their morals. Pepper, who uses Southern shift and nonstigmatized grammar, speaks to Mattie civilly after the gang captures her; in fact, he treats her with more respect than LaBoeuf does in their first few interactions. He promises Cogburn that he will return Mattie alive as long as the [illegible]ing is given time to escape and orders Chaney to keep her safe before de[illegible]arting with the rest of the gang. However, Chaney—a Southern speaker wi[illegible] a speech impediment who uses one instance of stigmatized grammar—im[illegible]ediately attempts to kill Mattie. As in *Cold Mountain*, questions of moralit[illegible] education, refinement, and class factor into *True Grit*'s character construc[illegible]on and its creators' choices for those characters' languages, and stigmatiz[illegible] grammar separates the educated from the ignorant, the refined from the coa[illegible]e.

2000's *The Patriot*, too, makes distinc[illegible]ns both between Southern and non-Southern speakers and among Sou[illegible]rn speakers. The film begins with the start of the Revolutionary War, a[illegible] though it takes place in South Carolina, almost none of the characters [illegible]e Southern speakers, including protagonist Benjamin Martin (Mel Gibso[illegible]. The film takes great pains to frame Martin as nearly without flaw both [illegible]thin the context of the time and in the eyes of the modern audience: for ins[illegible]nce, the Black people who work Martin's land explain quite pointedly tha[illegible]hey are freedpeople who work for Martin by choice, not his slaves. In fa[illegible]t, the first Southern speaker we meet is Danvers (Mark Twogood), the ow[illegible]er of an enslaved man whom he volunteers for service in the continental m[illegible]tia. Danvers, who uses two stigmatized features (*ain't* and adjectival *them* [illegible]n his brief appearance on screen, describes his "Negro" Occam (Jay Arlen [illegible]ones) as not "overly smart" but "strong as a bull"; after he signs Occam o[illegible]r to Martin, he's puzzled—even agitated—when Martin asks Occam to sig[illegible]is own consent as well: "Why? I just signed him over to you!" Martin respo[illegible]s by addressing Occam directly: "If you're willing, I'd like you to make yo[illegible]r mark." The film thus draws an obvious distinction between the slave own[illegible] and the protagonist through both their behavior and their language. The o[illegible] other Southern speaker in this film is John Billings (Leon Rippy), a ma[illegible] secondary character and close friend of Martin who is also framed by th[illegible]lm as a good guy and who uses nonstigmatized grammar.

However, no film may be more direct i[illegible]ts use of language for characterization than 2009's *The Blind Side*. We ex[illegible]nined this film and its depiction of Black English at length in Chapter 2, [illegible]t its stigmatization of "nonstandard" grammar is relevant to Southern [illegible]eakers as well. The film takes place primarily in Memphis and the prota[illegible]nist, Leigh Anne Tuohy (Sandra Bullock) uses Southern shift and the dom[illegible]ant culture's grammar, as do 20 of the other 21 Southern-speaking characte[illegible]. The only "nonstandard" user is a character credited as Milford Dad (Davi[illegible]Dwyer) who appears in a single scene and speaks only a few lines. At the [illegible]rst high school football game in which their adopted son Michael (Quinton [illegible]aron) plays, the Tuohy family is disappointed to see so many fans of the op[illegible]sing team, Milford, in the stands; Leigh Anne remarks drily, "You ever seen[illegible]o many rednecks in one place?"

Throughout the game, one of these "rednecks," Milford Dad, yells insults and slurs at Michael, exclaiming, "That ain't fair! They got a big ol' black bear playin' for them! What is this, a circus?" and bragging that his son is "kicking that blue gum's ass" until Leigh Anne threatens to "come up there and zip it for [him]." While he uses stigmatized grammar only once, he is, again, the only White Southern speaker to do so, and as we saw in Chapter 2, the film makes it clear that adoption of the dominant culture's grammar is a requirement for admission into refined, educated, upper-class life.

The only film in our dataset that subverts these patterns—to a degree—is 2011's *The Help*. As in previously discussed films, White characters are clearly segregated into "good" (a.k.a. nonracist) and "bad" (a.k.a. racist) categories, but in this case, a "nonstandard" grammar user is one of the good ones. While most of the wealthy White women of the film use racial slurs and treat their Black servants poorly, Celia Foote (Jessica Chastain) pays her cook and housekeeper Minny (Octavia Spencer) well, speaks to her as an equal, and invites her to sit at the family table. Celia hails from a small town called Sugar Ditch and she's shunned and called "trashy" by the suburban White women. She uses two stigmatized features, *ain't* and negative concord. Notably, though she's portrayed as more morally upstanding in the eyes of the audience, her character still falls prey to some negative Southern stereotypes: she is rural and uneducated—she hires Minny without her husband's knowledge because she's unable to care for her own home, despite having no other responsibilities—and she often comes across as quite naïve. In contrast, the other clearly "good" White character, the protagonist Skeeter Phelan (Emma Stone), has a college education and becomes a successful writer over the course of the film, and, of course, uses only "standard" grammar.

OTHER SOUTHERN-SPEAKING CHARACTER TROPES

In addition to the tropes of racism, ignorance, and bigotry, White Southern speakers (like Spanish and Spanish-influenced English speakers, as we'll see in the next chapter) tend to be overrepresented in a few very specific occupational tropes. The most common profession among Southern speakers in film who are clearly depicted to have or have had a specific job, by far, is that of protective service worker or member of the military. "Protective service occupations," according to the U.S. Bureau of Labor and Statistics (BLS), include correctional officers, police, detectives and private investigators, and security guards, among other professions;[14] these comprise 43 Southern-speaking characters in 27 films, or 6.7% of total characters. According to the BLS, in reality protective service workers make up 24.737 jobs per 1,000, or 2.5% of jobs on average across the 13 Southern states. The Southern state with the highest concentration of protective servic workers is Louisiana at 30.651 per 1,000 jobs, or 3.1% of total jobs.[15] T s comparison is, of course, not perfect, because these jobs numbers incl e all races of people while our list of Southern speakers includes only Wh e people and also includes many characters whose professions are never m e clear, but using these numbers to make an *approximate* comparison we ca safely say that protective service workers are overrepresented among South n speakers in film.

Furthermore, 17 of the 27 films that inc de Southern-speaking protective service workers do not take place in the S uth and most or all of the other characters do not use Southern speech; in ad, the protective service workers (usually police officers and quite often neriffs, but occasionally security guards or members of other law enforcem nt agencies such as the CIA) are the only or among the very few Southern s akers. For example, *Signs* (2002) takes place in rural Pennsylvania, but the ly cop in the film, Officer Paski (Cherry Jones), is a Southern speaker. This ttern indicates that the Southern cop is a trope found across mainstream fil *regardless* of the film's setting.

An additional 60 Southern-speaking ch acters in 30 films are or were members of the military, or 9.3% of total c aracters. Included in this number are three nonhuman characters who, tho h not literally members of the American armed services, behave like ste otypical gruff military officers: an uncredited pug drill sergeant in *Cats & Dogs* (2001); Dad's Fear (Carlos Alazraqui) in *Inside Out* (2015); and Sarg of *Toy Story 3* (2010), voiced by R. Lee Ermey, who was himself a U.S. m ine and played the stereotypical gruff Southern military and police officer c zens of times in film and on television, perhaps most famously in *Full Me Jacket* (1987). In fact, Ermey is almost certainly partly responsible for the eation of the stereotype; the pop culture wiki *TV Tropes* notes in their entr for "Drill Sergeant Nasty"—for which they provide hundreds of examples om film, television, advertising, comics, radio, and more—that the chara r "is usually played by R. Lee Ermey (who actually was a Marine drill in ructor for two years) or a Scary Black Man."[16]

A 2016 Department of Defense report und that while some Southern states are indeed overrepresented in the m tary relative to their populations (Alabama, Arkansas, Florida, Georgia, No and South Carolina, Tennessee, Texas, and Virginia), others are actua underrepresented (Kentucky, Louisiana, Mississippi, and West Virgini , indicating that the stereotype does not reflect the reality of military me ership. Indeed, according to the report the state most highly overrepresent in the military is Hawai'i,[17] yet we don't find tropes of Hawai'ian milita recruits or gruff Hawai'ian drill sergeants in our media.

In fact, using this Department of De se report, which provides data on military enrollment by race as well as y state, and the census data on the racial makeup of Southern states,[18] we can estimate that roughly 0.4% of White U.S. Southerners are members of the military. Combined, protective service workers and military members account for 16% of total Southern-speaking characters and nine out of 26 protagonists, or about 35%. This means that a White Southern-speaking film character is about 23 times more likely to be a member of the military than an actual White resident of the Southern U.S., and a protagonist is about 87 times more likely.

Where do these tropes come from? As noted above, R. Lee Ermey almost certainly had a hand in creating them, but beyond that, we can only speculate. It's possible that because the South is strongly associated with conservative views, including patriotism and support for "law and order" politics, film creators are more likely to funnel Southern actors into military and protective service roles, or to write military and protective service characters as Southern speakers regardless of the actors portraying them.

Notably, Southern-speaking law enforcement, security guards, and military characters are less likely to use stigmatized grammar and less likely to be depicted as racist, bigoted, or unintelligent. As we saw above, 27% of all Southern-speaking characters use stigmatized grammar, but only 14.4% of Southern speakers in these occupations do so. Additionally, 18% of all Southern speakers are portrayed as racist, homophobic, or stupid, while only 8.7% of protective service and military Southern speakers are portrayed this way. This may indicate that while mainstream Hollywood still considers it perfectly acceptable to depict Southern speakers using negative stereotypes, they are less comfortable doing so for law enforcement and military.

Sports players and other professions associated with sports (e.g., coaches, referees, announcers, and team owners) are also overrepresented, making up 39 Southern-speaking characters, or about 6.1% of the total. Football is the most well-represented with 18 characters (14 of whom appear in a single film, *Remember the Titans*), followed by NASCAR with 17 characters. In fact, throughout the film set, NASCAR is depicted as falling exclusively under the purview of the South, though in reality, on average the Southern U.S. states are no more enthusiastic about NASCAR than the rest of the country. Writing for World Sports Network in 2020, James Whitelock used data from Google Trends to analyze NASCAR popularity by state, and he found that while the top three states for NASCAR fandom are indeed Southern (West Virginia, North Carolina, and South Carolina), the remaining Southern states are situated more or less at random in the rankings, from Tennessee at number nine to Florida at 27 and Texas at 48.[19] Even Southern passion for NASCAR, then, is a stereotype that may have been created (or is at least perpetuated) by popular media.

A final, interesting note on the professions of Southern speakers: politicians are also surprisingly well-represented among them, accounting for 20 characters, or 3.1% of the total. This is due in part to the overrepresentation of Southern speakers among U.S. presidents in real modern history: Lyndon Johnson, Jimmy Carter, Bill Clinton, and George W. Bush all appear in at least one film (Carter and Bush appear in two), usually in the form of archival footage or audio clips. Additionally, two characters representing parodic versions of George W. Bush appear in two films—*Transformers* (2007) and *Get Smart* (2008). Together, U.S. presidents and their parodies comprise eight characters.

Where Are the Southern-Speaking Queer Characters?

A notable absence among Southern speakers in film are openly LGBTQ+ characters—in fact, Southern speakers are twice as likely to play a U.S. president as a queer person. As we shall see in the next chapter, six out of 336 Spanish-influenced English-speaking characters are openly gay (1.8%—still a depressingly small representation), while only four out of 644 Southern-speaking characters are gay, gay-coded, or transgender (0.6%). Of these, three are comedic or parodic representations that rely specifically on the character's queerness for humor and perpetuate harmful tropes about queer people. Let's examine each one.

2004's *Dodgeball: A True Underdog Story* features a character, credited as "Weird Guy with Monster Truck" (Jim Cody Williams), who is both the film's only Southern speaker and its only queer character. He appears on screen for less than 10 seconds at a car wash event organized by the protagonist's dodgeball team during which he watches one of the team's younger male members, high school student Justin (Justin Long), clad only in yellow underwear and on his hands and knees washing the wheels of his giant truck. He wears a black T-shirt under an open plaid flannel shirt and a red trucker cap, and his ginger hair and beard are long and unkempt—based on this appearance, his deep blue collar dialect, and his ownership of a pickup truck, he is classed as a stereotypical redneck in our data. As he fondles his own exposed potbelly and navel, he utters his only line, "That's it boy. Get in there nice and deep-like," while the large pit bull at his side snarls menacingly. He has been the team's only car wash customer that day, and his unpleasant behavior underscores their struggles, particularly to raise money. When the film cuts back to Justin's teammates, who are watching this bizarre scene, protagonist Peter (Vince Vaughn) remarks, "Yeah, that's not good," and teammate Steve the Pirate (Alan Tudyk) throws down a sponge angrily, exclaiming, "God, this sucks!" This portrayal falls in line with decades-old negative stereotypes about gay men preying upon young boys.

2015's *Pitch Perfect 2* includes a Southern-speaking gay-coded character who is named "Riff Off Host" in the credits and played by David Cross but credited as Sir Willups Brightslymoore, the character's name in the original script. He's a wealthy single man who lives in a large mansion and speaks with a stereotypical gay lisp, and in the one extended scene in which he appears, he hosts an extravagant acapella competition in his basement while wearing blue pajamas and a bright blue paisley floor-length dressing gown. After each round of the competition, he mocks the team that has been eliminated, for instance, telling a member of the Treblemakers, "What was that, y'all? That is *not* how you play the game. You think you're a better lyricist than Sir Mix-a-Lot. A man who was knighted by Queen. You know the band Queen?" The character is entirely comedic, and, like Weird Guy with Monster Truck, he is both the only Southern speaker and the only queer-coded man in his film.

22 Jump Street (2014) includes an even more problematic character, Southern speaker Mr. Walters (Rob Riggle), a high school track coach whose penis was shot off by one of the protagonists in the previous film. Now he is in prison for dealing drugs and has had vaginoplasty. During his one extended, crude scene, he behaves as though he believes himself to be a woman, while the other characters (his cellmate, Eric [Dave Franco], and the protagonists, Schmidt [Jonah Hill] and Jenko [Channing Tatum]) understand him to be a man. The film frames him as delusional and the other characters as rational:

> WALTERS: You know they gave me a vagina? It's awesome! You guys want to see it?
>
> SCHMIDT and JENKO: No no no!
>
> WALTERS: Alright. Eric's seen it. Eric's been all up in that shit! Isn't that right, Eric?
>
> ERIC: You guys gotta get me the fuck out of here.
>
> WALTERS: Hey, guess what. I'm Eric's bitch.
>
> ERIC: No, you're not!
>
> WALTERS: [shouting] Yes! I am! I'm your bitch! [softer] Oh, my god. I am so sorry, honey. I didn't mean that. You know that, right? [to Schmidt and Jenko] I am such a bitch when Aunt Flo shows up. It bleeds so much, it's crazy! It's like the elevator doors opening in *The Shining*.
>
> ERIC: Your vagina doesn't fucking work, man.
>
> WALTERS: Worked for you last night! [chuckles and makes a crude gesture with his tongue]
>
> SCHMIDT: You're so clearly forcing Eric into this relationship.
>
> WALTERS: Eric, am I forcing you into anything?

ERIC: Yes.

WALTERS: [smiling, to Schmidt] See?

Although Mr. Walters does not directly cla to be a woman and at no point requests to be addressed by a different na or using she/her pronouns, his character reinforces harmful tropes abou ransgender people, particularly trans women, being mentally ill or delud or being deceivers out to trick men into having sex with them.[20] This aracter is, again, both the only Southern speaker and the only queer chara er in his film.

Only one positive representation of S thern queerness appears in our film set in the character of Bobby Ray (Et Embry) of 2002's *Sweet Home Alabama*. When protagonist Melanie Sm er (Reese Witherspoon) returns to her small hometown of Pigeon Creek, labama, to seek a divorce from her estranged husband, Bobby Ray is one the first old friends she happens upon. He is funny and friendly, and though is closeted, we are led to understand early in the film that Melanie know e's gay. About halfway through the film, while drunk and angry in the l l bar, she outs him without his consent and he quickly leaves, the film c rly framing him as sympathetic and her behavior as inappropriate in this oment. She apologizes the next day and he forgives her, even helping her deceive her current fiancé into believing that she hails from a wealthier a by pretending that his family's large, historic home is hers and that he i er cousin. Later, the rest of the townspeople demonstrate their acceptance inviting him back to the bar and offering to buy him a drink.

Though perhaps a bit clumsily done, Bc y Ray's character and arc avoid the stereotypes and pitfalls often set for qu r characters in mainstream film: he is not flamboyant or promiscuous, no oes he prey on boys or straight men, and the film doesn't make jokes at hi xpense. In fact, the only time he is mocked is by Melanie herself when she uts him. The film also obliquely acknowledges that a queer person might ha good reason to remain closeted, particularly in a small, rural, conservative uthern town in the early 2000s, though it glosses over the potential conse ences of being outed by having the other characters unhesitatingly welco Bobby Ray back into their fold with nary a microaggression directed his v y.

The 2016 USC Annenberg report on versity on screen discussed in Chapter 1 found that only 2% of speaking named characters in television, film, and streaming series were coded as bian, gay, or bisexual, and less than 0.1% were transgender. "These findi ," they conclude, "tell the story of a group still fighting for inclusion in dia."[21] As our discussion above shows, this is equally true for Southern-sp king queer characters, especially Southern-speaking queer women and tra men, who are not represented at all. Remember also that although the stereotypical Southern redneck is associated with sexual deviance such as incest and bestiality, he is also associated strongly with homophobia; thus he is even less likely to be queer in film. Queer Southern audience members searching for representation on their screens simply will not find it in mainstream American film.

MOCKERY

As we saw in the previous chapter, film characters who do not speak a given dialect natively often appropriate that dialect for a variety of reasons. In the case of Black English, White characters appropriate it to affect the coolness they associate with Black people as well as to mock and disparage Black people. Southern speech doesn't carry the same cool or threatening connotations that Black English does, but non-Southern speakers do adopt fake Southern speech for the purpose of mocking actual Southern speakers, among other reasons—37 examples of Southern mockery appear in 33 films. However, perhaps the most surprising and interesting type of Southern mockery is the use of fake Southern to deceive others, which occurs 18 times in 17 films.

The Artless Southerner

Throughout our film set, non-Southern speakers affect Southern speech to assume a veneer of innocence in order to steal, to defraud, and to fake their identities in a variety of situations. For example, in 2006's *Superman Returns*, Lex Luthor (Kevin Spacey) and his henchpeople walk into a museum with the intention of stealing a collection of crystals; when a worker attempts to intercept him, telling him that the museum will close in ten minutes, Luthor uses fake Southern shift to put him at ease, assuring him, "We only need five." In an oddly parallel scene in 2018's *Ocean's 8*, professional thief Tammy (Sarah Paulson) uses fake Southern to ask a Metropolitan Museum of Art security guard for help in finding her way around the museum while in reality, she is casing it to rob it later. Later in the same film, actor Rene (Marlo Thomas) uses fake Southern while placing a stolen diamond ring up for auction, telling the appraiser that it was given to her mother by a Swedish prince "in exchange for her deflowering." In yet another museum theft scene, *National Treasure* (2004) protagonist Benjamin Franklin Gates (Nicolas Cage) poses as a security guard to enter the National Archives and steal the Declaration of Independence; he greets another security guard with "Howdy," which the *Dictionary of American Regional English* classes as chiefly Southern.[22]

Besides committing theft, non-Southern speakers frequently use fake Southern speech when taking on a fake identity. The titular character of

Rango (2011) is a domestic chameleon v ced by Johnny Depp who finds himself stranded in the desert, and when e happens upon a small, rough, Western town called Dirt, he uses Souther ronunciation and grammar as he pretends to be a hardened killer of outlaws d quickly gets himself appointed sheriff. He maintains this façade, including s Southern speech, through most of the film. Similarly, protagonist Frank A agnale, Jr. (Leonardo DiCaprio) of 2002's *Catch Me If You Can* begins his e as a con artist at a young age, affecting fake Southern pronunciation fo is first major job pretending to be a commercial airline pilot, which he co inues for several scenes. And in *xXx* (2002), in an elaborate scheme desig d to test the skills and reflexes of a recently arrested extreme sports ath e, government agents stage the robbery of a diner, during which one of m pretends to be a belligerent, Southern-speaking trucker (Tanner Gill).

Johnny Depp appears on this list again Officer Tom Hanson in *21 Jump Street* (2012), a DEA agent who is in dis ise and deep undercover with a drug-dealing gang known as the One Perc ters. In this role he wears a fake nose and a long beard and wig and uses f Southern speech, and even the audience is unaware of his true identity u he and his gang are forced into an armed standoff with the protagonists e in the film. *We're the Millers* (2013), which is discussed at length in C pter 4, also includes a scene in which a character uses fake Southern sh to gain access to drug dealers, though in this case she's operating on the o er side of the law: Rose O'Reilly (Jennifer Aniston) pretends to be part of normal, middle-class suburban family while smuggling thousands of po ds of cannabis from Mexico to the U.S., and in a scene in which she pre ds to pray with her faux family on a plane, she uses Southern speech and en feigns stereotypical Southern racism when she asks for everyone on the ane to be safe, "even the Jews."

After faking her own murder, the co- otagonist of *Gone Girl* (2014), Amy (Rosamund Pike), takes up residenc n a cheap resort, claiming to be from New Orleans and fleeing an abusive yfriend, and using fake Southern speech. *Chicago*'s (2002) Roxie Hart (Re Zellweger), on the other hand, uses fake Southern speech to appear innoc t before the press and the public eye as she attempts to avoid conviction a murder that she did, indeed, commit. And in the most dedicated act o eception in this discussion, Ted Winter (Liev Schreiber) of *Salt* (2010) a ears to be a Southern-speaking American CIA agent; we only learn late the film that he is actually a Russian spy who has been faking his Amer n identity for at least a decade.[23]

A final example comes from 2000's *M t the Parents* in which ex-CIA agent and father of the bride-to-be Jack (R ert De Niro) is secretly planning a honeymoon vacation to Thailand for the ung couple, though the audience is led to believe that something more sinist is occurring. While on the phone with his travel agent, Jack tells him, "Now you gotta be more careful when you call here. If anybody else answers, just use a Southern accent and ask for the vegetarian special, okay?" Though no Southern speech is ever heard in the film (and thus it's not included in the total of 18 above), these lines nonetheless fit into our established trope of characters pretending to be Southern while doing something deceitful.

The most logical explanation for this pattern involves a well-established Southern stereotype that we've already examined: that of the unintelligent or backward Southerner. If both film creators and audiences assume Southern speakers to be less intelligent than average, they might also assume these speakers to be more innocent and less likely to deceive others; thus the guise of an artless Southerner is, in creators' and viewers' minds, the best choice to avoid suspicion. An alternative explanation is that creators and audiences simply think of Southerners as more trustworthy. However, several of the examples discussed above indicate that the former explanation is the more plausible one. *Ocean's 8*'s Tammy, for instance, pretends to be a tourist to the big city, lost and overwhelmed, while asking for help, and *Meet the Parents*' Jack specifically instructs his travel agent to feign confusion about whom he is calling—these characters use Southern shift specifically to look dumb, while *xXx*'s trucker is rude and confrontational even before he begins robbing the diner—quite the opposite of trustworthy. He and Officer Tom Hanson also evoke redneck stereotypes, which are built primarily of traits that also do not elicit trust, e.g., bigotry, sexual deviance, etc. These examples, then, are further evidence that Southern speakers are more likely to be viewed as unintelligent compared to their EDC-speaking peers.

Mocking Real Southern Speakers

Non-Southern-speaking characters also use fake Southern speech to mock actual Southern speakers, both directly and in the abstract, and mockery of a specific Southern speaker can be good-natured or mean-spirited. For example, several soldiers and officers in *Black Hawk Down* (2001) use Southern speech natively, while others use it facetiously to mock the native speakers. In a comedic scene, Sergeant Pilla (Danny Hoch), a non-Southern speaker, is caught in the act of imitating his Southern-speaking superior officer, Captain Steele (Jason Isaacs), for the amusement of his fellow soldiers. While Steele remonstrates Pilla, it's clear that the imitation is in jest and Pilla suffers no real consequences. Similarly, in *Men in Black 3* (2012), Agent J (Will Smith) uses exaggerated Southern shift to mock his native Southern-speaking colleague, Agent K (Tommy Lee Jones), with whom he is often exasperated but ultimately has a strong relationship.

Examples of more malicious mockery in ıde *Remember the Titans* (2000), in which one of the few White non-South n speakers, high schooler Louie Lastik (Ethan Suplee), speaks to his Black ›otball teammate and mocks the White Southern racists who oppose the sch ›l's integration: "What you doin' in my school, boy?"; and in 2005's *The ›ngest Yard*, prison inmate Paul Crewe (Adam Sandler) uses fake Souther shift to mock Southern speaker Warden Hazen (James Cromwell) to his ıce when he accuses Hazen of planting a spy on Crewe's football team. *Mile*'s (2002) Rabbit (Eminem) uses fake Southern shift to mock his o ı mother in an impromptu rap after she gives him a beat-up car which i constantly broken down: "Here, happy birthday, Rabbit. Here's a brand-ne car. You can have it!" And Toby (Zachary Levi) of 2009's *Alvin and the C ›munks: The Squeakquel* mocks his own father—who never appears on s ›en—using fake Southern shift: "I'm not gonna be like, 'I know everythin nd you do this and you do that,' like my dad."

Non-Southern speakers additionally fal Southern speech to mock redneck stereotypes rather than specific Soutl n speakers. In a scene in 2002's *Austin Powers in Goldmember*, Dr. Evil (ike Myers), who usually speaks English with what is purported to be a Be an accent, combines this accent with fake Southern shift while talking on CB radio to his partner in crime, Goldmember (also Mike Myers). Banjo m ic plays in the background as he confers with Goldmember, exclaiming, "T -four there, Goldie Wang, this is Rubber Ducky. What's your ten-twenty? (er. . . . Yeehaw! Copy that, you son-of-a-bitch pile o' monkey nuts!" In t same film, Dr. Evil again uses fake Southern shift in a brief line as he re in his tiny human clone, whom he keeps on a leash: "Got me a marlin!"

Mike Myers appears in this section a s ond time as The Cat in 2003's live-action *The Cat in the Hat* in a bizarr xtended scene in which he pretends to be a "couch mechanic," wearing trucker cap and using exaggerated blue collar Southern pronunciation w le making "adjustments" to the family's couch. His fur sags below his son now human buttocks like poorly fitting pants and he passes gas audibly w le climbing into and under the couch; again, fast tempo banjo music plays ı the background. Another White male comic actor known for his farcical rformances, Jim Carrey, briefly uses fake Southern shift in his role as acto nd villain Count Olaf in *Lemony Snicket's A Series of Unfortunate Events* 004): while rehearsing with his theater troupe, he sits in an ornate, high-b ked chair and, in his usual pronunciation, announces, "This is a little pie I like to call 'electric chair.'" He sits motionless for a moment as the rest of e troupe gapes at him, then calls out loudly in exaggerated blue collar Sout n shift, "I think you might have to turn it up. . . . Is anybody *out there?*" n the final two words, his body tenses and jerks as though he is being elec ›cuted.

These sudden and apparently unelicited imitations of stereotypical "rednecks" demonstrate that rural, blue collar Southern people are still fair game for mockery and derision in pop culture. In their analysis of depictions of Southerners on television, Alison Slade and Amber J. Narro concur, claiming that "the fact remains the Southern stereotype is alive and well, prospering on both network and cable. New shows featuring the Southerner utilize myth narrative steeped in the dominant ideology of 'Southerners are stupid, lazy, and ignorant' to attract and maintain viewers."[24] However, it's important to point out that these stereotypes rely both on geography *and* class—while we see a number of examples of intelligent, well-educated Southern-speaking characters among the wealthy and privileged in our data (Leigh Anne Tuohy, John Nash, Leonard McCoy, Howard Hughes, etc.), the *redneck* stereotype—the "stupid, lazy, and ignorant" Southern speaker—is *always* blue collar or poor: the trucker, the mechanic, the inmate on death row, the trailer park resident.

Are Southern Accents Funny?

Finally, non-Southern speakers occasionally use fake Southern speech not to mock Southerners directly but simply for humorous effect. Examples include *Robots*' (2005) Fender (Robin Williams) switching to fake Southern shift for a single line—"Aunt Fanny, he needs a place to stay"—for no clear reason other than that he believes it sounds funny; *The Cat in the Hat*'s The Cat similarly using fake Southern pronunciation as he and the children ride their unconscious babysitter's body like a log on a flume ride; *The Incredibles* (2004) villain Syndrome (Jason Lee) using fake Southern shift for a single line when he is delighted to have unintentionally captured an entire superhero family; and *Rush Hour 2*'s (2001) Carter (Chris Tucker) uses fake Southern while wearing a huge cowboy hat and goofing around at a high stakes craps table: "Everything stays on the table. Don't nobody touch that table, you understand? [imitating Elvis] Thank you very much." Even Hannibal Lecter (Anthony Hopkins), a character known perhaps to be witty but rarely silly, gets in on this act: in 2002's *Red Dragon*, as he helps Detective Will Graham track a killer—before he himself is exposed as one—he uses fake Southern shift as he says, "You know I believe we're makin' progress."

As we shall see in the next chapter, while this Mock Southern doesn't appear nearly as often in the film set as Mock Spanish, it's not uncommon, signifying that American audiences consider Southern speech, like Black English and Spanish, to be inherently funny, apart from stereotypes and regardless of context. White Southern English—especially with "standard" grammar—is used by serious characters in serious situations far more frequently than Black English, but still significantly less frequently than EDC. This reinforces the pressure on Southern speakers, especially blue collar and

Appalachian speakers, to conform to Nortl n linguistic standards in order to be taken seriously in academia and the pro ssional world.[25]

CONSEQUE CES

Alison Slade, Dedria Givens-Carroll, and mber J. Narro begin their 2012 anthology *Mediated Images of the South: e Portrayal of Dixie in Popular Culture* with the words, "Poor white tr n. Racecar drivers. Drunkards. Racists. The South has heard all the stereot es. Often perpetuated in popular media, these classifications also are know o the world."[26] As we have seen in this chapter, these stereotypes attach the elves to Southern-speaking film characters *regardless* of the character's act l origin, meaning that the stereotypes rely not just on geography but on per ptions of Southern U.S. English dialects and the people who speak them.

While the literature on real-life, tangibl discrimination against Southern speakers is less robust than that on Bla English speakers, it stands to reason that when an individual must ov ome conscious or unconscious biases against an aspect of their identity— eir race, their gender or gender identity, their sexuality, or even their spee —this adds an additional hurdle in their path toward upward mobility and s -actualization. When this hurdle is combined with other hurdles such as p erty, it creates an intersectional barrier to entry that individuals must clear fore they can pursue their goals. Numerous researchers have shown that mericans, *including Southern speakers themselves*, believe Southern dial s to be less correct, less pleasant to listen to, less educated, and less intelli t.[27] As we discussed in Chapter 2, the solution is not as straightforward as mply learning and speaking the English of the Dominant Culture. Many uthern speakers cannot do this, and none of them should have to. Rather, it up to educators to dismantle the centuries-old belief that some forms of En sh indicate intelligence, wealth, and culture, while others signify stupidity, verty, and ignorance—that some forms are correct and others are not.

NOTES

1. William Labov, *Principles of Linguistic C ge: Internal Factors* (Oxford: Basil Blackwell, 1994), quoted in Guy Bailey and Tillery, "Sounds of the South," in *American Voices: How Dialects Differ from C st to Coast*, eds. Walt Wolfram and Ben Ward (Malden: Blackwell Publishing, 200 13.

2. William Labov, "The Organization of Dialect Diversity in North America," University of Pennsylvania, accessed September 8, 2021, https://www.ling.upenn.edu/phono_atlas/ICSLP4.html.

3. William Labov, Sharon Ash, and Charles Boberg, "A National Map of The Regional Dialects of American English," University of Pennsylvania, July 15, 1997, https://www.ling.upenn.edu/phono_atlas/NationalMap/NationalMap.html#Heading2.

4. United States Department of Health and Human Services, Substance Abuse and Mental Health Services Administration, *2019 National Survey of Drug Use and Health (NSDUH) Releases*, accessed September 8, 2021, https://www.samhsa.gov/data/release/2019-national-survey-drug-use-and-health-nsduh-releases.

5. *The American Heritage Dictionary*, online ed., s.v. "redneck," 2021, https://ahdictionary.com/word/search.html?q=redneck.

6. Patrick Huber, "A Short History of Redneck: The Fashioning of a Southern White Masculine Identity," *Southern Cultures* 1, no. 2 (1995): 145, https://doi.org/10.1353/scu.1995.0074.

7. Huber, "A Short History of Redneck," 148–49.

8. Huber, "A Short History of Redneck," 150.

9. "Larry the Cable Guy," IMDb, 2021, https://www.imdb.com/name/nm1249256/?ref_=tt_cl_t_4.

10. Elaine Wonhee Chun, "Listening to the Southern Redneck: Pathways Of Contextualization On Youtube," *American Speech* 93, no. 3–4 (2018): 441, https://doi.org/10.1215/00031283-7271261.

11. Judith T. Irvine and Susan Gal, "Language Ideology And Linguistic Differentiation," in *Regimes of Language: Ideologies, Polities, and Identities*, ed. P. V. Kroskrity (Santa Fe: School of American Research Press, 2000), 37.

12. Chun, "Listening to the Southern Redneck," 425.

13. Rogue (Anna Paquin) in *X-Men* (2000), *X2: X-Men United* (2003), and *X-Men: The Last Stand* (2006); Johnny Blaze (Nicolas Cage) and Caretaker (Sam Elliott) in *Ghost Rider* (2007); Fred Dukes (Kevin Durand) and Remy LeBeau (Taylor Kitsch) in *X-Men Origins: Wolverine* (2009); and Helen Parr/Elastigirl (Holly Hunter) in *The Incredibles* (2004) and *The Incredibles 2* (2018).

14. United States Bureau of Labor and Statistics, *Occupational Employment and Wage Statistics*, May 2020, https://www.bls.gov/oes/current/oes330000.htm.

15. United States Bureau of Labor and Statistics, *Occupational and Employment Wage Statistics*.

16. "Drill Sergeant Nasty," TV Tropes, accessed September 8, 2021, https://tvtropes.org/pmwiki/pmwiki.php/Main/DrillSergeantNasty.

17. United States Department of Defense, Office of the Under Secretary of Defense, Personnel, and Readiness, *Population Representation in the Military Services: Fiscal Year 2016 Summary Report*, 2016, https://www.cna.org/pop-rep/2016/summary/summary.pdf.

18. United States Census Bureau, *Population Estimates, July 1, 2019, (V2019)*, accessed September 8, 2021, https://www.census.gov/quickfacts/fact/table/US/PST045219.

19. James Whitelock, "NASCAR Most & ast Popular States [MAP]," World Sports Network, Rebel Penguin ApS, July 1, 20 , https://www.wsn.com/nascar/most -popular-states/.

20. Julia Serrano, "Trans Woman Manife ," *Whipping Girl: A Transsexual Woman on Sexism and the Scapegoating of Fen inity* (New York: Seal Press, 2007).

21. Stacy L. Smith, Marc Choueiti, and Kath ne Pierper, *Inclusion or Invisibility? Comprehensive Annenberg Report on Diversit Entertainment*. Institute for Diversity and Empowerment at Annenberg (IDEA) (l C Annenberg School for Journalism and Communication, 2016), 12.

22. *Dictionary of American Regional Englis Volume II* (1991), s.v. "howdy."

23. Other examples include: *The Cat in th Hat* (2003): Thing One (voiced by Dan Castellaneta) pretends to be a highway pa lman to pull over the protagonists' mother and delay her return home; though bo Thing One and Thing Two speak primarily in gibberish, in this brief scene Thin One can clearly be heard using fake Southern shift as it tells the mother, "Mekka d ka license, appa registration. You're one hot mama." *X2: X-Men United* (2003): Sha shifter Mystique (Rebecca Romijn) adopts the persona of a beautiful Southern w an in a bar to lure a prison guard into the bathroom so that she can drug him. *M dagascar 3: Europe's Most Wanted* (2012): An escaped zoo penguin uses Souther hift while pretending to be a circus animal (though none of the actual circus ani ls are Southern speakers). *Identity Thief* (2013): Diana (Melissa McCarthy), the ılar identity thief, uses fake Southern shift while chatting with a Georgia waitres ınd pretending to be the wife of the man who is actually her victim. *Minions* (2015 A convention of supervillains hides underground beneath the veneer of a fake bus ss, Billy Bob's Bait Shop, where a Southern voice on an intercom intercepts intru rs and admits attendees. *Boss Baby* (2017): The Boss Baby (Alec Baldwin) pretend o be an Elvis impersonator to sneak onto a flight to Las Vegas.

24. Alison Slade and Amber J. Narro, "An ceptable Stereotype: The Southern Image in Television Programming," in *Mediat Images of the South: The Portrayal of Dixie in Popular Culture*, eds. Alison Slade, edria Givens-Carroll, and Amber J. Narro (New York: Lexington Books, 2012), 17

25. Meredith McCarroll, "On and On: Appa hian Accent and Academic Power," *Southern Cultures* 22, no. 2 (2016): https://w .southerncultures.org/article/on-and -on-appalachian-accent-and-academic-power/.

26. Alison Slade, Dedria Givens-Carroll, an mber J. Narro, *Mediated Images of the South: The Portrayal of Dixie in Popular ture* (New York: Lexington Books, 2012), 1.

27. Dennis R. Preston, "Where the Worst En h Is Spoken," in *Focus on the USA*, ed. Edgar W. Schneider (Amsterdam: Benjam s, 1996). Valerie Fridland, Kathryn Bartlett, and Roger Kreuz, "Making Sense Of riation: Pleasantness and Education Ratings Of Southern Vowel Variants," *Ameri Speech* 80, no. 4 (2005). Valerie Fridland and Kathryn Bartlett, "Correctness, P santness, and Degree of Difference Ratings Across Regions," *American Speech* 81 o. 4 (2006), https://doi.org/10.1215

/00031283-2006-025. Dennis R. Preston, "Changing Research on the Changing Perceptions of Southern U.S. English," *American Speech* 93, no. 3–4 (2018), https://doi.org/10.1215/00031283-7271283.

Chapter 4

"You Need to Work on That Accent, Pablo"

Spanish, Spanish-Accented English, and Spanish-Influenced English

The 2013 comedy *We're the Millers* features a White low-level cannabis dealer, David Clark (Jason Sudeikas), who has been tasked by his White American supplier to smuggle a large amount of cannabis into the U.S. from Mexico to pay off a debt. To avoid attracting attention at the border, David rents an RV and enlists the help of three White neighbors—a middle-aged exotic dancer (Jennifer Aniston), a runaway teenage girl (Emma Roberts), and a well-meaning but naïve teenage boy (Will Poulter)—to pose as a vacationing family. The White pseudofamily works hard to appear unsuspicious, wearing conservative clothing in neutral colors and even getting haircuts to reflect what they believe to be mainstream White middle-class norms. (The film also includes a scene in which Anniston's character, Rose, uses fake Southern shift as part of their deception, which we discussed in Chapter 3.)

Importantly, *We're the Millers* goes to great lengths to distinguish the White English-speaking drug traffickers from their Latinx Spanish-speaking counterparts: David's White supplier (Ed Helms) is a businessman with a lavish office who wears expensive suits, and though David himself is, prior to his makeover, unkempt, he is explicitly depicted as unarmed, nonthreatening, and at the mercy of some neighborhood thugs who rob him. The Mexican suppliers, on the other hand, are heavily armed, clad in black leather, and quick to resort to violence. The lead henchman, credited as One-Eye (Matthew Willig), is tall, imposing, and has a facial deformity. David's first interaction with One-Eye proceeds as follows:

DAVID: Hola, hola, me llamo David.

ONE-EYE: *Que*? . . . You are the White gri) with the haircut of a donkey.

DAVID: Yeah, si. Yeah, mucho White-o, ve very gringo. . . . That's my family. Mi familia.

David's words work to differentiate an(listance him from the Mexicans supplying him with drugs; though they an(e are engaged in the same transaction with the same goal—smuggling d gs into the U.S. for sale—he is quick to emphasize his Whiteness and for(nness, indicating that he is nonthreatening and out of place in this Mexica lrug compound, while One-Eye, who speaks Spanish and Spanish-accented nglish, is threatening and potentially dangerous. David, too, uses Spanis words but makes no attempt at authentic pronunciation or grammar—as a /hite person working to distance himself from real Spanish speakers, he ca not reveal too much familiarity with Spanish. Jane H. Hill calls this speech lock Spanish, and we'll examine it in more detail below. First, let's define t other types of speakers we will discuss in this chapter.

DEFINING A SPAN H ACCENT AND SPANISH IN LUENCE

A number of characters in the film set)eak Spanish, Spanish-accented English, Spanish-influenced English, or so combination. Spanish-accented English is the version of English spoken y native Spanish speakers who learned it as a secondary language, whil Spanish-influenced English can refer to any dialect of English strongly i uenced by Spanish vocabulary, pronunciation, and/or grammar, such as icano English, Cuban English, Puerto Rican English, etc. For the purpose f our analysis, Spanish-accented English and Spanish-influenced English wi be grouped together and referred to collectively as Spanish-influenced Eng h or SIE. This is done primarily for two reasons. First, the average m(olingual audience member cannot distinguish between a Spanish accent nd a Spanish-influenced dialect spoken by a native English speaker who ay or may not also speak fluent Spanish; instead, they tend to assume that a such speakers are simply speaking Spanish-accented English.[1] Second, in any cases the actors in question are performing—with varying degrees of nsistency and success—accents or dialects that they themselves do not sp k natively, and this often makes it difficult for even a trained ear to ascerta which type of accent or dialect they're attempting to reproduce. Unlike ack English and Southern U.S. English speakers, SIE speakers in film ten to use "standard" grammar with very few exceptions—the "nonstandardnes of their speech is found instead entirely in their pronunciation. We'll examine Spanish speakers alongside SIE speakers because there's a great deal of overlap between the two categories: many Spanish- and SIE-speaking characters code-switch between Spanish and English. Additionally, we will not consider Spanish and SIE speakers' country of origin in the analysis because it is rarely made explicit; in fact, as we shall see, some films make it a point of *not* telling the audience where a Spanish-speaking character was born.

SPANISH AND SIE SPEAKERS IN THE FILM SET

A total of 336 characters who unambiguously speak Spanish, SAE, and/or SIE appear in 120 films, or about 24.3% of the 493 films examined. (The film *Coco* [2017] alone comprises 45 of those characters, or about 13.4%, as discussed in more detail below.) Only eight films feature Spanish- or SIE-speaking protagonists representing 1.6% of total films and about 1% of total protagonists. This is far below the proportion of U.S. residents who speak Spanish at home, which the U.S. Census estimated at 13.5% in 2019[2] and which does not account for SIE speakers who do not speak Spanish at home, indicating, unsurprisingly, that Spanish and SIE speakers are significantly underrepresented among mainstream film protagonists relative to the population. Additionally, 65 films include only a single Spanish- or SIE-speaking character (54.2% of films with Spanish- and SIE-speaking characters), and 29 films feature only minor or background characters who speak Spanish or SIE (24.2% of the films with Spanish- and SIE-speaking characters).

As these data show, the number of roles, especially major roles, for Spanish and SIE-speaking characters is quite limited; furthermore, these characters tend to be funneled into a specific and rigid set of stereotypes and archetypes. Perhaps the most problematic is that of the Spanish- and SIE-speaking criminal. Seventy-nine of the 336 Spanish- and SIE-speaking characters represented in the film set—about 23.5%—are inmates or ex-convicts, or are unambiguously engaged in criminal activity during the course of the film. (When *Coco* is omitted from the data, this number jumps to 27.1%; when minor and background characters are also omitted, it jumps to 32.7%.) This includes three characters who are adult relatives, specifically wives and mothers,[3] of those engaged in crime who do not directly participate in the criminal acts but are complicit in and benefit from them. Of these 79 characters, 35 are specifically involved with drugs: growers, dealers, traffickers, users, and their employees, wives, and mothers, or about 10.4% of Spanish and SIE speakers (compared to 4.9% of Black English speakers and less than 0.3% of White Southern speakers). Most but not all of these criminals are antagonists or villains in their respective films; indeec wo protagonists are included in their number: Chato Santana a.k.a. El Diab (Jay Hernandez), co-protagonist of the ensemble cast of *Suicide Squad* (2 6), and Puss in Boots (Antonio Banderas), protagonist of *Puss in Boots* (2 1).

In addition to criminals and other type of drug dealers, we find Latinx people overrepresented in a number of s eotypical occupations, some of them perhaps a bit unexpected. Service v kers, predictably, are well represented among Spanish- and SIE-speak characters: domestic workers comprise 15 characters in 12 films and i lude maids, nannies, janitors, a butler, a servant, a home health worker, a g lener, and a pool boy. Two of the eight Spanish-speaking protagonists are or is list: Marisa Ventura (Jennifer Lopez) from *Maid in Manhattan* (2002) d Marta (Ana de Armas) from *Knives Out* (2019).

Interestingly, "protective service occupa ns," which according to the U.S. Bureau of Labor and Statistics (BLS) inc de correctional officers, police, detectives, and security guards,[4] are heavi overrepresented in the film set. Twenty-four characters in 14 films appear this list, including several police detectives, DEA agents, and a secret servi agent, representing about 7.1% of Spanish- and SIE-speaking characters. ecret agents and spies were not included in this category—they comprise characters in five films, namely the *Spy Kids* trilogy [2001, 2002, and 2003] *ie Another Day* [2002], *G-Force* [2009], and *Fast & Furious Presents: Hob & Shaw* [2019]. Combined, protective service workers, secret agents, and pies account for about 10.4% of Spanish- and SIE-speaking characters.) T BLS reports, however, that in 2020 only about 1.8% of Hispanic and Lati people worked in this industry.[5] Hispanic and Latino people are, of cours not a perfect proxy for Spanish and SIE speakers as they do not all speal panish, but as the BLS doesn't track Spanish and SIE speakers specifical across occupations, it's the best comparison available. In "Latino Represe ation on Primetime Television," Dana E. Mastro and Elizabeth Behm-Mor itz include the "law enforcer" in their list of historical stereotypic characte ations that have been identified through analyses of Latinx people in me ,[6] indicating that this on-screen overrepresentation of the demographic in otective service is not new. *Why* this overrepresentation exists is a difficul uestion to answer, but I would argue that it may be partly a result of the ersection between the excess of law enforcement roles in media in gener nd the likelihood that a Latinx actor will be cast in a secondary role rather an as a protagonist. Because the plots of so many films and TV shows rev e around criminal activity, cops and detectives, security guards, etc. are o represented among occupations relative to their actual share of the popul n. These are usually secondary or minor characters who have only a few nes or a few minutes of screen time. Spanish- and SIE-speaking charact , too, appear almost entirely in secondary and minor roles, resulting in a significant overlap between these two groups. We saw a similar effect in White Southern speakers, though as we discussed in Chapter 3, they were more heavily overrepresented as members of the military.

Other types of service workers comprise 18 characters in 12 films and include a "whale wash" employee (like a car wash but for anthropomorphic sea creatures), a car dealership employee, a roadside fruit stand vendor, a shoe shiner, a tour guide, and a number of hospitality workers such as waiters, bartenders, restaurant kitchen staff, doormen, hotel concierges, and a caterer. Altogether, service workers represent 60 Spanish-and SAE-speaking characters, about 17.9%. This is slightly below the BLS's estimate of 22% of Hispanic and Latino people employed in these occupations in 2020.[7]

Religious figures, i.e., priests and nuns, are also overrepresented among Spanish- and SIE-speaking characters, comprising seven characters in seven films, or about 2.1%. The BLS. estimates that in 2020, about 1.4% of Hispanic and Latino people were employed in "community and social service occupations,"[8] which includes counselors and social service specialists in addition to religious workers.[9] (The BLS doesn't provide data on the number of Hispanic and Latino people employed in religious services alone.) Notably, the National Hispanic Media Coalition points out that religiosity is one of "the most common positive stereotypes about Latinos."[10]

Other occupations of note for Spanish and SIE speakers in film include pirate (five characters in three films) and actor/soap opera star (six characters in four films). The remaining characters whose occupations are made clear in their films make up a broad and seemingly random assortment and include, for example, a pilot, a pop star, an emergency services operator, a sex worker, a flamenco instructor, a news anchor on a Spanish-language newscast, several nurses, a circus ringleader, etc. However, perhaps even more interesting are the professions *not* represented in the data.

In the 493 films examined, there are no Spanish or SIE-speaking scientists, no astronauts, no lawyers or politicians, no writers, no professional (or even collegiate or high school) athletes or coaches, and no university professors. Only two high school teachers are represented (*X-Men Origins: Wolverine* [2009] and *Spider-Man: Homecoming* [2017]), and both teach Spanish. The data also include only two Spanish- and SIE-speaking doctors: Manny (Benjamin Bratt) from *Cloudy with a Chance of Meatballs* (2009), an immigrant who worked as a doctor in Guatemala but came to the U.S. "for a better life" and now works as a cameraman for a local television news show, and an unnamed police psychologist (Ivelin Giro) in *Bad Boyz II* (2003) who is sleeping with her male patient and has only one line, discussed in further detail below in the section "The Fiery Latina."

Hispanic people—again, not a perfect p y for Spanish and SIE speakers but the best one we have—are underrepres ted in these professions not only in film but also in real life. For example, National Center for Education Statistics reports that in 2018, only 6% of l-time faculty in degree-granting postsecondary institutions were Hispanic nd for full-time professors the number drops below 3%.[11] In the same yea ess than 6% of active physicians identified as Hispanic according to the sociation of American Medical Colleges.[12] Pew Research found that onl 7% of workers in STEM fields are Hispanic and, again, 6% of those wi a bachelor's degree or higher.[13] Studies have found that having race- an ender-matched role models has positive impacts on student achievement,[1] nd mainstream film *could* be an opportunity for young Hispanic people to d those role models when they don't encounter them at school or at work, t at present audiences hoping to see diverse representations of Spanish and E speakers in prestigious professions on screen are forced to look elsewhe .

Spanish and SIE speakers are also dra ally underrepresented in superhero films. Superhero films have been a st le of mainstream Hollywood for decades, accounting for billions of dolla n ticket sales annually. Spanish and SIE speakers appear in 15 of them, ab t 23.8%, accounting for 28 total characters, only *two* of whom are actually perheroes—they are even more poorly represented in this regard than B k English and White Southern speakers. The rest comprise minor, back und, and secondary characters, including most of the tropes discussed ab —drug dealers, gang members, ex-cons, domestic workers, service worke military and security guards, a priest, and both of the Spanish teachers fo d in the film set. In other words, Spanish and SIE speaker representation in perhero films mirrors representation in other genres.

The first superhero in this demographic, Diablo of *Suicide Squad*, might be better termed an antihero; he appeare in our list of Spanish-speaking criminals above and he represents one of t eight Spanish and SIE-speaking protagonists in the data. He is a native Span speaker and speaks SIE, though the film never explicitly states where he w born. The plot features a group of inmates incarcerated for a range of crim who are unwillingly recruited by Amanda Waller (Viola Davis) to perform vert and extralegal assignments on behalf of the U.S. government. Due to ability to create and control fire at will, El Diablo is imprisoned in a thick tal tank where he can be quickly doused with water. We later learn the rea n for his incarceration: prior to the start of the film, after his wife accus him of criminal acts, including possibly killing several people in an act of son, he burned her and their two children to death in a fit of rage. He then su ndered himself to the police and expressed remorse, refusing to use his fire wers until coerced into doing so by another member of the squad. He event lly sacrifices himself to stop one of the film's main antagonists who is attempting to destroy modern civilization. Although this character is, indeed, a superhero, he still falls prey to the stereotypes common among other SIE-speaking characters.

Miles Morales (Shameik Moore) of *Spider-Man: Into the Spider-Verse* (2018), who was also discussed briefly in Chapter 2, is a more positive representation of Spanish-speaking superhero protagonists. A high school student who has recently begun attending an exclusive boarding school, he speaks Spanish at home with his mother and with at least one school friend as well as unaccented American English. Another Spider-Man already exists in Miles's universe, but when Miles is bitten by a radioactive spider in traditional Spider-Narrative fashion, he gains similar abilities. After the original Spider-Man is killed Miles attempts to take his place, and when a villain creates a portal allowing people to cross over from other universes, Miles meets unique Spider-People from those universes who mentor him in all things Spider. Unlike El Diablo, Miles is smart, likable, sympathetic, and relatable, and the film was praised by critics for its diverse cast among other attributes. We can safely say that it represents the exception rather than the rule in portrayals of Spanish speakers, including Spanish-speaking protagonists, on screen.

While these two protagonists represent opposite ends of the superhero spectrum, the major portion of that spectrum is occupied by "standard" English-speaking White men, including the most well-known characters who appear in multiple films in the film set: Batman, Superman, Iron Man, Captain America, all other representations of Spider-Man (appearing in a total of ten films), etc. Furthermore, until 2016 there were *no* Spanish- or SIE-speaking superheroes in mainstream American film. Clearly, much work is left to be done to improve diversity in this genre.

The other six Spanish- and SIE-speaking protagonists in the film set include hotel maid Marisa Ventura (Jennifer Lopez) of *Maid in Manhattan* (2002); Juarez (Penélope Cruz) of *G-Force* (2009), a sexualized female guinea pig secret agent; Puss in Boots (Antonio Banderas) of *Puss in Boots* (2011), a feline gentleman thief; Cassian Andor (Diego Luna) of *Rogue One: A Star Wars Story* (2016), a Rebel pilot who sacrifices himself in the quest to steal the plans for the evil Empire's Death Star; Miguel (Anthony Gonzalez) of *Coco* (2017); and home health worker Marta Cabrera (Ana de Armas) of *Knives Out* (2019). Note that 25% of Spanish- and SIE-speaking protagonists are animals, and female Spanish and SIE speakers consist of two domestic workers and a guinea pig. As noted above, Spanish and SIE speakers are vastly underrepresented among protagonists, particularly relative to their proportion of U.S. residents, and with only eight representatives in the film set, it is impossible for this brief list to present a diverse picture of Spanish- and SIE-speaking characters.

COCO

The 2017 Disney/Pixar film *Coco* contai by far the greatest number of distinct and unambiguously Spanish- and S -speaking characters in a single film at 45 (the next highest is *Puss in Boots* ith 19 speakers), or about 13.4% of total Spanish and SIE speakers in the lm set. The film takes place in Mexico and features a young boy named M guel who belongs to a family of shoemakers but longs to be a musician like s idol, deceased actor Ernesto de la Cruz (Benjamin Bratt). However, Migue family has been forbidden from playing music for generations since Migu s great-great-grandfather left his family to pursue his musical career and n ver returned. On the Day of the Dead, Miguel steals de la Cruz's guitar fro his mausoleum and is magically transported to the Land of the Dead, where learns that de la Cruz murdered his great-great-grandfather, Hector, when H ctor decided to quit their musical partnership and return to his family. When Miguel returns to the Land of the Living, he reveals the truth and his famil ifts the ban on music, enabling him to pursue his dream.

Nearly every character on screen in *Coc* speaks Spanish and/or SIE, providing not only the largest collection of sp kers in a single film, but also the greatest diversity of positive representatio Only 14 other films feature four or more Spanish and/or SIE speakers, and majority of these characters are negative or stereotypical representations– ke the Bolivian dictator and his henchmen in *Quantum of Solace* (2008), t numerous drug dealers and corrupt cops in *Traffic* (2000), or the inmates d gangsters in *S.W.A.T.* (2003)—or minor/background characters with lit or no characterization at all. However, *Coco*'s story centers around art d music; in addition to Miguel's shoemaking family, we see a number of s cessful and aspiring musicians, dancers, artists (including Frida Kahlo), a actors, as well as townspeople and other minor and background character n a variety of occupations in the Lands of both the Living and the Dead.

But while we might look to *Coco* as strong example of positive and diverse representation of this dialect grou it is only a single film. The fact that one film out of 493 contains over 13 of the characters in this dialect group is in itself problematic; a single fil with a concise focus like *Coco* cannot present a *truly* diverse picture of an group. In order to represent accurately the huge range of life experiences an professions intrinsic to any large demographic group, we simply need more ilms featuring more fully developed Spanish- and SIE-speaking charact s. Mastro and Behm-Morawitz also point out that "constructive Latino ch acters may be presented in such programs, [but] they are not likely to intera with white peers—consequently removing Latinos from cultural inclusion." *Coco* takes place in Mexico and all of the characters are Latinx (as are the human characters in *Puss in Boots*); they never interact with White people. Thus while these films do present a comparatively diverse picture of Spanish and SIE speakers (at least relative to other films), this picture is painted at a safe distance outside of American borders, segregating these speakers from their majority White English-speaking audience. As noted in Chapter 2, White EDC-speaking men are hugely overrepresented among protagonists relative to their proportion of the U.S. population. Until these numbers become more balanced, speakers of marginalized dialects will continue to be marginalized in film.

LATINX STEREOTYPES IN SPEAKERS OF SPANISH AND SIE

In addition to the overrepresentation of drug dealers and other criminals among Spanish and SIE speakers in the film set, other well-worn stereotypes of Latinx people appear frequently among this dialect group.

The Fiery Latina

The stereotype of the fiery Latina is that of a loud, dramatic, or easily angered woman who often also dresses provocatively or behaves promiscuously. We see 12 examples in the film set, about half of whom are minor or background characters who receive no development at all beyond the characteristics of the stereotype. Note that although other Spanish- and SIE-speaking female characters in the film set are sexualized—displayed nude or in revealing clothing or have their bodies fetishized by the camera's gaze—they're not included in this category unless they also exhibit other characteristics of the fiery Latina. Several of these depictions are worth examining individually.

One of the female SIE-speaking protagonists in the film set falls into the "fiery Latina" trope, and it is not one that readers might expect: Juarez of *G-Force*, a genetically altered hyperintelligent guinea pig who has been trained as a secret agent, is sexualized by both the camera and her fellow guinea pigs, and uses her sexuality to her advantage. We first see her climbing out of water in the midst of a mission. As a male guinea pig watches wide-eyed, she shakes herself dry in slow motion while Latin music plays in the background and the camera pans slowly up the length of her body, reminiscent of any number of similar scenes featuring human women emerging from oceans and pools, such as the famous scene in *Fast Times at Ridgemont High* (1982) starring Phoebe Cates in a now iconic red bikini. Juarez speaks Spanish-accented English with occasional Spanish words and enjoys using her sexuality to cause jealousy between t male guinea pigs. Importantly, she is not physically anthropomorphized: er body is shaped more or less realistically as a guinea pig's. The sexu zation of her character and her male colleagues' reaction to it is a parody the trope that appears repeatedly among human female characters in other ms—one must be familiar with the trope in order to get the joke. Juarez al has a fiery temper, at one point threatening to turn a male guinea pig "int a smokeside of bacon" after he makes a sarcastic comment to her. He resp ds, "Well, you are sizzling hot." The important point here is that Juarez is t really Latina—she is a guinea pig, and therefore has no race—but she i *oded* as Latina by her Spanish accent, without which she could not partic ate in the fiery Latina trope.

Chris Sanchez (Michelle Rodriguez) o 2003's *S.W.A.T.* is also a major character—though not a protagonist—in r film. She is a police officer who has repeatedly applied for and is ev ually accepted on the S.W.A.T. team, and when she's introduced, we see bare midriff first as she sits on a hospital gurney being treated for minor juries. The camera pans slowly up her torso to her face—notice the simil ty to the introduction of Juarez the guinea pig—and the S.W.A.T. leaders king for her are surprised to discover that she's female. She speaks very htly Spanish-influenced English with occasional Spanish and Chicano slan in her first scene, she remarks, "I'm sick and tired of these bullshit com ints because some *vato* doesn't like gettin' thrown to the pavement by a w nan," indicating that she's eager to use physical force on a suspect, i.e., an er Latina character with a fiery temper. After she is admitted to the S.W.A. team she has considerably fewer lines than the male members of the team; also quickly begins dating one of her colleagues, and most of her lines ur during her interactions with him. She receives no other character dev pment beyond her fiery temper and her availability as a love interest.

Meet the Fockers' (2004) Isabel Villalo s (Alanna Ubach) is the former housekeeper of and current caterer for th Focker family, whose adult son Greg (Ben Stiller) has brought his fiancée d her family home to meet them. Isabel speaks Spanish and Spanish-accent English and we hear her before we see her, yelling loudly in Spanish o screen when someone inquires where the vegetables are. She is conventic lly attractive; when we first see her, she's wearing a low-cut, close-fitting ghtly colored dress with a tropical pattern. She greets Greg dramatically a kisses him several times on the cheek, and when Greg remarks that she lo s good, she responds bluntly, "I had a boob job." We learn that Greg was e mored with Isabel as a teenager and that the two had sex when Greg was 1 -an example of the fiery Latina's stereotypically promiscuous behavior—an a running joke ensues in which the other characters try to discover whet r Isabel's teenaged son is also Greg's son. Like Chris Sanchez, her chara erization is made exclusively of her fiery temper and her sexual availability. Isabel is discussed further in the section below, "Racial and Linguistic Derision."

Isabella Molina (Roselyn Sanchez) of *Rush Hour 2* (2001) also dresses provocatively, and her body is highly sexualized by both the camera and the film's protagonists. We first meet Isabella at a yacht party; she is conventionally attractive, wears a low-cut black dress, and speaks Spanish-accented English, purporting to be from San Juan. Co-protagonist Carter (Chris Tucker) immediately begins hitting on her and propositions her with sex within a few moments of their meeting. She taunts him before turning him down, and later, Carter and Lee (Jackie Chan), suspecting that she has a connection to the primary antagonist, spy on her through the window of her hotel room using binoculars and ogle her as she undresses. We soon learn that she is an undercover secret service agent who has been using her sexuality to infiltrate the antagonist's organization; interestingly, she has more in common with Juarez the guinea pig than any other character. Like many of the other women on this list, her sexuality is apparently her only personality trait.

Another fiery Latina who is also a major character in her films is Roxanne Chase-Feder (Salma Hayek) of *Grown Ups* (2010) and *Grown Ups 2* (2013). Roxanne is the fashion designer wife of protagonist Lenny Feder (Adam Sandler) and appears in a number of scenes in both films. She speaks Spanish-accented English and, as is common among Spanish-speaking characters, switches to Spanish when angry. She dresses fashionably but not provocatively, but this doesn't prevent the other male characters from staring at her body even as the group is attending a funeral, one calling her a "sexy senorita." An older Black female character, upon first meeting her, remarks to Lenny, "What a spicy quesadilla you got yourself." These remarks indicate that we are conditioned to sexualize and view Spanish- and SIE-speaking women as "sexy" and "spicy" even when their appearance and behavior do not merit it more so than do other characters.

Fiery Latinas also comprise a number of smaller roles, most of which overlap into other stereotypical SIE speaker tropes. For example, in *Bad Boys II* (2003), protagonist police officer Mike's (Will Smith) police psychologist (Ivelin Giro) appears on screen for only a few seconds during a brief flashback. In the film's current time, Mike mentions that he once attended mandatory therapy, and the film flashes back to a shot of him and his therapist having sex on a couch during the therapy session. The therapist speaks one line of Spanish-accented English and calls Mike "*papi*." We don't even get a clear look at her face. Notably, although she is credited as a psychologist, the text of the film does not state her actual title and does not indicate whether she has a medical license—her inclusion in the film is simply a joke used to emphasize Mike's masculinity and characterization as a "ladies' man."

The final two examples of this trope ar erhaps the most blatant. On his first day working in the mailroom at a lar tech company in *Transformers: Dark of the Moon* (2011), protagonist Sa Witwicky (Shia LaBeouf) witnesses a brief but tense interaction betw two coworkers, a White male who sits on a yoga ball behind a desk and attractive Latina woman (Leidy Mazo) who stands before him wearing a t ht, cleavage- and midriff-baring white outfit. This exchange follows:

> MAN: What is this hoochie mama outfit?
>
> WOMAN: [Answers him in unsubtitled Spa h.]
>
> MAN: No, this is the aerospace division, ok we do not allow that here.
>
> WOMAN: [Continues in unsubtitled Spanis speaking over him while walking away angrily. We hear her continuing to con ain in Spanish in the background during the next lines.]
>
> MAN: [turning to Sam] New guy, you see th ? That's a Latin meltdown, okay? You ever show up in my office with a hoo e mama outfit, you're fired. You got that?

Sam is wearing a conservative button- wn shirt and tie and has shown no propensity for wearing revealing clot ng; the White man's comment serves no purpose other than to mock an er provocatively dressed Latina with a fiery temper. The lack of subtitl indicates that her words—her perspective—do not matter. The scene, w ch has no bearing on the plot, exists only for the amusement and gratifica on of the presumed White, male, EDC-speaking audience.

Finally, *Jumanji: The Next Level*'s (20 Lady in Red (Dania Ramirez) presents certainly the most literal use of t fiery Latina trope. The story—discussed in more detail in Chapter 5—fea res several people who are transported bodily into a video game and must c nplete the game to escape it. The Lady in Red is a non-player character (NP who, in the world of the game, is the ex-girlfriend of a player, Bravestone Dwayne Johnson). After another NPC gives the group a mysterious piece o dvice—to "follow the flame" to find an important clue—they discover the dy in Red in a dimly lit bar. She speaks Spanish-accented English, is conv tionally attractive, and wears a low-cut, off-the-shoulder red dress; the ly "The world was on fire and no one could save me but you" from Chris Is k's "Wicked Game" plays in the background when we first see her. She ap oaches Bravestone and tells him softly that she needs to speak to him priva ly; then, to entice him to follow her, she slaps his face and runs away. He re arks, "Fiery!" The group follows her outside where she confesses to Braves ne that if her husband knew she was talking to him, he would "be dead by rning" before revealing the next step required to complete the game. She then kisses Bravestone passionately twice before they part. It might be fair to say that the Lady in Red is not a character at all but is rather pure embodied trope, an SIE-speaking Latina who is fiery, sexualized, and nothing else.

The Latin Lover

The stereotypical Latin lover is typically depicted as a handsome, passionate, and romantic SIE-speaking man with sexual prowess; he is also often a serial seducer. We find three examples in the film set, but unlike the fiery Latina stereotype, these are parodies of the trope rather than direct depictions.

The Proposal (2009) features a White female Canadian immigrant editor in chief of a major publishing company, Margaret Tate (Sandra Bullock), who is at risk of deportation and blackmails White male employee Andrew Paxton (Ryan Reynolds), forcing him to marry her so she can remain in the U.S. When she travels to his remote Alaskan hometown to meet his family, his female relatives take her to a strip club where a short, potbellied Latino man named Ramone (Oscar Nuñez) performs an exotic dance to raucous cheers from the entirely White audience as several women shove money into his pants. He then pulls Margaret on stage to perform a lap dance for her, thrusting his pelvis repeatedly into her face while Andrew's grandmother (Betty White) encourages Margaret to "smack his ass." Ramone appears in several other scenes and we learn that he is also a caterer and runs the island's general store, and he later also performs Margaret and Andrew's wedding ceremony. He speaks with a strong Spanish accent and continues to flirt with Margaret whenever they interact exclusive of her wedding. Ramone displays all the traits of the Latin lover except the conventionally handsome physique; the joke lies in the fact that these isolated White island women react to his dance as though he is, indeed, very attractive, implying that *all* "Latin" men are passionate and skilled lovers, regardless of their appearance.

Toy Story 4 (2010) includes a subplot, described in more detail in the section "Mock Spanish" below, in which co-protagonist and toy space ranger Buzz Lightyear (Tim Allen) is accidently switched to "Spanish mode." For a major portion of the film, he speaks Spanish (voiced by Javier Fernández-Peña) and behaves like a parody of the stereotypical Latin lover: he collapses to his knees at the sight of toy cowgirl Jessie (Joan Cusack) and professes his feelings passionately for her; later he dances around her using exaggerated movements while Latin guitar music plays. At the end of the film, after he has been returned to his normal English-speaking personality, he finds his hips twitching involuntarily when Jessie plays Latin music on the radio. His Latin lover personality springs forward again, and the two dance together while Jessie clutches a rose between her teeth. Nadia Lie, in "From Latin to

Latino Lover: Hispanicity and Female De e in Popular Culture” points out that “[t]he association between Latin Love and dance” is “a fixed one”[16]—indeed, in this film the Latin music bring ut Buzz’s inner Latin lover like a full moon bringing out a werewolf. A n, the joke lies in the contrast between the behavior of the character and is image: while he performs the role of Latin lover, he is, in fact, a plastic wearing a bulky space suit and bulbous helmet with a limited range of mo n. The humor cannot land unless the audience is already familiar with the L n lover stereotype.

The final example bears great similar to the previous: the character Puss in Boots (Antonio Banderas) appear n four films in the film set, but his characterization as a Latin lover is mo prominent in his own film, *Puss in Boots* (2011). Puss speaks Spanish and panish-accented English, and in the opening scene of this children’s film, meet him sneaking away from a bed where a female cat sleeps whose name e has already forgotten. Later he “dance fights” a rival cat thief in an extend scene while, again, Latin guitar music plays; when he discovers this rival i emale, he propositions her: “Let me buy you some *leche*! I am a lover, n a fighter.” This rival later comments on Puss’s reputation with women. In e final voiceover narration, Puss describes himself as “an outlaw dedicated justice and a lover of beautiful women. A great, great lover. Really, it is zy.” The joke once again lies in the framing of the character as a Latin lo within his own story while the audience doesn’t actually see him as phy ally attractive because he is, of course, a cat. Lie points out the direct co parisons between Puss’s characterization in *Shrek 2* (2004) and the classi atin lover character Zorro, also played by Banderas in *The Mask of Zorr* 1998) and *The Legend of Zorro* (2005)—in addition to being played by th same actor, Puss carves his first initial into a tree using a sword, and the bl rings around his eyes evoke the idea of a mask. But in *Shrek 2*, Lie notes, xcept for his constant flattering of Shrek and one suggestive pass to [prin ss] Fiona (‘I could be Shrek to you, baby’), all that remains of his Latin L r capacities is this ability on the dance floor.”[17] It is not until *Puss in Boot* hat he realizes his full potential in this trope.

Why is the Latin lover trope only paro d among the SIE-speaking male characters in our film set while the fiery tina trope is fully realized and, indeed, shamelessly employed, among the E-speaking women? The paucity of women in behind-the-camera roles may ovide one explanation. The 2016 USC Annenberg study on diversity in me found that only 10.8% of film writers and 3.4% of film directors were wo en;[18] in other words, mainstream film is still very much an artefact of the m gaze. Under this gaze, the Latin lover trope becomes a source of comedy, le the fiery Latina trope remains very much intact.

The Immigrant and the Refugee

The Spanish-speaking undocumented immigrant or refugee character appears seven times in five films and, with one exception, serves two specific roles: as a source of humor and/or as a direct or indirect threat to the protagonist. For example, in *Fun with Dick and Jane* (2005) White protagonist Dick (Jim Carrey) joins a large group of undocumented Latino men waiting for work. When a White man pulls up in a truck and asks for one worker who knows how to paint, the entire group runs after him. Dick manages to grab the back of the truck, but another man punches him and knocks him off in a moment of physical comedy. Only three other men speak in the scene—Carlos, Eduardo, and Gustavo (Dario Gonzalez, Emilio Rivera, and Jullian Dulce Vida; Dick uses their names but they are all credited as "Day Laborer")—using Spanish and Spanish-accented English, and they are kind to Dick, reassuring him that his injury does not look bad. Later we see the four of them playing cards together; just as Dick decides to leave for the day, INS arrives and Dick is rounded up with the group in a misunderstanding discussed further in "Mock Spanish" below. In this instance, the humor is found not in mocking the Spanish speakers directly, but in the fact that a White man is treated as one of them; the incongruous images of Jim Carrey huddled despondently with the men against a wall, seated at their card game, and being roughly herded onto a bus with them are meant to be comedic. The men also fulfill the role of the indirect threat, as being treated like an undocumented Latino Spanish speaker is horrifying to the White protagonist and, by proxy, the presumed White audience.

A Latina immigrant seen only briefly on screen serves a similar role in *The Proposal*. After convincing Andrew to pretend to be her fiancé, Margaret and he rush to the immigration office to file the appropriate paperwork. As an immigration officer threatens them with deportation, prison time, and fines if their visa application is fraudulent, a straight-faced Andrew watches a uniformed White man drag away a struggling Latina woman shouting in Spanish outside the office. The implication is that Andrew could suffer the same fate if his and Margaret's scheme is discovered; again, this is unthinkable to the protagonists and to the audience.

Pitch Perfect 2 (2015) centers around an all-female college acapella group which includes a comedic immigrant character, Flo (Chrissie Fit), who speaks Spanish-accented English. Nearly every line spoken by or about Flo is a joke about the stereotypical difficulties of life in her home country, which is never positively identified—this, too, is part of the joke. Flo is first introduced backflipping across the stage during a performance, prompting commentator John (John Michael Higgins) to joke, "She may need to do that flip right over the fence and back into Mexico." His fellow commentator Gail (Elizabeth

Banks) replies, “I think she’s Guatemala to which John responds, “Oh, none of that matters”: a message clearly r ant for the audience as much as for Gail. Later, after the group is banned f m competing due to a wardrobe malfunction, another member, Chloe (Britt y Snow), remarks despondently, “This is the worst thing that’s ever happen to any of us!” Flo replies drily, “Before coming to Barden I had diarrhea f seven years. But yes, this is terrible.” A later scene repeats this joke, Chl exclaiming, “This is the biggest challenge that any of us have ever faced! and Flo retorting, “When I was nine years old, my brother tried to sell me r a chicken, so . . . ” Still later, when the group considers admitting anoth member, Flo points out, “Good to have an extra body in case someone get kidnapped”; and during a camping scene, when the other members discu their postgraduation plans, Flo says, “After I graduate there’s a chance I w be deported. I will try to reenter this country, but there’s a chance I will die sea.” No one reacts to this. The stereotype of Mexico and Central Americ countries as dirty, poor, dangerous, and homogenous and the contrast of White characters’ ignorance of and apathy toward this reality are the sou e of comedy surrounding Flo’s character, and she receives no character velopment beyond them. In this film the immigrant character is exclusivel humorous prop.

Knives Out (2019) also features a run ng joke in which the wealthy, privileged White family does not know at country their elderly father’s Latina home nurse, Marta, comes from: e claims she is from Ecuador, another from Paraguay, a third from Braz We the audience never actually learn where she and her family immigrate rom, indicating that, as in *Pitch Perfect 2*, it’s not important—the gag fun ons to mock the ignorant White characters and for this purpose, one Spa h-speaking domestic worker is, apparently, as good as another. Marta, how er, is not the undocumented individual in this example; it is her mother, w se undocumented status is used to threaten Marta directly when the family arns that their recently deceased patriarch left his fortune to her. Both Marta d her mother speak Spanish and Spanish-accented English, and her mother ppears on screen for only a few moments; she is yet another minor Spanis speaking character whose presence in her film functions only as a tool to rther the plot.

The exception to this pattern mentione bove appears in *Cloudy with a Chance of Meatballs*, which features Ma , cameraman for the local television news. Manny appears on screen r larly but doesn’t speak until a rather serious scene late in the film in wh a child is injured. Manny then reveals that he is a doctor—to everyone’s prise, including his reporter colleague—and saves the child. We soon dis ver that he is also a pilot; after this he jokes that he is also a particle phy cist, which is not true. Like the other characters described above, he rece s very little character development (though we do learn that he is from uatemala), but the film doesn’t joke at his expense. Rather, he uses his piloting and medical skills to aid the White characters in reversing a catastrophe caused by the White protagonist, his status as an immigrant being incidental to the plot. He represents the only positive, nonstereotypical portrayal of a Spanish-speaking refugee in the entire 493-film set.

QUEER IN SIE

Our film set includes six openly gay SIE-speaking characters representing 1.8% of total Spanish and SIE speakers—a small number, but considerably higher than the percentage of Southern English speakers represented as queer, and slightly higher than the percentage of Black English speakers. In some cases the character's sexuality is relevant to their role, while in other cases it is incidental, but none of these characters is portrayed as exclusively positive or even particularly nuanced; instead, they form a collage of gay and SIE-speaking stereotypes.

2000's *Traffic* features Francisco Flores, a.k.a. "Frankie Flowers" (Clifton Collins, Jr.), a gay Mexican hitman for hire whose character is primarily a one-dimensional pawn who bounces from location to location furthering the plot as needed. His sexuality is mostly irrelevant aside from a scene in which Mexican police officer Javier Rodriguez (Benicio del Toro) is able to kidnap him easily by flirting with him at a gay bar, an unfortunate example of the stereotype of gay men as promiscuous and opportunistic when it comes to sex.

2001's *Legally Blonde* includes the character of Enrique Salvatore (Greg Serano), a pool boy who lies about having an affair with a wealthy older woman so as to help her stepdaughter frame her for murder. In a key scene during a break in the trial, Salvatore, who wears a loud, brightly colored sequined jacket with the Virgin Mary on the back and speaks SIE with a lisp, cuts in front of protagonist Elle (Reese Witherspoon) at a water fountain. Elle taps her foot impatiently, and Salvatore stands up and turns to her, saying, "Don't estomp your little last-season Prada shoes at me, honey." As he walks away, Elle says to herself, "They're not last season"; her eyes then widen in an epiphany as she realizes that Salvatore is gay, and therefore must not have actually been involved in this affair. Salvatore's lisp, flamboyant clothing and mannerisms, and knowledge of fashion represent several gay stereotypes rolled into one, which is par for early 2000s representations of gay characters. *Anger Management* (2003) also includes a flamboyantly gay SIE speaker with a lisp, Lou (Luis Guzmán), a member of the protagonist's support group, discussed again in "Racial and Linguistic Derision" below, who is mocked by other characters for both his sexuality and his race. He has corn rows and wears see-through mesh shirts, crop tops, a a single large hoop earring, and when he speaks, he uses stereotypical exa erated hand gestures.

A minor comedic character appears in Hitch (2005) in Raoul (Maulik Pancholy), a doorman at protagonist Hitch (Will Smith) apartment building who appears in two brief scenes, talks op nly about his male partner, and calls Hitch "*papi*" despite Hitch's objectio s. He has no impact on the plot and appears to serve merely as intermitter omic relief, the combination of his sexuality and his Spanish accent appar tly meant to be enough to make his character funny. (We'll discuss the im cation that Spanish is inherently funny in more detail below.)

In 2012's *Skyfall*, part of the James nd franchise, the villain, Silva (Javier Bardem) is implied to be gay or b exual in his first encounter with Bond (Daniel Craig). Bond has been tied t a chair, and as Silva interrogates him, he unbuttons the top buttons of Bond white shirt and caresses his neck and thighs in a tense moment. In an intervi v with *The Hollywood Reporter*, screenwriter John Logan acknowledged th he wrote the character this way to intentionally unnerve viewers: "[T]he s been so many ways to do a cat-and-mouse and intimidate Bond, and w thought, what would truly make the audience uncomfortable is sexual intim ation; playing the sort of homo-erotic card that is sort of always there subt tually."[19] Though Logan himself is gay, the implication that a gay villain i imidating Bond sexually would make the audience more uncomfortable th n a straight female villain doing the same thing betrays the overt hetero ga e of the mainstream Hollywood camera. Indeed, Lauren Spungen compar the scene to similar scenes of nonconsensual heterosexual seduction in revious Bond films, and argues that the tying of Bond's hands intensifies t villain's menacing aspect: "The decision to have Bond's arms tied up whi receiving unwelcomed physical contact from Silva makes the villain seem e more of a monster than in past Bond films and portrays homosexuality a a larger evil that is being forced upon the 'good' in society."[20] Beyond th scene, Silva's sexuality has no bearing on his character or the plot.

Finally, 2013's *We're the Millers* inclu s a comedic scene in which the faux Miller family, who are attempting to muggle thousands of pounds of cannabis from Mexico into the U.S. in a RV, are stopped by a Mexican cop (again played by Luis Guzmán) who fers to let them go in exchange for a bribe:

> DAVID: How much we talkin', a hundred, t hundred?
>
> COP: One thousand.
>
> DAVID: A thousand? What, are you buyin' a ouse down here? We don't have that sort of cash on us right now.

COP: Hm. You see, that's gonna be a problem. Maybe you can offer me something else. Say, uh, something a little more personal.

DAVID: Oh. I gotcha. [turning to his "wife"] Rose, suck his dick.

ROSE: Fuck you! I'm not sucking anything.

DAVID: Come on, will you be a team player?

[. . .]

COP: *Señora*, no need to be alarmed. See, I'm, how you say, a man who prefers the company of other men.

DAVID: Oh.

ROSE: Oh. David, suck his dick.

David then quickly volunteers his teenaged "son" Kenny, who is about to go through with the act until the family realizes that the cop wants a thousand pesos rather than a thousand dollars. This scene, again, depicts the gay character as menacing, as predatory, reinforcing decades of stereotypes about gay men preying upon young boys.

Why are there proportionately more gay SIE-speaking characters than Black English- or Southern-speaking characters? Arguably, the difference in queer representation between SIE speakers and Black English speakers (1.8% versus 1.3%) is actually negligible. As we discussed in Chapter 2, these characters exist at an intersection of race, language, and sexuality encompassing three underrepresented minority groups and thereby compounding the underrepresentation. We will not have more complex and nuanced queer SIE-speaking characters on film until we have both more queer characters and more SIE-speaking characters in general. Regarding the comparison to queer Southern speakers, as we saw in Chapter 3, the Southern-speaking "redneck" stereotype is associated with sexual deviance but almost never with homosexuality, perhaps because it is trumped by the more pervasive stereotype of the bigoted, homophobic Southerner. This stereotype, too, will not change until we see broader representations of blue collar Southern speakers on our screens.

MOCKERY

The use of Spanish by native English-speaking film characters for purely practical purposes—i.e., to communicate with native Spanish speakers without humor or denigration—is surprisingly rare in the data set, appearing in only a few brief words or lines in each of about 12 films (this doesn't include films in which the native English speaker exchanges only a greeting in Spanish). As we shall see in the following sections, English speakers in mainstream film use Spanish and fake Spanish accents *far* more frequently for comedic effect than for actual communication.

Mock Spanish

In her 2008 book *The Everyday Language of White Racism*, Hill defines Mock Spanish as

> a set of tactics that speakers of American English use to appropriate symbolic resources from Spanish. In Mock Spanish Spanish loan words like *macho* "male," *cerveza* "beer," and *mañana* "morning, tomorrow," expressions like *hasta la vista* "until we meet again," and even a few morphological elements such as the Spanish definite article *el* and the masculine singular suffix *-o* are assigned new pronunciations, new meanings and new kinds of cultural value (Agha 2003).[21]

This "covert racist discourse," she argues, props up and reinforces negative stereotypes about Spanish speakers. As an iconic example she cites the famous line from the 1991 film *Terminator 2: Judgment Day*, "Hasta la vista, baby." The Terminator (Arnold Schwarzenegger) says the line before shooting and destroying the antagonist, the T-1000 (Robert Patrick), indicating that it is "not a sincere farewell," and "the pleasure of the phrase requires access to a negative stereotype of Spanish speakers as treacherous and insincere, the kind of people who would tell you politely 'Until we meet again' and in the next instant blow you away."[22] Mock Spanish, Hill continues, converts Spanish grammar and vocabulary into a form of English, subtly changing its meaning and tone. Mock Spanish can be pejorative or comedic, but it is never formal.[23]

Hill further claims that "Mock Spanish works to create a particular kind of 'American' identity, a desirable colloquial persona that is informal and easy going, with an all-important sense of humor and a hint—not too much, but just the right nonthreatening amount—of cosmopolitanism, acquaintance with another language and culture."[24] For example, in the dialogue we examined at the beginning of this chapter from *We're the Millers*, David uses Mock Spanish as he speaks to One-Eye: his pronunciation is hyperanglicized, and he adds the suffix *-o* to an English word, *wee-te*. The primary conceit of *We're the Millers* is the White family's efforts to appear easygoing and nonthreatening, whether they are avoiding unwanted attention from law enforcement or interacting with their Mexican suppliers, and David's use of Mock Spanish to do so aligns with Hill's observations. Hill further notes, "At the same time that Mock Spanish helps to constitute this identity, it assigns Spanish and its speakers to a zone of foreignness and disorder, richly fleshed out with denigrating stereotypes."[25] David's territory is safe, orderly White America. David is cultured enough to have a passing familiarity with Spanish, but his hyperanglicized pronunciation of Mock Spanish indicates that he does not *truly* speak it. The territory of Spanish speakers, on the other hand, is dusty, chaotic, and dangerous. As we have seen, the depiction of both Spanish speakers and Spanish-influenced English speakers in the film set is loaded with these stereotypes.

Mock Spanish appears in at least 87 of the 493 films examined—over 17%, more than seven times the number of films that feature English speakers using real Spanish for practical purpose only. Hill points out that Mock Spanish "is a staple of humor in films, and especially in television cartoons aimed at children,"[26] and indeed, of the 87 films noted, 26 are rated G or PG and targeted at children. Hill identifies four tactics by which Spanish loan words are transmogrified into Mock Spanish, all of which, we shall see, appear in our film data set. We shall also use Hill's methods for transcription: true Spanish is italicized, while Mock Spanish is not italicized nor does it use diacritics such as accents or tildes because it is truly a type of English, not a type of Spanish.

The first tactic Hill describes is "semantic pejoration," in which "Spanish words of neutral or even positive meaning are moved down into a semantic space that ranges from the merely jocular to the deeply negative and insulting." Goodbyes such as "adios" and "hasta la vista" and terms of address such as "amigo," "senor," etc. might be used merely for humor, or they might be used insultingly or threateningly, but they can never be used formally.[27] This is the most common Mock Spanish tactic that appears in our film set. We see numerous examples of native English speakers—usually, but not always, White—using Mock Spanish to insult, degrade, or harass both Spanish speakers and non-Spanish speakers as well as using it simply for comedic effect. For instance, in *Suicide Squad*, prison guard Griggs (Ike Barinholtz), who has been shown repeatedly abusing prisoners physically and verbally, addresses the Spanish-speaking prisoner El Diablo in an overtly racist manner: "Yo ese. Hola amigo. Put that burrito down, you got visitors man." In this scene, Diablo is not actually holding a burrito nor any kind of food; rather, Griggs is mocking him. Later, after Diablo asks fellow squad member Deadshot (Will Smith) what Deadshot considers to be an offensive question—how many people he has killed—Deadshot calls Diablo "ese." In another superhero film, 2017's *Logan*, a White female motel manager (Maureen Brennan) rudely scolds Mexican nurse Gabriela (Elizabeth Rodriguez) after Gabriela's ten-year-old ward accidentally breaks a window with a ball, calling Gabriela "mamacita." Later, in a scene ostensibly filmed covertly with a cell phone in an illicit genetic research facility in Mexico, a Whit 3ritish doctor (Richard E. Grant) chastises a Mexican nurse in English, then risively asks her, "Comprende?" Gabriela comments on this obviously patrc zing behavior in voiceover, saying, "They thought we were too poor and ıpid to understand."[28]

Examples of English speakers using M ıck Spanish to insult or harass non-Spanish speakers are somewhat less ommon but by no means rare. They include a scene in 2003's *Charlie Angels: Full Throttle* in which White antagonist Madison Lee (Demi Moc), thinking that she has defeated one of the three protagonist "angels," says the remaining two, "Looks like one of the three amigos has gone adios." A that moment, the missing angel, Dylan (Drew Barrymore), appears behind r and attempts to kick her in the head. Lee catches Dylan's foot without ning and greets her mockingly with "Hola." Yet another example appe in *Spider-Man: Homecoming* when the villain, Adrian Toomes (Michael eaton), in preparing to fight hero Spider-Man/Peter Parker (Tom Holland) g ts him with, "Hey Pedro." He is reminding Peter that he knows his secret ic ntity, thereby threatening Peter's loved ones.

The use of Mock Spanish for purely cc edic effect is even more extensive throughout our film set. Non-Spanish peakers—again, usually but not always White—insert Mock Spanish wor and phrases into conversation without prompting in dozens of examples, ıd as Hill posits, these examples never appear in formal or serious conte s. Non-Spanish-speaking characters often refer to each other as "amig or "compadre" and use words such as "vamanos" and "andale" in place f their English equivalents. The well-known phrase "Mi casa es tu casa" o appears in some form in two separate films.

In some cases, the Mock Spanish in given film consists of a single word. For instance, in *Ice Age: Continenta Drift* (2012), Sid the Sloth (John Leguizamo) exclaims, "Oh my whole fam a!" when reunited with his family. In *Juno* (2007), teenaged protagonist uno (Elliot Page) responds to a drug store clerk (Rainn Wilson) who is ocking her with "Silencio, old man!" In other cases, Mock Spanish appe in numerous or extended interactions. A running joke in the 2005 film *un with Dick and Jane* features Dick (Jim Carrey) and Jane's (Téa Leoni) oung son Billy (Aaron Michael Drozin) frequently speaking Spanish beca e he spends more time with the Spanish-speaking maid than with his overv rked parents. For instance, when he protests losing his TV privileges, he s s, "Don't take my Telemundo! SpongeBob Pantalones!" Later in the film a scene we discussed above in the "Immigrant and Refugee" stereotype, Dick is looking for work and is waiting with a group of Latino constructio workers, implied to be undocumented immigrants, when INS agents arriv and begin arresting them. Dick's mouth is swollen after being punched ir he face and he speaks with an impediment, pronouncing his wife's name as "Yane" rather than "Jane," which one INS agent interprets as a Spanish accent. The agent mocks Dick for this, saying, "You need to work on that accent, Pablo." In an attempt to prove his citizenship (and his English-speaking ability), Dick asks the agent to call his home, but Billy answers the phone with "Hola?," further cementing the agent's suspicions.

The Lego Batman Movie (2017) also features a running gag between Batman/Bruce Wayne (Will Arnett) and Robin/Dick Grayson (Michael Cera) using Mock Spanish. At a fancy party, orphan Dick asks fellow orphan Bruce Wayne for advice in getting adopted:

> Dick: How about eyeliner or a foreign language?
>
> Bruce: Try both.
>
> Dick: Bueno.

While at the party, Bruce unwittingly agrees to adopt Dick himself, but later, in his guise as Batman, feels uncomfortable when Dick calls him "Dad." They agree on "Padre" as a compromise since, according to Batman, it can also mean "friend" or "pal," and Dick addresses him as such throughout the rest of the film. At the end of the film, Batman finally accepts Dick as his son and refers to him as "mi hijo," clarifying for the non-Spanish-speaking listeners in the film and in the audience, "It's Spanish for 'son.'"

The second tactic for Mock Spanish creation identified by Hill is euphemism, in which "Spanish words that are insulting, lewd, or scatological in Spanish are substituted for vulgar English words."[29] She cites the specific examples of *loco*, *caca*, and *cojones*, describing the latter as "especially offensive to Spanish speakers."[30] We find all three of these usages in our film set, specifically, three uses of *loco*, one of *caca*, and three of *cojones*. Interestingly, all three uses of *loco* appear in children's films: one example in *Alvin and the Chipmunks: Chipwrecked* (2011), a second in *Happy Feet* (2006), and a third in *Despicable Me 2* (2013).

English-speaking characters also use nonvulgar Spanish words in place of English profanity for comedic effect, a form of euphemism not specifically identified by Hill. In *Cloudy with a Chance of Meatballs* (2009), protagonist Flint Lockwood (Bill Hader) accidentally destroys an amusement park and wreaks havoc on a town after his scientific invention malfunctions. When the mayhem ends and the dust settles, Flint says only, "Ay, papi." Similarly, in *Dr. Dolittle 2* (2001), Archie the bear (Steve Zahn), after being told he has been sold to a Mexican circus, responds, "Ay chihuahua." And finally, in *The 40-Year-Old Virgin* (2005), protagonist Andy (Steve Carell) tries not to swear while having his chest waxed, and instead pews out a slew of random nonsense: "Sweaty pie hole! Como se llama! lly Clarkson!"

The third tactic that Hill identifies is "t add Spanish morphology, especially the definite article 'el' and the suff '-o' . . . to English words. The most common example is 'No problemo from English 'No problem.'"[31] This tactic, too, appears regularly in the ta set. "Problemo" in particular occurs three times: "No problemo" in *Re Dragon* (2002) and *Night at the Museum* (2006) and "Problemo solved" *Madagascar: Escape 2 Africa* (2008). Other forms of this tactic includ in example from *Mamma Mia!* (2008) in which friend of the protagonist anya (Christine Baranski) calls protagonist Donna (Meryl Streep) "el roc chick supremo," as well as two examples from *Meet the Fockers* (2004), oth provided by Bernie Focker (Dustin Hoffman), the father of the prota nist. In the first, he explains to houseguests that "[t]he upstairs bathroom s on el fritzo"; in the second, he speaks to his toddler grandson, saying, "Y have to question everything El Stiffo Grandpa Jack says."

We're the Millers' David also uses Hill's ourth tactic, "hyperanglicization and the closely related tactic of bold mispr unciation."[32] In the lines quoted at the beginning of the chapter, he uses merican English pronunciation with no attempt to mimic accurate Spanish honemes. "Mock Spanish," Hill argues, "with its relentlessly anglicized an even hyperanglicized and boldly mispronounced phonology and pidgin gra mar, assigns native Spanish fluency to the realm of the 'un-American.'" David is making every effort to appear the epitome of the White middle-c ss American, and as such, he is not permitted to pronounce Spanish words orrectly.

While most of the examples of Mock Sp ish in the film set use anglicized and hyperanglicized pronunciation, some d use the more overtly racist "bold mispronunciation," which parodies real Sp nish pronunciation. We also find many examples of an exaggerated and par ic imitation of Spanish-accented English that has close parallels with the or graphic "visual accent" of Lupe Vélez discussed in Chapter 1. These imita ns are not intended to represent authentic pronunciation of either Spanish r Spanish-accented English but rather distorted caricatures of both that ve been popularized in White media over the course of decades. Exampl include an extended scene in *22 Jump Street* (2014) in which undercover p ice officer Schmidt (Jonah Hill) uses parodic grammar and pronunciation Spanish and Spanish-accented English while pretending to be a Mexica drug dealer, hoping to infiltrate what he believes to be a group of suppliers lso Mexican. The scene features a number of lines of this, including "You S epy! Everyone say in the barrio, Sleepy, he like the Mexican Wolverine and it. . . . My partner here, he want to see the product." Schmidt's partner, Jenk (Channing Tatum), also attempts to use this accent when pressed by the suspicious suppliers (who, incidentally, are dealing not in drugs but in exotic animals), but is able to mutter only a few halting words. This—not Schmidt's obviously satirical performance—is what tips off the suppliers in this comedy. In *Rango* (2011), chameleon protagonist Rango (Johnny Depp) utilizes both parodic mispronunciation and the Latin lover stereotype in describing his ability to assume many false identities: "And if you desire romance, I will become the greatest lover the world has ever known! Hola /hola/. . . . You know the womens /wimənz/ find me uncomfortably good looking."[34]

Anglicization and hyperanglicization of Mock Spanish serve to distance (usually White) English speakers from Spanish, indicating that they have a familiarity with it but, importantly, are *not Spanish speakers*, while parodic mispronunciation of Spanish and Spanish-accented English are used to directly make fun of Spanish and Spanish speakers. A foil to these two types of usage is hypercorrect pronunciation, in which English speakers go out of their way to emphasize Spanish pronunciation to a degree that calls attention to itself. We see two examples in the film set.

The first appears in *Spy Kids* (2001), one of the exceedingly rare films to feature several Spanish-and Spanish-accented-English-speaking major characters whose ethnicity and speech are not subjects of humor and who do not fall into the stereotypes we typically see assigned to such speakers. Though the young protagonists (Alexa PenaVega and Daryl Sabara) speak EDC, their father, Gregorio Cortez (Antonio Banderas), and several other positively depicted characters speak Spanish-accented and Spanish-influenced English. However, White English-speaking villain Fegan Floop (Alan Cumming) mockingly calls Cortez "Mr. Corteth" /koɾtɛθ/, using hypercorrect pronunciation. (Cortez himself and the other native Spanish speakers pronounce the name "Cortes" /koɾtes/, while other native English speakers, including Mrs. Cortez (Carla Gugino), pronounce it "Cortez" /kɔɹtɛz/.) It's unclear whether this mispronunciation is intentional on the part of the character—is he mocking Cortez's Spanish heritage or is he simply ignorant of the correct pronunciation? In either case, his distance from Latinx culture and the Spanish language set him apart and differentiate him as an outsider in an unusual negative depiction.

We find the second example of hypercorrect Spanish pronunciation in buddy cop film *The Heat* (2013), in which White FBI agent Ashburn (Sandra Bullock) repeatedly pronounces the name of a low-level drug dealer, Rojas, with an exaggerated rolled *r*. Ashburn is uptight and by the book; her colleague Mullins (Melissa McCarthy) mocks her neatly pressed pantsuits, her refusal to use physical threats when interrogating an inmate, and her disdain for profanity. Ashburn is also eager to earn a promotion and her superior officer, Hale (Demián Bichir), is a native Spanish speaker who also speaks

English with a Spanish accent. Ashburn uses the hypercorrect pronunciation of "Rojas" as well as a few other Spanish words ("*lo siento*," "*señor*," "*perdón*") when speaking to Hale, and based on her characterization we can interpret this not as mocking Hale or the Spanish language, but as a misguided attempt to impress her boss. Hale is another unique positive depiction of a Spanish-speaking character whose speech and race are not a source of jokes and, like *Spy Kids*, the Anglo character's ignorance of Spanish pronunciation is used to mock the Anglo rather than the Spanish speaker.

AMERICANS THINK ALL FOREIGN LANGUAGES ARE SPANISH

Another interesting pattern appears across a number of films in which an American English speaker mistakes another language for Spanish or vice versa. This is most frequently played for laughs in comedies, as in 2007's live-action *Alvin and The Chipmunks*, in which villain Ian (David Cross), who wishes only to exploit the singing chipmunks for profit with no regard for their well-being, commissions cheap, ugly, foreign-language-speaking stuffed versions of them to sell. When Ian first presents one to the chipmunks' human guardian Dave (Jason Lee), the toy speaks a line in what is clearly Japanese, but Ian remarks, "It's Spanish! It's funny." In *The Karate Kid* (2010), Dre (Jaden Smith) is a young American boy who has recently immigrated to China. In trying to make himself understood to his apartment building's Chinese-speaking maintenance man, he says "No hot agua," as though this will somehow be clearer to the man than English. And in *Pokémon Detective Pikachu* (2019), while examining a container of drugs he has found, Pikachu (Ryan Reynolds) says, apparently seriously, "This is what a Frenchman would call, 'caliente fiesta.'" The joke, of course, is that Americans are notoriously inept at learning secondary languages relative to the rest of the world, and that what little secondary language exposure they do have is likely to be to Spanish; therefore, White Americans assume that all foreign languages are Spanish. We see another version of this joke in *Ghostbusters* (2016): after demonic forces attack hotel janitor Fernando (Jaime Pacheco) on the job, the Ghostbusters are called to investigate. They arrive as Fernando is carried out on a stretcher muttering in Spanish; no subtitles are provided but the word *diablo* is clearly repeated several times. Ghostbuster Erin Gilbert (Kristen Wiig) translates: "There's a chicken frying itself in the library," and Ghostbuster Patty (Leslie Jones) responds, "That is not what he said."

Note that in three of the four examples discussed above, it is a protagonist who makes the mistake and shows their ignorance of other languages. We can infer, then, that while the audience might find this ignorance funny, they don't find it shameful; the filmmakers almost certainly assume that much of the audience shares this ignorance themselves. We might even interpret this phenomenon as cousin to Mock Spanish, as it demonstrates Hill's "all-important sense of humor and a hint—not too much, but just the right nonthreatening amount—of cosmopolitanism, acquaintance with another language and culture."[35] These speakers indeed have no more than a hint of familiarity with another language, and because their audience presumably shares their ignorance, we are permitted to laugh both at and with them and, by proxy, ourselves.

In fact, many filmmakers take advantage of this ignorance in their casting and writing decisions. As discussed earlier in this chapter, actors are often called upon to use accents and dialects that they don't speak natively; for example, in *Quantum of Solace*, former Bolivian secret service agent Camille is played by Ukrainian actor Olga Kurylenko; in *Pirates of the Caribbean: On Stranger Tides* (2011), King Ferdinand of Spain is played by English actor Sebastian Armesto. In addition, Spanish actors are frequently cast to play Mexican and Central American characters—the reverse is less common but not unheard of—and Spanish-speaking and Spanish heritage actors of many nationalities sometimes play Brazilian characters. We find a number of examples of this in *Rio* (2011) and *Rio 2* (2014), which take place in Brazil, including, for instance, actor Carlos Ponce, a native of Puerto Rico who plays Marcel, the primary antagonist in *Rio*. (These characters are not counted in the data on Spanish and SIE speakers because in the worlds of their films, they are Portuguese speakers, not Spanish speakers.)

Furthermore, *Rio* and *Rio 2* contain no instances of major characters speaking intelligible Portuguese *other* than a few brief lines that are lexically and grammatically identical to Spanish, including some which resemble Mock Spanish. For instance, in *Rio 2*, Gabi (Kristin Chenoweth), a poison dart frog who speaks EDC, says, "Wow, Nigel is muy macho," and Roberto (Bruno Mars), a Spix's macaw who also speaks EDC, says, "Mi casa es su casa." Again, these data are not counted as Mock Spanish because in the world of the film the characters are Brazilian, but in these lines the writers are clearly relying on the audience's familiarity with both Spanish and Mock Spanish; therefore we might categorize these examples as a different subset of mockery, perhaps Mock Portuguese. A similar example appears in *Signs* (2002) during which White English speaker Merrill (Joaquin Phoenix) watches a news broadcast that features a home video taken at a children's birthday party in Brazil. The children are blocking the view of an alien, and Merrill in frustration yells at the television, "Move children! Vamanos!" Many non-Spanish-speaking Americans would understand the word *vamanos* but might not realize that the word is the same in Portuguese; indeed, Merrill himself might not realize or care that the ildren are speaking Portuguese, not Spanish. Again, this is evidence of th ilmmakers' assumption that the presumed White American audience is norant of languages other than English; in short, it is evidence that these ns are made for White monolingual English speakers.

A final, odd example comes from *Clo y with a Chance of Meatballs*, appearing not in the film itself but in th closed captions. While flying a plane, Manny, the SIE-speaking camera n/doctor/pilot discussed earlier, exclaims quite clearly, "*Was ist das*?"—Ge an for "What is that?" However, the film's closed captions interpret this a "[speaking Spanish]." It seems, then, that not only do audiences think that foreign languages are Spanish; closed caption generators do as well.

RACIAL AND LINGUI IC DERISION

In addition to Mock Spanish, we see a nu er of instances in the film set in which a Spanish or SIE speaker's race o nguage are mocked or insulted directly, a form of overt racism apparen still acceptable in mainstream American media. In some instances this is ne by another character; in others the audience is invited to laugh at the eaker when the film's gaze calls attention to their language.

The number of instances of non-Lat , non-SIE-speaking characters openly mocking or insulting Spanish and speakers' race and/or language that appears in the film set is perhaps surpri g—at least 12 in 11 films. These do *not* include the examples listed in "Mo Spanish" in which non-Spanish speakers mock Spanish or Spanish-accent English by performing an anglicized or exaggerated version of it. Notabl most of the characters doing the mocking are not antagonists and the mock is usually not framed as wrong or explicitly racist; instead, it's framed a omedic banter. For instance, in *America's Sweethearts* (2001), Hector (H k Azaria) is the new boyfriend of a movie star recently separated from he usband. He speaks English with an exaggerated Spanish accent, lisping ev *s* sound, and also falls into the next category, characters whose language framed as inherently funny by the film itself. The movie star's sister Kiki lia Roberts) derisively calls him "Ricky Ricardo," while most of the other ajor characters simply call him "The Spaniard."

The *Transformers* franchise is notorious r its use of racial stereotypes and racist jokes—we examined several examp in Chapter 2, and in the section "The Fiery Latina" above, we discussed the ene in *Transformers: Dark of the Moon* (2011) in which a White man calls angry Latina woman a "hoochie mama" and describes her as having a " tin meltdown." Additionally, in

Transformers (2007), a Spanish and SIE-speaking soldier credited only as Ranger Team (Luis Echagarruga) occasionally uses Spanish during conversations with his English-speaking compatriots (no subtitles are provided), and they chide him for it, reminding him that they don't speak Spanish. In an early scene he protests that it's "his heritage," and another soldier responds, "Go with the Spanish, whatever," but in a later scene they again scold him for speaking Spanish. In the same film, Spanish- and SIE-speaking used car dealership employee Manny (Carlos Moreno, Jr.) expresses confusion about a car that seems to have appeared on the lot suddenly and mysteriously, exclaiming, "That's *loco*!" His boss, Bobby Bolivia (Bernie Mac), replies, "Don't go Ricky Ricardo on me, Manny. Find out [where the car came from]!" And in *Transformers: Revenge of the Fallen* (2009), Skids (Tom Kenny), a minor Autobot (the robot "good guys") who speaks in a parody of Black English discussed in Chapter 2, calls Leo, a human speaker of Spanish and EDC, a "shrimp taco."

The *Grown Ups* franchise also takes every opportunity to mock the Spanish- and SIE-speaking wife of the films' protagonist. Her character, Roxanne, is discussed in the "Fiery Latina" section and she appears in an example of Mock Spanish used to deride Spanish speakers. Further, in *Grown Ups* (2010), when Roxanne becomes angry and begins ranting in Spanish, her friend Deanne (Maya Rudolph) imitates her, not in Spanish or Mock Spanish but in gibberish, and the other women present laugh. And as noted above, an older woman also refers to her as a "spicy quesadilla." In *Grown Ups 2* (2013), after telling his son that he shouldn't be afraid of women, protagonist Lenny (Adam Sandler) goes on to say that he did not ask his wife if his son could play football because "I was scared. I'm afraid she's gonna yell at me in that accent that no one understands." In fact, Roxanne's English is only lightly accented but in both *Grown Ups* and *Grown Ups 2* she speaks Spanish when angry, so it's unclear whether Lenny is mocking her use of Spanish or her accented English.

Anger Management's Lou, whom we discussed in the section "Queer in SIE," is also a target of derision for both his race and his sexuality: his fellow anger management support group member, Chuck (John Turturro), calls him "little Spanish fruit topping." And in yet another Adam Sandler film, *Mr. Deeds* (2002), antagonist Chuck Cedar (Peter Gallagher) insults butler and sympathetic character Emilio Lopez (John Turturro, this time on the receiving end of the racist comments). Emilio speaks Spanish and Spanish-accented English and Chuck at one point tells him, "As soon as that moron goes back to Cowpie Falls, you are out of here on your fat, Puerto Rican ass." Emilio—who is actually tall and lean—is indeed offended, responding, "I hail from Spain, sir." We've already mentioned the racist comments in *Pitch Perfect*

2 that are directed toward SIE-speaking i nigrant Flo—"do that flip right over the fence and back into Mexico"—a in *Pokémon Detective Pikachu,* Pikachu again demonstrates his ignoranc of Spanish when he encounters shirtless SIE-speaking antagonist Sebasti "All I hear are consonants and all I see are nipples." Finally, *Bad Boys II,* addition to the use of the "Fiery Latina" trope mentioned above, contains number of jokes and humorous scenes based in racist stereotypes, such as ie banter between SIE-speaking Detectives Mateo Reyes (Yul Vázquez) d Marco Vargas (Jason Manuel Olazábal) and the two protagonists, Dete ves Mike Lowrey (Will Smith) and Marcus Burnett (Martin Lawrence). ring one such conversation, for instance, Mike says, "Hey, isn't Ricky rtin having a concert?" Reyes responds, "You always gotta go racial, man and Vargas adds, "It's sad, man."

We can quickly spot a pattern in the li above: four of the 11 films are directed by Michael Bay, and another four ar Adam Sandler, who is known for using an improvisational style of com y in his films rather than sticking to scripts written by others. This migh empt us to write off these racist jokes as the bad habit of two powerful Ho wood men, but these eight films combined to sell almost 250,000,000 tic ts. As we've discussed, media portrayals of human behavior influence a lience's attitudes toward demographic groups, and when a film frames rotagonist or other sympathetic character's use of racist insults as normal even funny, it sends a message to those hundreds of millions of viewers t their culture also considers this normal or funny—a highly problematic m sage to continue perpetuating in the twenty-first century.

We also find a number of examples of e film itself framing a Spanish- or SIE-speaking character's language or havior as inherently funny and worthy of mockery. Several of these chara rs have already been examined, such as *America's Sweetheart*'s Hector, v ose exaggerated Spanish accent is treated as comedic, and *Meet the Foc s'* "fiery Latina" Isabella, who addresses a toddler that she believes to l Greg Focker's son, remarking, "He's a handsome little Focker!," pronou ing it quite clearly as "fucker." The dinner party guests exchange uncom table glances at this pronouncement while the audience, presumably, lau s. A nearly identical joke occurs when the housekeeper of *Fun with Dick a Jane*, Blanca (Gloria Garayua), insists on calling Dick "Mr. Richard." In r Spanish-accented English, the name sounds like "retard." Dick reacts w a pained expression so that the audience has time to appreciate the joke, ien reminds Blanca to call him "Dick." *The Proposal*'s "Latin lover" Ram e is also mocked by the framing of his film for speaking Spanish, in this ca in a scene that occurs during the credits. Here, an unseen immigration offi interviewing several characters asks Ramone to spell his name. Ramone do so using Spanish pronunciation,

"/ere-a-ɪm-o-ɪn-e/," and the interviewer immediately asks him to "do that again in English, please." The camera cuts away before he can respond. In this fast-paced montage of interviews, every character's answers to the interviewer's questions is comedic, but in Ramone's case, the use of Spanish itself is presumed to be funny.

Million Dollar Baby's (2004) mockery of SIE speaker Omar (Michael Peña) is rather more mean-spirited. Omar is one of a pair of bullies who frequents the boxing gym where the film spends much of its time and he speaks SIE with exaggerated pronunciation and grammar and regularly harasses a young, poor, skinny White Southern boy, Danger Barch (Jay Baruchel). When female protagonist Maggie (Hilary Swank) begins working out at the gym, Omar and his fellow antagonist, Shawrelle (Anthony Mackie), turn their attention to her, arguing that she and Barch should fight each other, because, as Omar says, "It's perfect . . . cause you know why? Cause she and you, you could fight to him and then you could kiss to him, and then you fight to him one more time." Omar fits the profile of the historical Latinx stereotype that Mastro and Behm-Morawitz call "the buffoon," "characterized by a heavy accent, laziness, secondary status, and lack of intelligence"[36]—the film depicts him as Shawrelle's lackey, constantly loitering about this boxing gym but never actually competing in a fight, and instead spending his time pestering or outright assaulting the other athletes.

This type of mockery is, of course, not limited to human characters nor to films aimed at adults. The 2006 film *Happy Feet*, for instance, includes an entire group of major secondary characters whose Spanish and SIE are used for comedy—the Adélie penguins. The film centers around a community of talking emperor penguins living in Antarctica for whom singing is a significant (arguably the only) part of their culture, but the protagonist, Mumble (Elijah Wood), cannot sing and prefers to dance. When he is ostracized by his species, he leaves in search of acceptance elsewhere, and he soon meets a community of Adélie penguins, five of whom speak SIE and quickly become his friends and accompany him through a major portion of the film. Four of the five are voiced by Latino actors, but the fifth, Ramon, is voiced by Robin Williams, who performs an exaggerated parody of Spanish-accented English for comedic effect. Ramon has the most significant role of the five Adélie penguins and is the only one who is visually distinguishable from the others; he uses both exaggerated pronunciation and "nonstandard" grammar for comedy throughout his screen time. For example, he repeats the line "Let me tell something to jou /dʒu/" three times, emphasizing the pronunciation of /dʒu/ for humor—an iconized Spanish accent feature—while using the "standard" English pronunciation of "you" at other points in the film. The character is framed as funny not simply because of what he says, but primarily because of how he says it. (Though this character is created by a White English-speaking actor pretending to speak with a Spanish a nt, he is not included in the data on Mock Spanish because in the world of e film, he is not White—he is a penguin—and he is not using Mock Span ı; he is speaking his native dialect.) This holds true for the other four Ad e penguins as well.

Interestingly, the four secondary Adélie enguins are among the few SIE speakers in our data that use "nonstandar grammar, frequently employing a grammatical feature that is actually one the most recognizable features of Black English—zero copula—as in th ollowing lines: "Everyone a bit down," "He with us," "You dangerous, by," "He never wrong," "You a bird, ain't you?" "You in tragic shape nan," "He the guru," "He *loco* maniac!" (As these four penguins look nea identical, sound quite similar to each other, frequently talk over each other, d do not use each other's names, it's impossible to attribute every line to speaker with any certainty and therefore impossible to say whether any gi n penguin uses this feature more than the others.) It should be noted that Sp sh is not a zero copula language, so if we are to interpret these Antarctic bir as native Spanish speakers, this is not an example of native language inte rence. As we saw in Chapter 2, White audiences associate proximity to Bl ness with coolness, and it's possible that the filmmakers intended this fea e to give the penguins this sense of coolness, as they express extreme con ence in their dancing and their ability to attract female penguins—stereot s associated with both the Latin lover and hypersexual Black masculinity.

I admit that I was a bit surprised by th widespread acceptance of overt racial derision of Spanish and SIE speak s in twenty-first century mainstream American film. These characteriz ons—both of the SIE speakers themselves and of the White EDC speak who mock them without consequence or even negative framing—are ainly racist, yet filmmakers and filmgoers have clearly decided that this rm of racism is not a problem in the pursuit of entertainment. It betrays e extreme degree to which the White EDC-speaking gaze still dominate ur media, despite the marginal gains in representation in front of the cam . To buy a ticket to a big budget Hollywood film as a stigmatized speaker i face the fact that you are quite likely to see your language (and by exte on your race and/or your class) openly disparaged on screen by characters hom the film will frame as sympathetic or even heroic.

CONSEQUE CES

The numerous representations of Spanish d SIE speakers in stereotypical roles such as criminal, inmate, drug deal domestic worker, fiery Latina, and undocumented worker illustrate wh Margaret M. Russell calls the "dominant gaze," "the tendency of mainstream culture to replicate, through narrative and imagery, racial inequalities and biases which exist throughout society."[37] White Americans, broadly, *believe* Spanish and SIE speakers to be criminals, inmates, drug dealers, domestic workers, etc.; therefore mainstream film tends to depict them that way. And, the evidence shows, these depictions create a cycle of stereotypes, reinforcing these beliefs in the White audiences from which they stem. Ediberto Román argues that "while stereotyping in film and other media may at first blush appear to be innocuous, such metaphors as the hot-blooded lover, gang member or illegal immigrant help shape how society perceives a group that it considers as outsiders, and thereby justifies treating such groups as different or foreign."[38] A spate of U.S. laws and policies enacted in recent years that disproportionally harm minorities—voter ID laws, family separation policies, refusal of most asylum claims—demonstrate that in the twenty-first century, dominant White America does indeed still "treat[] such groups as different or foreign."

A 2012 study by the National Hispanic Media Coalition on *The Impact of Media Stereotypes on Opinions and Attitudes Towards Latinos* reinforces Román's claim. They tested the effects of stereotypical depictions of Latinx people in media, presenting short representations of Latinx people that could be categorized as either clearly positive or clearly negative to 3,000 non-Latinx viewers. They found that regardless of the medium—fiction entertainment, TV news, talk radio, or print—viewers who were exposed to negative representations of Latinx people consistently rated that real-world demographic lower in metrics such as honesty, neighborliness, and patriotism than did viewers who were exposed to positive representations, and higher in metrics such as being less educated, relying on welfare, having a "culture of crime and gangs," taking American jobs, and being "illegal immigrants." They also found that "[e]xposure to just *one* negative cue predicts higher rates of negative Latino stereotyping in terms of criminal activity, families being too large, and impressions of them being 'illegal immigrants.'"[39] In other words, viewers who watched a fictional clip of Latinx people engaging in crime, for example, were *also* more likely to believe other negative stereotypes about them. The 79 Spanish- and SIE-speaking inmates and criminals in our film set, then, are not only encouraging negative stereotyping of this demographic as criminal, but also as having too many children and entering the country without documentation.

On the other hand, viewers in the study who saw positive representations of Latinx people were significantly less likely to hold to negative stereotypes. It is not enough, then, to reduce or eliminate stereotypical depictions in media; they must be replaced with Spanish- and SIE-speaking protagonists, major characters, and secondary characters who are more fully developed, who have character traits beyond simply being an immigrant, a drug dealer, or a maid, and who can fully represent the complex p ure of Spanish and SIE speakers in modern America.

NOTES

1. Carmen Fought, "Talkin' with mi Gente (C ano English)," in *American Voices: How Dialects Differ from Coast to Coast*, eds. lt Wolfram and Ben Ward (Malden: Blackwell Publishing, 2006), 233–35.

2. United States Census Bureau, *Language S en at Home*, accessed September 8, 2021, https://data.census.gov/cedsci/table?q= 2spanish%20at%20home%22&tid =ACSST1Y2019.S1601&hidePreview=false.

3. *Suicide Squad* (2016), *Traffic* (2000), and *d Boys II* (2003).

4. United States Bureau of Labor Statistics, *L or Force Statistics from the Current Population Survey*, accessed September 8, 2(, https://www.bls.gov/cps/cpsaat13 .htm.

5. United States Bureau of Labor Statistics *l or Force Statistics*.

6. Dana E. Mastro and Elizabeth Behm-M rawitz, "Latino Representation on Primetime Television," *Journalism and Mass ommunication Quarterly* 82, no. 1 (2005): 111.

7. United States Bureau of Labor Statistics, *bor Force Statistics*.

8. United States Bureau of Labor Statistics, *bor Force Statistics*.

9. United States Bureau of Labor Statistics *Data for Occupations Not Covered in Detail*, *Occupation Outlook Handout*, acce d September 8, 2021, https://www .bls.gov/ooh/about/data-for-occupations-not- vered-in-detail.htm#Transportation %20and%20material%20moving%20occupatio .

10. *The Impact of Media Stereotypes on Op ons and Attitudes Towards Latinos*, National Hispanic Media Coalition, 2012, 1 https://www.chicano.ucla.edu/files/ news/NHMCLatinoDecisionsReport.pdf.

11. United States National Center for Educa n Statistics, *Race/Ethnicity of College Faculty*, accessed September 8, 2021, h s://nces.ed.gov/fastfacts/display.asp ?id=61.

12. "Diversity in Medicine: Facts and Fig s 2019," Association of American Medical Colleges, 2021, https://www.aamc. /data-reports/workforce/interactive -data/figure-18-percentage-all-active-physician ace/ethnicity-2018.

13. Cary Funk and Kim Parker, "Diversity i he STEM Workforce Varies Widely Across Jobs," Pew Research Center, January 2019, https://www.pewresearch.org/ social-trends/2018/01/09/diversity-in-the-stem orkforce-varies-widely-across-jobs /.

14. Sabrina Zirkel, "Is There A Place for Me Role Models and Academic Identity among White Students and Students of Color, *eachers College Record* 104, no. 2 (2002), https://doi.org.10.1111/1467-9620.001

15. Mastro and Behm-Morawitz, "Latino Re esentation," 125.

16. Nadia Lie, "From Latin to Latino Lov Hispanicity and Female Desire in Popular Culture," *Journal of Popular Romanc Studies* 4, no. 1 (2014), http://www

.jprstudies.org/2014/02/from-latin-to-latino-lover-hispanicity-and-female-desire-in-popular-cultureby-nadia-lie/.

17. Lie, "From Latin to Latino Lover."

18. Stacy L. Smith, Marc Choueiti, and Katherine Pierper, *Inclusion or Invisibility? Comprehensive Annenberg Report on Diversity in Entertainment*. Institute for Diversity and Empowerment at Annenberg (IDEA) (USC Annenberg School for Journalism and Communication, 2016), 3–4.

19. John Logan, quoted in Jordan Zakarin, "New Bond Goes Old School: Exploring 007's Past and Playing With 'Sexual Intimidation,'" *The Hollywood Reporter*, November 6, 2012, https://www.hollywoodreporter.com/movies/movie-news/james-bond-gay-flirtation-parental-386864/.

20. Lauren Spungen, "When Can Homophobia Live and Let Die?: An Examination of Sexual Deviance in the James Bond Franchise," *Film Matters* (2017): 15, https://fms.wustl.edu/files/fms/imce/fm_spungen_article.pdf.

21. Jane H. Hill, *The Everyday Language of White Racism* (West Sussex: Wiley-Blackwell, 2008), loc.1974, Kindle.

22. Hill, *The Everyday Language*, loc. 1853–9.

23. Hill, *The Everyday Language*, loc. 2057.

24. Hill, *The Everyday Language*, loc. 1957.

25. Hill, *The Everyday Language*, loc. 1979.

26. Hill, *The Everyday Language*, loc. 2048–53.

27. Hill, *The Everyday Language*, loc. 2061.

28. Additional examples of Mock Spanish used to degrade or threaten both Spanish and non-Spanish speakers can be found at www.lindseyclouse.com.

29. Hill, *The Everyday Language*, loc. 2089.

30. Hill, *The Everyday Language*, loc. 2093.

31. Hill, *The Everyday Language*, loc. 2098.

32. Hill, *The Everyday Language*, loc. 2114.

33. Hill, *The Everyday Language*, loc. 2226.

34. Additional examples of parodic mispronunciation can be found at www.lindseyclouse.com.

35. Hill, *The Everyday Language*, loc. 1957.

36. Mastro and Behm-Morawitz, "Latino Representation," 111.

37. Margaret M. Russell, "Race and the Dominant Gaze: Narratives of Law and Inequality in Popular Film," *Legal Studies Forum* 15, no. 3 (1991): 244.

38. Ediberto Román, "Who Exactly Is Living La Vida Loca: The Legal and Political Consequences of Latino-Latina Ethnic and Racial Stereotypes in Film and Other Media," *The Journal of Gender, Race & Justice* 37 (2000): 48, https://ecollections.law.fiu.edu/faculty_publications/313/.

39. *The Impact of Media Stereotypes on Opinions and Attitudes Towards Latinos*, 12–17.

Chapter 5

"It's like Whatever"

Gendered Speech Patterns and Mock White Girl

Jumanji: Welcome to the Jungle (2017) and *Jumanji: The Next Level* (2019) are direct sequels to the 1995 film *Jumanji* starring Robin Williams, and through the plot device of body swapping, the two films give us valuable insight into not only how screenwriters, directors, and audiences perceive gendered speech patterns (GSP), but how actors do as well. *Welcome to the Jungle* begins in 1996 when the Jumanji board game magically transforms into a video game to lure in modern, tech-savvy teenagers; shortly thereafter, a high school student named Alex disappears. Viewers familiar with the original film know that, like Alan Parrish before him, he has been trapped in the world of Jumanji.

The film then fast-forwards twenty years and introduces us to a motley group of teenagers who, *Breakfast Club*-style, have been given detention together. Fridge (Ser'Darius Blain) is tall, athletic, and popular; he speaks Black English with common features such as zero copula. His former friend Spencer (Alex Wolff) is physically slight and bookish and has been doing Fridge's homework for him. Martha (Morgan Turner) is also studious and uninterested in athletics; when we meet her, she is in P.E. complaining that the class is a waste of time. She and Spencer speak EDC. Bethany (Madison Iseman) is obsessed with social media and her phone—we see her meticulously arranging her environment for an Instagram photo and video chatting with a friend in the middle of a class quiz. Throughout the film, several other characters describe her as self-absorbed, and she acknowledges that this assessment is "fair." She uses frequent creaky voice (a.k.a. "vocal fry") and the friend with whom she video chats uses modern (for 2016) teenage girl slang: "gorge" (gorgeous) and "rando" (random person). As we shall see in this chapter, in mainstream film these GSP are usually associated with young women who, like Bethany, display negati traits stereotypically associated with teenage girls like self-absorption and cial media obsession.

During detention, while rummaging aro d a dusty storage area inside the school, the teens come across an old gam g console with the Jumanji cartridge inside it. Spencer connects the cons e to a television and each of the teens picks up a controller and chooses a vatar, and as soon as the game begins, they are physically sucked into the onsole.

The group then finds themselves insid the game inhabiting the bodies of their chosen avatars: Spencer has be me tall, muscular Dr. Xander "Smolder" Bravestone (Dwayne Johnso the game protagonist, while Fridge is his smaller, slower sidekick, zo ogist Franklin "Mouse" Finbar (Kevin Hart). Martha is now living in the dy of Ruby Roundhouse (Karen Gillan), an athletic assassin who wears re aling clothing typical of female video game characters. Finally, Bethany i ow Professor Sheldon "Shelly" Oberon (Jack Black), a cartographer and, a Bethany herself puts it, "an overweight middle-aged man."

Spencer → Bravestone
Fridge → "Mouse" Finbar
Martha → Ruby Roundhouse
Bethany → Sheldon Oberon

Thanks to Spencer's extensive video ga e knowledge and the exposition provided by a helpful NPC (nonplayer ch acter) who arrives in a Jeep, the group quickly discern their circumstances nd learn that not only must they beat the game to escape it, but that their avatars have a fixed number of "lives," and that too many fatal mistakes n the game might result in their actual deaths. Thus prepared, they set abo playing the game.

Importantly, though each character no possesses a set of abilities and weaknesses unique to their avatar (Bethany or example, is the only character who can read the map), internally they ar still themselves. Spencer's body is that of a professional athlete, but his m d belongs to a skinny, awkward teenager who is shy around girls. The act s playing their avatars, then, are tasked with projecting this inner personalit through their language and mannerisms. In their own bodies, Spencer an Martha speak EDC, and as their avatars, they continue to do so. Similarly, idge, in the body of Kevin Hart, continues to use Black English pronuncia n and grammar, including zero copula, negative concord, *ain't*, and elisi of word-final consonants, as in "zoologis."

However, Madison Iseman's and Jack ack's versions of Bethany's dialect are less consistent with each other. ile Iseman's primary gendered feature is creaky voice, Black relies more n uptalk (rising intonation at the end of a phrase or sentence, similar but not identical to the intonation of a question), slang, and frequent uses of *like* and *literally* to gender his character, and rarely uses creaky voice. Compare these examples, in which underlined words mark creaky voice and ↑ marks the rising intonation of uptalk:

Iseman:
"Yeah, I don't think that's gonna work."
"She's not big on fun."
"This may be the lamest thing I've ever done."
Black:
"I, like, can't even with this place."
"Oh my god, you guys, there is like *literally* a penis attached to my body right now."
"Can you not judge me for like two seconds?"
"Does anyone have any like money I'm literally starving."
"I'm a map doctor↑, and I have this map that has like a missing piece."
"I feel like since I lost my phone my other senses have kind of heightened."

Whether the provenance of these differences is the script or is simply different interpretations of the character by different actors, it is significant that both actors use GSP throughout the film for this unlikable character, who displays stereotypical negative gendered traits such as vanity, self-absorption, and lack of concern with academics, whereas the more serious, intellectual female character of Martha doesn't use these speech patterns, regardless which actor represents her.

As the characters make their way through the game, they face and overcome personal weaknesses, confess their inner struggles to each other, and bond as a group. Spencer becomes braver and more confident; Martha risks her peers' rejection to befriend them; and Fridge learns to rely on his mind rather than his physical prowess. At one point the self-absorbed Bethany voluntarily sacrifices one of her avatar's lives to save Alex, the boy who disappeared into the game twenty years ago. Alex has run out of lives and faces real death, and in giving up one of her lives, Bethany puts herself at a greater risk of real death, redeeming her character in the eyes of the audience—yet this does not impact her dialect; both Black and Iseman continue to use their pre-established speech habits for the character until the end of the film. However, in the subsequent film, *Jumanji: The Next Level*, both Iseman's and Black's portrayals of the character have changed.

The Next Level takes place about two years after the first film. The four teenagers are now college freshmen and have parted ways to attend different universities, but have kept in touch and plan to reunite for the holidays.

Shortly before their reunion Spencer disap ars, and the rest of the group discover that he has begun playing Jumanji a n and has been transported back into the game. Knowing that he can't beat game and survive without their help, they attempt to reenter it too. Howe , before they are able to choose their avatars, the console malfunctions an ucks in Fridge and Martha, but not Bethany. Instead, Spencer's unsuspecti Grandpa Eddie (Danny DeVito) and his retired friend Milo (Danny Glover) e transported into the game with the teens. When they land in the jungle, M ha is back in the avatar of Ruby Roundhouse while Fridge now finds himse in the body of Professor Oberon; Grandpa Eddie is Dr. Bravestone and Mil s "Mouse" Finbar.

Grandpa Eddie → Bravestone
Milo → "Mouse" Finbar
Martha → Ruby Roundhouse
Fridge → Sheldon Oberon

Jack Black must now project the charac r of Fridge, a young Black man who, in the previous film, used Black En ish pronunciation and grammar. But while Black does consistently elide w d-final consonants (for instance, he pronounces "zoologist" with no final *t*, Kevin Hart did in his portrayal of Fridge), he uses almost no Black En sh grammar features. With the exception of a single line with zero cop a—"Ya dead"—his grammar is "standard."

We might speculate that the optics of W te actor Jack Black using blackvoice are the reason behind this choice, it at one point in the game the characters find a way to switch avatars w each other, and Fridge briefly inhabits Ruby Roundhouse before eventua returning to his familiar avatar of "Mouse" Finbar. Yet at no time in th ilm does he use Black English grammar aside from the single line mentic ed above, even when in his own body outside the game. Both films are dir cd by Jake Kasdan, so we can't attribute the change in Fridge's speech to change in directors; the fact is simply that the character of Fridge has gr vn and matured since the previous film, and also no longer uses Black glish grammar. The change fits the pattern we established in Chapter 2: s ous characters almost never use Black English in film.

Bethany's language has also changed. t the beginning of the film she mentions that she has spent the semeste building houses in Costa Rica, indicating that she's no longer self-absorb l and, like Fridge, has matured. She spends more of this film outside the g ie and in her own body, and she no longer uses creaky voice or other GSP ile outside the game. When her friends are transported into the game, Be any seeks the help of Alex, the teenager who spent twenty years inside J anji and is now an adult living outside the game with a family, to reenter the game to help her friends. Together she and Alex are able to reenter the game, and this time she finds herself in the avatar of a horse. Because the avatar of "Mouse" Finbar is able to speak to animals, the elderly Milo (who currently inhabits Mouse's avatar) translates for her, Kevin Hart delivering the lines in Milo's slow, reserved manner: "Oh my god, right. Like I'm a total horse. I can't believe we found you guys." Here we again see the gendered use of *oh my god* and *like*, a return to the familiar speech patterns Bethany used in the first film. Later, when the characters switch avatars and Bethany is once again in the avatar of Professor Oberon and the body of Jack Black, she uses *like* in a similar way: "It feels like this isn't a perfect, like, moment."

We can again speculate about the reasons for these inconsistent depictions of Bethany's speech; perhaps the creators worried that without clear GSP, the audience would be confused about which avatar represented Bethany—a reasonable concern given the complexity of the plot. Or perhaps they believed that hearing Kevin Hart and Jack Black speak in a stereotypically feminine manner is simply funnier. Regardless of the reasons, like Fridge, she uses a stigmatized dialect far less—and not at all when in her own body—as her character has grown and become more serious. These two films are a commentary on how mainstream film represents GSP that are identified by researchers as iconically associated with young White women and girls, including creaky voice, uptalk, and certain types of slang[1] (defined in more detail below): first, film creators are more concerned with meeting audience expectations than with authentic portrayals, and second, GSP and the people who use them are usually depicted negatively or comically. Tyanna Slobe describes the stereotypical user of these patterns as "young, vapid, expressive, linguistically innovative, attached to her phone, and constantly socializing with her peer social group"[2]—all traits that apply to Bethany in the first film.

TYPES OF GENDERED SPEECH

It's crucial that we first acknowledge that these speech patterns are not only gendered, but also associated with a specific class and race: middle class and upper-middle class White girls and young women. As Slobe points out, discussions and performances of these patterns "perpetuate the erasure of girls of color from representations of girlhood by attributing the style simply to 'girls,' despite being grossly limited in its representation of girls' language."[3] Hollywood itself is already complicit in its erasure of girls of color simply through severely inadequate representation of women of color of all ages, and Black women most egregiously.[4] But because the GSP identified by Slobe and others as iconically associa l with middle and upper-middle class White girls are, indeed, used with ve few exceptions[5] exclusively by White women and girls in the film set (incl ing nonhuman characters voiced almost entirely by young White women ar girls), our analysis of these patterns must necessarily focus on these use with the acknowledgment that these users are not broadly representative "girls" in reality.

Creaky Voice

In his *A Dictionary of Language*, linguist vid Crystal defines *creaky voice* thus: "A vocal effect produced by a very w vibration of only one end of the vocal folds; also called creak or lar gealization. Because the sound somewhat resembles that of frying, the ect has also been described as 'vocal fry.' Filmstar Vincent Price produ d excellent creaky voice in his especially menacing moments."[6] Indeed, ile creaky voice was once associated with masculinity and authority, rece research has shown that, at least in American English, young women now it more frequently than young men.[7] Those unfamiliar with the term have netheless undoubtedly heard the feature in use as it's widespread among A rican English speakers of many ages, genders, and races, and in the last de de it has attracted a great deal of media attention, particularly among comm tators intent on policing the language of young women and especially you White women.[8] Because people of all ages and genders use creaky voice t ome degree, in order for it to be considered evidence of a gendered speech ttern in our analysis, the character must use it in an exaggerated or exces e manner that calls attention to itself, or it must be paired with one or more f the other GSP discussed below.

Uptalk

In *Uptalk: The Phenomenon of Rising tonation*, linguist Paul Warren defines the feature as "a marked rising into tion pattern found at the ends of intonation units realized on declarative utt ances, and which serves primarily to check comprehension or to seek fe back."[9] In simpler terms, uptalk involves a rising intonation used at the enc of words, phrases, and sentences that are making statements rather than a ng questions. Some lay people interpret uptalk as intoning a statement as it is a question, but this explanation is not strictly accurate—in English he intonation patterns of uptalk and those of questions are often quite diffe nt.[10] Like creaky voice, uptalk is more strongly associated with White fema speakers[11] and has been vilified by public commentators for decades.

Slang

Slang is the most difficult feature to define—even for those who study it professionally—as the concept is so fluid and popular slang changes so rapidly. However, some patterns are discernible in our film set: namely, some slang words and structures such as *like* and *totally* are used more frequently by young female characters who also use other GSP as well as by the people who mock them. These will be expanded upon below.

GENDERED SPEECH USERS IN THE FILM SET

Like users of Black English, Southern speech, and Spanish or Spanish-accented English, individual characters are often inconsistent in their use of GSP throughout a given film. In our set of 493 films, 48 characters use some combination of the GSP discussed above at some point in their films. Of these, 45 are earnest users and three are young White women who are mocking other women. The earnest users include: 37 young women and girls (including one cartoon troll, three animals, and two anthropomorphic cars), one middle-aged woman, one teenage boy, one middle-aged man, and five characters or actors who are pretending to be young White women because some kind of body swap has occurred (a situation that arises more frequently in mainstream film than one might expect). Characters who are represented by multiple actors in a single film are counted as separate characters; for example, as discussed above, in *Jumanji: Welcome to the Jungle*, the character of Bethany is played by both Madison Iseman and Jack Black, who differ somewhat in their portrayals, thus they are counted as two characters. The GSP features we see in these 48 characters' dialogue are shown in Table 5.1. Let's examine the earnest users of these features first.

NEGATIVE DEPICTIONS OF EARNEST GSP USERS

The majority of the characters who use GSP in earnest—30, or about 67%—are depicted comically or negatively by their films. This is unsurprising considering that the majority of high-grossing mainstream films are not primarily targeted at an audience of young women, and a number of researchers have demonstrated that, broadly speaking, adult men and women do not like the way young White women speak.[12] (Likely for this reason, female characters who are framed as desirable to male protagonists, such as the *Transformers* franchise's Mikaela [Megan Fox], do not use GSP.) These characters are rarely depicted as evil; rather, they are selfish, self-absorbed, silly, ditzy,

Table 5.1. Gendered Speech Patterns Appearing e Film Set

Feature	*Number of Users*	*Sample User*	*Filn*	*Usage*
creaky voice	19	Joni Thrombey (Toni Collette)	*Kni Out* (19)	"I feel simultaneously freed by and supported by them."
uptalk	9	Jessica (Anna Kendrick)	*Twi ht* (2008)	"They're, um, Dr. and Mrs. Cullen's ↑foster kids."
like as a discourse marker	33	Crystal (Chrissy Teigen)	*Ho 1 nsylvania 3* (18)	"This is like the nicest hotel I've ever been to."
total/totally	11	Lorraine (Hilary Duff)	*Ch per by the L zen* (2003)	"Up 'til now, I've been like totally mellow about this."
you know as a tag question	5	Jessica (Anna Kendrick)	*The wilight S a: New M on* (2009)	"It's not funny, you know? And like, is it supposed be a metaphor for consumerism? 'Cause don't be so pleased with your own like self-referential cleverness, you know?"
oh my god/ gosh	4	Allyson (Andi Matichak)	*Ha ween* (18)	"Oh my gosh I wish that you were here."
like and/or *all* as a dialogue tag	3	Heather (Avril Lavigne)	*Ov the Hedge* (06)	"She's all like, 'wow.'"
whatever	3	Guinevere (Latifa Ouaou)	*Shr the Third* (07)	"It's like whatever. She's just totally into college guys and mythical creatures and stuff."
seriously	2	Becky (uncredited)	*Sin* 2016)	"Ugh, seriously, she's not even that good."

Source: Lindsey Clouse

dumb, or simply very young and immatu . The character of Bethany discussed above, for instance, is described by other character as self-absorbed, and as we saw, she uses fewer gendered f ures after her character matures and becomes selfless. Other rude, selfis and self-absorbed GSP users include Bethany's friend Lucinda; *Sing*'s ecky, a porcupine who "steals" another porcupine's boyfriend and make nide comments about that porcupine's singing ability; Taffyta (Mindy ling and Melissa Villaseñor) of

Wreck-It Ralph (2012) and *Ralph Breaks the Internet* (2018), a sentient video game character who bullies another young girl character in her game; *Thor*'s (2011) Darcy (Kat Dennings), an intern who equates the confiscation of her iPod with the loss of a scientist's lifetime of work; and *Gran Torino*'s (2008) Ashley (Dreama Walker), who wears a crop top to her grandmother's funeral and longs to get her hands on her grandfather's vintage car when he dies. All of these characters are teenagers or younger.

GSP users who are depicted in a more sinister light include *Get Out*'s (2017) Rose Armitage (Allison Williams) a young White woman whose family, we later learn, is kidnapping Black people, stealing their bodies, and implanting elderly White people's brains into them with Rose's help; *22 Jump Street*'s (2014) Mercedes (Jillian Bell), a college student who's assisting her father in supplying drugs to other college students; *Little Fockers*' (2010) Andi Garcia (Jessica Alba), a young pharmaceuticals rep who sexually assaults a married man; and *Knives Out*'s Joni Thrombey, a middle-aged woman who has been defrauding her wealthy father-in-law and who describes herself as a "lifestyle guru." Note that all of these characters are at least college-aged—the implication is that GSP becomes less forgivable as one gets older, and therefore in older characters is associated not just with self-absorption but with actual villainy.

Finally, the earnest GSP users who are portrayed as simply silly, ditzy, dumb, or immature comprise 14 female characters of a range of ages, from roughly grade school aged (age is sometimes difficult to determine because several of these characters are animals or anthropomorphic cars) through young adults. A few representative examples deserve further discussion.

At times, film creators go out of their way to make it clear to the audience that a character or characters are unintelligent. This occurs among a number of users of GSP. For instance, 2003's *Anger Management* features a pair of characters, Stacy (Krista Allen) and Gina (January Jones), who attend the anger management support group with the protagonist. They are adult film stars and lovers, and they use a significant amount of creaky voice in their lines. Throughout their film, they frequently begin kissing each other passionately in public places and wear shockingly revealing clothing to a fine restaurant, and the film makes a point of showing that they are dumb in a scene in which they mistake Rudy Giuliani for Regis Philbin. Another 2003 film, *Cheaper by the Dozen*, includes the character of Lorraine, a teenage girl who, when chided for wearing black for a Christmas card photo, responds, "Black works, Mom. Jesus like had his funeral on Christmas." Her brother then mockingly calls her "Barbie," an insult that implies that her ignorance is directly connected to her gender and appearance, including her blonde hair. Another GSP user depicted as ditzy and naïve is Kymberly (Laura-Leigh) of *We're the Millers* (2013), a new exotic ıncer working alongside veteran Rose (Jennifer Aniston). When Rose advi ; Kymberly on choosing a stage name and asks if she has a nickname, K ıberly responds, "Totally!" and folds down the front of her skirt to reveal attoo that reads "Boner Garage" with a downward arrow. "Is that not, like, e hottest?" she raves.

Again, these depictions reinforce perce ons of GSP that already exist in the public mind: Anderson, Klofstad, May v, and Venkatachalam found, for example, that young adult women who use reaky voice are perceived by listeners as "less competent [and] less educat ";[13] indeed, one need only survey the popular public discourse on the evils c creak (which Slobe describes as a "moral panic"[14]) to confirm the study's ndings. Other researchers have found similar results in studies of uptalk. An interesting example of GSP use from our film set comments on these ceptions in the character of Girl in Alley (Rebel Wilson) from 2007's *Gho Rider*. She appears in only two scenes—in the first, our hero the Ghost Ri r (Nicolas Cage) saves her from a mugger, and in the second, a local telev on news crew interviews her as an eye witness to the unusual event:

> REPORTER (Eva Mendes): Could you tell about the good Samaritan?
>
> GIRL: Oh, I'll never forget him, that's for e. He was tall, broad shoulders, and thin, really thin, like bony↑, and he hac ıis rad chopper. It was all flames and stuff. Oh, and his face was a skull↑, an t was on fire.
>
> [The reporter makes eye contact with the cameraman (Grant Carter), who crosses his eyes and stifles a laugh.]
>
> REPORTER: [skeptically] On fire?
>
> GIRL: Yeah, like [makes blowing noises an vaves her hands around her face] like that much fire↑, and I know it sounds ird but it looked okay on him. I mean, it was an edge look but he totally pul l it off.
>
> REPORTER: Not sure what to add to that!

We, the audience, know that Girl in Alley recounting the story accurately: the Ghost Rider's head is indeed a flamin skull, and he does indeed ride a rad chopper. However, the outlandishness her story coupled with her use of multiple GSP features (creaky voice, alk, and *like*) combine to make her seem completely uncredible to her liste rs, enabling them to dismiss her out of hand. Based on what we know abo how GSP affects listeners' perceptions of speakers' credibility, we might eculate that if she were older, or male, or used more "standard" language, reporter and cameraman might take her at least a bit more seriously.

Another comedic user of GSP, the only adult man in the film set who uses it, also deserves scrutiny. He is Woody Stevens (John Travolta) of *Wild Hogs* (2007), and his use of GSP features calls attention to centuries-old stereotypes about female hysteria. While on a motorcycle road trip, Woody and his three friends have a run-in with a rough biker gang who call themselves the Del Fuegos. After the four are humiliated and leave the Del Fuegos' favorite bar in disgrace, Woody, feeling his masculinity has been threatened, convinces the other men to stop so he can return and have it out with the gang. He leaves his friends on the side of the road and heads back to the bar where he surreptitiously cuts the gang's motorcycles' gas lines and accidentally blows up the building. He hides this information from his friends, but throughout the remainder of the film seems constantly in a rush to put as much distance between himself and the Del Fuegos as possible, and gets anxious when he believes they're getting near. At last, when the Del Fuegos arrive in town, he is forced to admit his actions to his friends, and when he does so, he uses GSP, pitching his voice higher than usual and using dramatic hand gestures as he recounts what happened during and after the group's encounter with the gang:

> WOODY: Dudley, you're like, "I'm all stupid. Take my bike and give me a piece of junk and I'm happy," and you guys are all, "I'm scared. Let's get out of here," whatever. The Del Fuegos are all like, "You're nothin,'" you know? "We're real bikers."
>
> DOUG (Tim Allen): This isn't about us. What did you do to them?
>
> DUDLEY (William H. Macy): What did you do, Woody?
>
> WOODY: I . . . [hesitating] I cut the gas lines of their bikes and I . . . maybe blew up their bar.

The multiple GSP features are unmistakable: both *like* and *all* as dialogue tags, *you know* as a tag question, the dismissive *whatever*. In this moment Woody is panicking, and in his panic the filmmakers choose to represent him as a young girl, counting on the contrast between Woody's appearance—a large, middle-aged man in a black leather jacket and bandanna—and his words, voice, and behavior for humor. The comedy relies on the audience's prior familiarity with both GSP and stereotypical White gender roles; if they don't understand that Woody is using language typically associated with young women, then they won't get the joke: that the sight of an adult man reacting hysterically like a young woman is funny, at least in the eyes of the filmmakers.

Positive and Neutral Depictions of E iest GSP Users

While the majority of the films that depic GSP at all do so negatively (24 out of 35 films), about a third defy this trer . This includes another film that, like the *Jumanji* films, relies on body swap ng and the humor inherent in an adult using the stereotypical language of a eenage White girl, but this time, the joke is not at the girl's expense. *Frea Friday* (2003) is about a White middle-aged mother, Tess (Jamie Lee C tis), and her teenage daughter, Anna (Lindsay Lohan), who magically sw bodies. As they go about their day, they attempt to keep their family and ends in the dark about what has occurred, which results in some humorou moments. Tess—now in Anna's body—attempts to talk like a teenager and so doing, actually *overuses* GSP features: "I mean, like, how could I, like, t an F?" The humor is at Tess's expense, not Anna's, because Anna doesn actually speak in such an exaggerated way. Meanwhile, Anna—now in he nother's body—draws a puzzled reaction from her mother's fiancé by using r own natural GSP: "Could you, like, chill for a sec?"

The film, which is rated PG and targets primarily female audience, also features two teenage friends of Anna wh use some GSP (one of whom is among the very few girls of color in the fil set who use it), namely *like* as a discourse marker ("You told her this chan would like never come again?") and *totally* ("Your mom is totally ruining ur lives!"). These usages are not exaggerated and the film doesn't treat ther as comedic; they are simply part of ordinary conversation between Anna a her friends. Significantly, none of the GSP users in the film are mocked fo heir language use or depicted as excessively self-absorbed or unintelligent. t the beginning of the film Anna and Tess do not get along, but the film ma s it clear that both are equally to blame, and by literally walking in each oth 's shoes, they learn to empathize with the other's feelings and their relation p is ultimately strengthened.

This film is part of a pattern: of the 11 ns in which GSP is not depicted negatively or comedically, eight are target to young women or girls. These include *Legally Blonde 2* (2003), *Pitch P ect 2* (2015), *Trolls* (2016), and four of the films in the *Twilight* franchise (08, 2009, 2010, and 2011). Like *Freaky Friday*, each of these films feature GSP users whose usage is natural, unexaggerated, and not treated as a s ce of comedy, and who are not depicted as especially selfish or dumb. Fo nstance, the *Twilight* franchise's Jessica (Anna Kendrick) is the first to b iend protagonist Bella (Kristen Stewart) at her new school, and upon their aduation in a later film, we learn that she is the valedictorian. She uses creak voice, uptalk, *like* as a discourse marker, *totally*, *seriously*, and *you know* a tag question. In *Pitch Perfect 2* and *Trolls* Anna Kendrick plays the pr gonist and continues to use her likely natural creaky voice; in the former n she also uses *like*.

Because the eight films discussed above are targeted to the very individuals who use GSP the most, it's logical to assume that the filmmakers would wish to avoid depicting those individuals negatively, and research shows that young women and girls have a more positive view of GSP than do other listeners, especially older listeners. In *Uptalk*, Warren discusses studies on listener attitudes toward uptalk, including Di Gioacchino and Crook Jessop's conclusion that while "younger listeners fail to hear uptalk as extraordinary," older listeners find it "jarring."[16] Warren also notes that "female listeners are less likely than male listeners to associate uptalk with some of the more stereotyped meanings such as uncertainty."[17]

Perceptions of creaky voice are somewhat less well understood, due in part to the limitations of the studies conducted on it. In their *PLOS ONE* meta analysis of creaky voice studies through 2019, Katherine Dallaston and Gerard Docherty found the literature to be insufficient to either support or refute the claims that use of creaky voice has become more widespread among American women in the last ten years.[18] However, several studies have demonstrated that among young (generally college-aged) listeners, use of creaky voice by young women is associated with authority,[19] particularly when used only on the final phrase of an utterance.[20] Additionally, in a 2010 study (one of the first in creaky voice research), Yuasa found that a small majority of participants under the age of 25, about 60%, described a single female creaky voice user positively using terms such as "professional" and "a graduate student."[21] Anderson et al., who found largely *negative* reactions to creaky voice usage in their *PLOS One* study, cite age range as an explanation for the discrepancy between Yuasa's results and theirs.[22]

Hollywood, it would seem, is quite savvy in its depictions of GSP: reinforcing negative beliefs about GSP users in older viewers who already hold those beliefs, and avoiding those negative portrayals when marketing films to GSP users themselves.

MOCKERY

Gendered speech patterns, like other marginalized languages including Black English, Southern speech, and Spanish and Spanish-influenced English, are subject to mockery by nonusers. Tyanna Slobe refers to this as Mock White Girl (MWG), a performance which creates a parodic white girl persona using linguistic features such as creaky voice, uptalk, *like*, *oh my god*, etc.[23] As we saw in the previous chapters, linguistic mockery tends to associate a group of speakers with the most negative, stereotypical beliefs about that group; for instance, Mock Southern relies on "redneck" stereotypes of stupidity, backwardness, and bigotry to deride or insult Southern speakers of blue collar dialects. Similarly, Slobe notes that in the M ck White Girl performances she analyzed, users associated the stereotypic White girl's GSP with characteristics such as "infantile" and "unprofes nal."[24] We find only three brief examples of Mock White Girl in our film s , but all three follow the patterns that Slobe identified.

In *How to Lose a Guy in 10 Days*, co- otagonist Andie (Kate Hudson) writes for the "How-to" section of a wome s magazine but longs to become a more serious journalist. As she complai about the subjects she is forced to write about, she briefly uses MWG (indi ted in italics), affecting a higher pitch and stereotypical Valley Girl pronu iation: "God, I busted my butt in grad school to be Andie Anderson, 'H -to' girl, and write articles like, 'How to Use the Best Pick-Up Lines' and ' *Blondes, Do They, Like, Really Have More Fun*?'" This brief performativ ine tracks with a genre of Mock White Girl that Slobe refers to as "Savior WG," in which successful adult women profess both concern and disdain f he language of young (primarily White) women as a supposed barrier to en to male-dominated professional worlds.[25] In this case, Andie is concerne or her *own* career, worried that she'll be stuck writing unimportant, nonse us articles about stereotypically feminine topics rather than the analyses of obal politics she prefers to write and considers more respectable. Her Mock hite Girl performance indicates that she associates GSP with that very lac f seriousness and respectability that she fears.

This is our first glimpse into Andie's (ar the film's) Not-Like-Other-Girls mentality, in which stereotypically femini activities and qualities, such as attending a Celine Dion concert rather thar n NBA game, preferring to write about fashion rather than politics, and pro sing strong feelings too early in a romantic relationship are repeatedly deri d by both the framing of the film and the protagonists. It's unsurprising, the that the film and the protagonist also have a negative attitude toward GSP d the people who use it, though it is somewhat unusual that such an attitu appears in a romantic comedy, a genre typically targeted at women. Th are two potential explanations for this. First, the director (Donald Petrie) d two of the three screenwriters (Brian Regan and Burr Steers) are male– ndie's negative attitude toward GSP may simply be a reflection of the fi makers' attitudes. On the other hand, White adult female audiences (incl ing young adults) who identify with Andie and also have or aspire to prof sional careers might sympathize with her attitude toward GSP, whether or r they use it themselves.

The second and third examples of Moc White Girl, which both occur in 2001's *Legally Blonde*, are even more int sting, especially when analyzed alongside the first. In the film, protagonis lle Woods (Reese Witherspoon) applies and is admitted to Harvard Law Sc ol in the hopes of winning back her ex-boyfriend. The film establishes earl n that Elle is intelligent when a saleswoman, assuming she is a "dumb blonde," attempts to trick her into overpaying for an outdated dress and fails conspicuously. At Harvard, however, Elle quickly finds herself feeling out of place, not because she's not smart enough to grasp the material, but because her bright pink clothing and accessories (including her purse-sized chihuahua), bubbly persona, resistance to the school's cutthroat practices, and refusal to tolerate her professor's sexual harassment put her at odds with her peers and superiors. When she attempts to join a study group of other students, two of them, Claire (Samantha Lemole) and Enid (Meredith Scott Lynn), use Mock White Girl as they turn her away:

VIVIAN (Selma Blair): Our group is full.

ELLE: Oh, is this like an RSVP thing?

CLAIRE: No, it's, *like*, a smart people thing↑. And as Viv said, we're full.

[. . .]

ELLE: Oh, okay. I'll just leave then.

ENID: Hey, maybe there's like a sorority you could like join instead like.

Note that whereas Elle uses *like* as a preposition (not a gendered usage) and the rising intonation common in questions, Claire uses *like* as a discourse marker and the rising intonation of uptalk; in other words, she uses GSP to mock Elle even though Elle does not use them herself. Enid, on the other hand, overuses *like* in an unrealistic manner, again mocking Elle. It's important to point out, though, that while Elle has a naturally high-pitched voice, she *does not use GSP* in the film. The young women who are rude to her attribute these linguistic characteristics to her because they attribute the stereotypical qualities that come with them to Elle—"youthful, vapid, irrational, and flamboyantly feminine" according to Slobe.[26] Elle is, indeed, flamboyantly feminine (in the study group scene she wears a bright pink paisley top and pink skirt and carries a basket of homemade muffins), and of course all of the students are youthful, but she is far from vapid or irrational; her classmates simply perceive her this way *because* of her flamboyant femininity. This observation also aligns with our introductory discussion of listener perceptions in the orthography of Mexican actress Lupe Vélez's accent and the speech of interviewees in the WPA slave narratives: listeners hear what they expect to hear. Elle's classmates hear GSP in her speech because they expect to hear it, even though it is not actually there.

Unlike *How to Lose a Guy in 10 Days*, *Legally Blonde* is a celebration of all things girly: although Elle briefly attempts to match her style to the dark, conservative clothing worn by the other women, by the end she returns to her true, brightly colored self, gets the sexual harasser fired, befriends one of her rivals, helps her mentor win an important urder trial, and graduates at the top of her class. And although Elle herself es not use GSP, those characters who mock her and deride GSP are clearly picted as bullies, indicating that the film itself does not view GSP negative

CONSEQUE CES

Negative depictions of GSP are, at their c e, not about language but about gender. Creaky voice, for instance, has b n common among English language users for decades, but public com ntary on its ills didn't begin in earnest until it became more common a ng young women than among other demographics. Crystal's 1999 defin n of creaky voice used Vincent Price as an example, while Yuasa's study, blished in 2010, found creak to be a "new type of American *female* voice q lity."[27] Unsurprisingly, a Google Books Ngram Viewer search of both *crea voice* and *vocal fry* shows sudden, sharp upticks in usage of both terms s rting in 2009, marking the point at which the public began to notice and c plain about young women's use of creak. As Stanford linguistics professo 'enny Eckert told NPR in 2015, "People are busy policing women's langua and nobody is policing older or younger men's language."[28]

Writing in their *PLOS ONE* article, A erson et al. advise that "young American females should avoid using voc fry speech in order to maximize labor market opportunities."[29] Although th may be a valid piece of advice for any individual young woman desperate be employed, the point that we have made repeatedly throughout this boo stands: speakers of marginalized dialects *should not have to change their sp ch* to suit society's racist, sexist, classist, and ever-changing standards. Furt rmore, because our beliefs about a given dialect are proxy for our beliefs ab the people who speak it, as long as our culture clings to implicit race, gen r, and class biases, all the voice training in the world will not eliminate the crimination that people of color, women, and poor people face in every asp of society. Hollywood's continual reinforcement of these biases via stere pical depictions of marginalized speakers is but one small part of this enor us problem.

NOTES

1. Tyanna Slobe, "Style, Stance, and Social eaning in Mock White Girl," *Language in Society* 47 (2018): 547–8, https://doi. /10.1017/S004740451800060X.
2. Slobe, "Style, Stance, and Social Meanin 543.
3. Slobe, "Style, Stance, and Social Meanin 546.

4. Stacy L. Smith, Marc Choueiti, and Katherine Pierper, *Inclusion or Invisibility? Comprehensive Annenberg Report on Diversity in Entertainment*. Institute for Diversity and Empowerment at Annenberg (IDEA) (USC Annenberg School for Journalism and Communication, 2016), 7–9.

5. These exceptions are: Maddie (Christina Vidal) of *Freaky Friday* (2003); Woody Stevens (John Travolta) of *Wild Hogs* (2007); Jessica the ostrich, voiced by Columbian American actor Laura Ortiz in *Horton Hears a Who!* (2008); Andi Garcia (Jessica Alba) in *Little Fockers* (2010); Crystal the invisible woman, voiced by Chrissy Teigen in *Hotel Transylvania 3: Summer Vacation* (2018); and teenage boy Dave (Miles Robbins) in *Halloween* (2018).

6. David Crystal, *A Dictionary of Language* (Chicago: University of Chicago Press, 1999), s.v. "creaky voice."

7. Ikuko Patricia Yuasa, "Creaky Voice: A New Feminine Voice Quality for Young Urban-Oriented Upwardly Mobile American Women?," *American Speech* 85, no. 3 (2010): 325, https://doi.org.10.1215/00031283-2010-018.

8. Jessica Grose, Penny Eckert, and Susan Sankin, interview by Terry Gross, "From Upspeak To Vocal Fry: Are We 'Policing' Young Women's Voices?," *Fresh Air*, NPR, July 23, 2015, https://www.npr.org/2015/07/23/425608745/from-upspeak-to-vocal-fry-are-we-policing-young-womens-voices.

9. Paul Warren, *Uptalk: The Phenomenon of Rising Intonation* (Cambridge: Cambridge University Press, 2016), 2.

10. Warren, *Uptalk*, 26–8.

11. Warren, *Uptalk*, 113.

12. Warren, *Uptalk*, 148. Slobe, "Style, Stance, and Social Meaning," 543–44. Jessica Grose, Penny Eckert, and Susan Sankin, interview by Terry Gross, "From Upspeak To Vocal Fry." Rindy C. Anderson et al., "Vocal Fry May Undermine the Success of Young Women in the Labor Market," *PLOS ONE* 9, no. 5 (2014), https://doi.org/10.1371/journal.pone.0097506.

13. Anderson et al., "Vocal Fry May Undermine."

14. Slobe, "Style, Stance, and Social Meaning," 544.

15. Warren, *Uptalk*, 158.

16. Warren, *Uptalk*, 161.

17. Warren, *Uptalk*, 162.

18. Katherine Dallaston and Gerard Docherty, "The Quantitative Prevalence of Creaky Voice (Vocal Fry) in Varieties of English: A Systematic Review of the Literature," *PLOS ONE* 15, no. 3 (2020), https://doi.org/10.1371/journal.pone.0229960.

19. Sarah Greer and Stephen Winters, "The Perception of Coolness: Differences in Evaluating Voice Quality in Male and Female Speakers," *Proceedings of the 18th International Congress on Phonetic Sciences*, Glasgow, August 2019, 4, http://www.internationalphoneticassociation.org/icphs-proceedings/ICPhS2015/Papers/ICPHS0883.pdf. Robert J. Podesva, "Gender and the Social Meaning of Non-Modal Phonation Types," *Proceedings of the 37th Annual Meeting of the Berkeley Linguistics Society*, Berkeley, 2013, 436, http://journals.linguisticsociety.org/proceedings/index.php/BLS/article/viewFile/832/615. Nicole Hildebrand-Edgar, "Creaky Voice: An Interactional Resource for Indexing Authority" (master's thesis, University

of Victoria, 2014), 47, https://dspace.librar vic.ca/bitstream/handle/1828/7437/Hildebrand-Edgar_Nicole_MA_2016.pdf?sequ ce=1&isAllowed=y.

20. Sarah Greer, "The Perception of Coolne : Voice Quality and Its Social Uses and Interpretations" (master's thesis, Universit of Calgary, 2015), 61, https://prism.ucalgary.ca/handle/11023/2238.

21. Yuasa, "Creaky Voice," 329.

22. Anderson et al. "Vocal Fry May Underm e."

23. Slobe, "Style, Stance, and Social Meani " 547–8.

24. Slobe, "Style, Stance, and Social Meani " 542.

25. Slobe, "Style, Stance, and Social Meani " 549.

26. Slobe, "Style, Stance, and Social Meani " 545.

27. Yuasa, "Creaky Voice," 331.

28. Grose, Eckert, and Sankin, "From Upsp : to Vocal Fry."

29. Anderson et al. "Vocal Fry May Underm e."

Chapter 6

"We Ain't Come This Far"

Conclusions

> "The proper use of language is to use proper language always. . . . Standard English is English; everything else is slang. Slang should never be considered appropriate by educators. We should encourage our children to speak English in class and on the playground."—C. Mason Weaver, member of the National Advisory Committee of the African-American Leadership Group Project, April 21, 1997[1]

Linguistic discrimination is real. And because our beliefs about marginalized dialects are actually proxy for our beliefs about the people who speak them, linguistic discrimination can and does occur anywhere that other types of discrimination occur—in education, in housing, in employment, and in the criminal justice system.

LINGUISTIC DISCRIMINATION IN REAL LIFE

In an early, still famous example of a court acknowledging the reality of linguistic discrimination in the classroom, a U.S. District Court judge ruled in favor of 11 Black English-speaking children whose parents had sued their school district in *Martin Luther King Junior Elementary School Children et al. v. Ann Arbor School District Board*, the 1979 case that became known as the Ann Arbor Black English trial. The children had been diagnosed by a speech pathologist as "linguistically handicapped" and, as a result, had been improperly placed in special education classes. In his ruling, Judge Charles Joiner acknowledged that the children spoke Black English at home, and that "unconscious but evident attitude of teachers toward the home language causes a psychological barrier to learning by the student." The school had failed in its duty to help the students ov [illegible] come this and other barriers to learning.[2]

However, while the court recognized t [illegible] injustice that had been perpetrated on the students because of their race [illegible] t failed to challenge the prevailing beliefs about Black English that caus [illegible] l the misdiagnosis of linguistic handicapping in the first place. "'Black En [illegible] sh' is not a language used by the mainstream of society black or white," the [illegible] pinion read. "It is not an acceptable method of communication in the edu [illegible] tional world, in the commercial community, in the community of the arts [illegible] d science, or among professionals. It is largely a system that is used in ca [illegible] al and informal communication among the poor and lesser educated."[3] Th [illegible] school's duty was not to uphold Black English, the judge ruled, but to reco [illegible] ize it as a barrier to learning the standard, "acceptable" language of mainstr [illegible] m society. This opinion perpetuated the idea that Black English and othe [illegible] tigmatized varieties, systematic and rule-governed though they may be, a [illegible] still inferior to EDC, still inappropriate in serious, educated, and profess [illegible] al spaces.

The Ann Arbor case raised a lot of cor [illegible] oversy in public spaces, largely due to misrepresentation of the facts of th [illegible] case in the media. However, no controversy over Black English in educati [illegible] reached the level of indignation, outrage, and, as Rosina Lippi-Green puts [illegible] "moral panic" that the Oakland "Ebonics" controversy of 1997 achieved.[4]

The "Ebonics" controversy stemmed fr [illegible] n the well-intentioned Oakland school board's attempt to address the di [illegible] arities in educational outcomes between Black and White students, but [illegible] he resolution that they passed in December 1996 sparked a massive b [illegible] klash due to a combination of poor wording (it states, for example, tha [illegible] "African language systems are genetically-based and not a dialect of Eng [illegible] sh,"[5] a claim that is misleading at best), inaccurate media reporting of the [illegible] ontent and intent of the resolution—some of which led the public to belie [illegible] that teachers would be required to teach in Black English—and the public [illegible] reaction to the notion that Black English should be recognized as a legitin [illegible] te language rather than a failed attempt to speak "standard" English. "T [illegible] 'Ebonic Plague' has reached epidemic proportions," conservative Blac [illegible] commentator C. Mason Weaver railed. The California State Department of [illegible] lucation's notion that "standard" English was not the only correct way to [illegible] eak was "nonsense." "Standard English is English," said Weaver. "[E]very [illegible] ing else is slang."[6]

It seems the public attitude toward Blac [illegible] English has changed little in the intervening years. When in 2010 the DE [illegible] put out a call for linguists fluent in other languages, including nine lin [illegible] ists who understood "Ebonics," *Washington Post* opinion writer Jonathan C [illegible] pehart joked that he'd be quitting to seek a new job as a DEA agent. "After al [illegible] I can lop off words and run them together with the best of them," he wrote, arguing that "Ebonics" might be a dialect, but it's certainly not "a real language."[7]

Despite the attempt by the Ann Arbor case to rectify the harm done by teachers' conscious or unconscious biases toward Black English and other stigmatized dialects, evidence shows that it continues to affect student outcomes today. In their 2001 study "Pre-Service Teacher Attitudes Toward Differing Dialects," Cross, DeVaney, and Jones surveyed over 100 university-enrolled preservice teachers, asking them to rate recorded voice samples of five different speakers: an EDC speaker, White Southern speakers with strong and weak Southern shifts ("High White" and "Low White," respectively), and Black speakers with strong and weak Black English pronunciation ("High Black" and "Low Black"). They began this study in part, they note, because they had "observed in the university community and in the public schools a uniform commitment to standard English and the demeaning and correction of variant dialects, particularly AAVE and the 'uneducated' Central Southern common to rural Alabama. Remedial English programs at the university seemed specifically created to eradicate secondary dialects, and most students forced to enroll in these programs were African American."[8] They sought to determine whether teacher attitudes toward stigmatized dialect groups had a hand in these pedagogical realities, and they found that both Black and White respondents in their study rated the EDC speaker higher than any other speaker on *every metric* that they tested: "intelligence," "education," "considerate," "honesty," "friendliness," "trustworthy," "ambition," and "social status"—and the stronger the "nonstandard" pronunciation among both the White Southern and Black speakers, the lower their ratings.[9]

"Low White" Southern speakers were rated the lowest across several metrics by both Black and White respondents despite the fact that 71% of the respondents reported hailing from the Southeastern U.S.[10] In intelligence, the "Low White" speaker scored an average of 2.19 points on the 4-point scale, compared to 2.78 points for the "Low Black" speaker and 3.11 points for the EDC speaker. In the metrics "friendliness" and "considerate," surprisingly, the "Low White" speaker outscored only the "High Black" speaker, while the reverse was true for the measure of "social status," indicating that supposedly positive stereotypes about friendly Southerners and cool Black people don't necessarily translate to real-life attitudes. Although Black respondents tended to score the Black speakers slightly higher than the "Low White" speaker, they, like the White respondents, still scored the Black speakers lower than the "standard" speaker on every metric, indicating that it is not only White people who would benefit from better education in the field of linguistic diversity.[11]

Cross, DeVaney, and Jones point out that attempts by teachers to eradicate or "correct" Black English and other "nonstandard" dialects in the classroom often have the opposite of their intended ef[illegible]t, increasing children's self-consciousness and hindering their efforts to le[illegible],[12] and they fear that "[t]eachers' preconceptions of students may be reflect[illegible] in students' grades and impact their self-perception, beginning a cycle o[illegible]elf-fulfilling prophecy that contributes to eventual academic failure of s[illegible]akers of nonstandard dialect."[13] This attitude among twenty-first century p[illegible]service teachers mirrors the one we saw in working teachers in the Ann Ar[illegible]r case over thirty years prior.

In 2013, Newkirk-Turner, Cooper [illegible]lliams, Harris, and Whitfield McDaniels surveyed 38 undergraduate pr[illegible]ervice teachers, most of whom were Black, on their attitudes toward Bla[illegible] English and its effects on children's learning. Over 60% reported that t[illegible]y believed that Black English is not "an adequate language system" and o[illegible]r 70% said that speaking Black English "affects students' performance i[illegible]anguage Arts." And over 40% agreed or strongly agreed with the staten[illegible]t, "Teachers are likely to have lower expectations of speakers of [Black [illegible]glish] compared to speakers of [standard English]."[14] These results align [illegible]th the results of dozens of other studies that show that even members of ma[illegible]nalized communities themselves consider marginalized dialects to be inferi[illegible] and inadequate. "The findings," the authors write, "is [sic] noteworthy b[illegible]ause of the potential damaging effects such attitudes can have on teach[illegible], learning, and student-teacher interactions."[15]

Arnetha Ball and Ted Lardner agree th[illegible] these fears are well-founded. In their examination of the Ann Arbor case [illegible]d its implications for pedagogy, they discuss "teacher efficacy," which "s[illegible]aks to the cumulative effect of teachers' knowledge and experience on t[illegible]ir feelings about their students and their own ability to teach them."[16] "T[illegible]n as now," they write, "research on language attitudes consistently indica[illegible]s that teachers believe African American English-speaking children are [illegible]nonverbal' and possess limited vocabularies. Speakers of African Americ[illegible] English are often perceived to be slow learners or uneducable: their spee[illegible] is often considered to be unsystematic and in need of constant correction [illegible]d improvement."[17] And teachers who believe that a given group of stude[illegible]s are less educable—less intelligent, less ambitious, less friendly—whe[illegible]er it is Black English speakers, White Southern speakers, or English langu[illegible]e learners, create "self-fulfilling prophec[ies]"[18] for these students. In the A[illegible] Arbor case, specifically, "teachers expected less and their students not sur[illegible]isingly lived down to these lowered expectations."[19] A teacher's personal *[illegible]lief* about their ability to educate a given student, Ball and Lardner argue, h[illegible] a direct impact on that student's educational outcomes.

In housing, too, linguistic discriminatio[illegible]remains widespread. In research conducted by linguist John Baugh in the Sa[illegible]Francisco Bay area, Baugh made phone calls to landlords advertising apart[illegible]ents for rent using either Black

English, Chicano English, or EDC, all of which he is proficient in. He found that when using EDC, his success rate in scheduling an appointment to see an available apartment remained mostly consistent, about 60 to 70%, regardless which neighborhood he was inquiring in. When using Black English, his success rate leapt to 80% in the majority minority neighborhood of East Palo Alto and fell below 30% in the predominantly White neighborhood of Woodside. And when using Chicano English, his success rate peaked at just over 60% in East Palo Alto and bottomed out at barely 20% in Woodside.[20] Landlords in White neighborhoods consistently agreed to show apartments to the EDC speaker and consistently denied showing those very same apartments to the Black English and the Chicano English speaker, who were, unbeknownst to them, all the same individual.

These practices are, of course, blatant violations of the Fair Housing Act, and even the U.S. Department of Housing and Urban Development recognizes that they are happening. An advertisement from the agency reproduced in Lippi-Green's *English with an Accent* advises readers, "What matters is how you look on paper—not how you sound over the phone. Judging you by your national origin or race instead of your qualifications is discrimination. . . . The best way to stop housing discrimination is to report it."[21] The problem is that often, people don't know they're being discriminated against.[22] If a Black English or Spanish-accented English speaker is turned down for an apartment over the phone, they may have no way of knowing whether their dialect is the culprit or the reasons are more legitimate, and they may be hesitant to report discrimination without being certain.

Not only are "nonstandard" speakers less likely to be able to find a place to live, they're also less likely to find a job. In "Is Your Money Where Your Mouth Is?: Hiring Managers' Attitudes Toward African-American Vernacular English," Anita Henderson tested the reactions of 42 hiring managers, roughly half of whom were Black and half of whom were White, to recordings of potential job candidates of a variety of linguistic backgrounds, including White New Englanders and Midwesterners; a White Southerner; Black speakers using "standard" English; Black speakers using minimal, moderate, or strong Black English features; British English speakers; and non-native English speakers whose first language was Korean, Chinese, Spanish, or French.[23] Henderson asked the respondents to rate the speakers on personal characteristics such as "Ambitious, Confident, Friendly, Intelligent, Kind, and Trustworthy," as well as to identify the highest job for which they would recommend the speaker, the options being

5 = Trial Lawyer
4 = Corporate Trainer
3 = Office Manager

2 = Security Guard
1 = Cook/Dishwasher (Kitchen Help).[24]

As by now we should expect, the respo nts ranked the American EDC speakers and British English speakers hi est in intelligence, confidence, and ambitiousness; the two Black speaker ho used EDC also fared well in these metrics, though not as well as the W e speakers. The White Southern speaker was ranked highly in friendline kindness, and trustworthiness, but in intelligence, confidence, and amb ousness, he was ranked below the White and Black EDC speakers, the tish English speakers, and even a clearly disfluent native French speaker. ack English speakers who used minimal Black English were rated as more elligent than both Black English speakers who used more Black English fea res and native Spanish speakers; these latter two groups, on average, recei d the worst scores in perceived intelligence.[25]

The respondents' job recommendation lso follow this predictable pattern: the British English speakers and both e White and Black EDC speakers were all recommended, on average, fo Corporate Trainer or above. The White Southern speaker, too, managed to hieve this average recommendation, though just barely. Conversely, *none* the Black English or non-native English speakers received average recom ndations above Office Manager, with the French speakers again outscoring ack English speakers and native Spanish speakers. The male native Spanis speaker received the lowest recommendations, averaging out to only a Se rity Guard.[26]

Interestingly, one other White native En sh speaker was ranked as poorly as the speakers of Black English and Spani -accented English in intelligence and confidence, and nearly as poorly fo ob recommendation—a female speaker who spoke a strong South Philad hia dialect. In fact, she was the only White native English speaker who recommended, on average, for a job no higher than Office Manager. The udy took place in Philadelphia, and Henderson points out that the speaker dialect is clearly evident in both her pronunciation and her vocabulary— ch diverge from the "standard" in noticeable ways—and that after hearing multiple respondents remarked that they "hate that South Philadelphia acc ." Clearly, Henderson notes, like the Southern speaker's English, the Sout Philadelphian's English "do[es] not represent high status for the subjects rated the speakers"[27]—in other words, it's not EDC. This is further evid e that *any* divergence from the prestige dialect will be punished by liste rs, though, at least in this case, not quite as severely as the more stigmati dialects associated with speakers of color.

Gendered speech patterns, too, may aff t hirability. In their 2014 *PLOS ONE* study (mentioned in Chapter 5), And on et al. surveyed 800 American adults on their perceptions of creaky voice ("vocal fry"), particularly as it relates to characteristics of employability. They recorded seven young adult men and seven young adult women speaking the sentence "Thank you for considering me for this opportunity" both with and without creak on the final phrase. Survey participants then listened to the pairs of sentences and selected which voice they "considered to be more educated, competent, trustworthy, attractive, and which speaker they would hire." The researchers found that while listeners consistently preferred the noncreaky samples of both the male and the female speakers, "the negative perception of vocal fry was significantly stronger when listeners judged *female* voices [emphasis added]" for every metric except attractiveness, and female listeners judged creak even more harshly than male listeners.[28] Contrary to Yuasa's results in her limited study,[29] they also found negative perceptions of creak among all age groups, though older listeners did rate creak more negatively than younger listeners specifically in the metric of competence. As a result, the authors suggest that "young American women should avoid vocal fry in order to maximize labor market perceptions, particularly when being interviewed by another woman."[30] Of course, changing the way one speaks isn't quite so simple, and as we've discussed in previous chapters, speakers of stigmatized dialects shouldn't *have* to change the way they speak in order to be taken seriously, just as people of color shouldn't have to conform to White European beauty standards to be considered attractive. The popular mindset that leads people of all ages and genders to judge speakers as less intelligent and less competent based only on their voices is the problem at issue, not the voices themselves.

Finally, and perhaps most disturbingly, linguistic discrimination shows up in our criminal justice system, both directly and indirectly. Linguist John Baugh points out that economic injustice is the primary contributor to judicial injustice,[31] and marginalized speakers are more likely to suffer economic injustice due in part to the inequitable education and hiring practices discussed above. But, Baugh points out, beliefs that marginalized speakers are less intelligent, credible, and trustworthy can also have a direct impact in the courtroom when juries and judges have less confidence in their testimony.[32]

In "Language and Linguistics on Trial: Hearing Rachel Jeantel (and Other Vernacular Speakers) in the Courtroom and Beyond," John R. Rickford and Sharese King discuss examples of legal cases in which the testimony of Black English speakers was disregarded by juries, from the 1955 trial of the murderers of Emmett Till, to a 1965 self-defense case in which the Black English-speaking defendant was convicted after jurors considered most of his testimony "incomprehensible"; they also point to a 2015 case in which a recorded call made by a Black English-speaking suspect in a San Francisco jail was patently mistranscribed by police, leading the suspect to appear as though he was admitting guilt.[33]

In their look at the acquittal of Geor Zimmerman in the killing of Trayvon Martin, Rickford and King exam e reactions to the prosecution's key witness, Black English speaker Rach Jeantel, who was described by online commentators as "a dullard, an id , an individual who can barely speak in coherent sentences," "who speaks laitian hood rat," who is "unemployable and another welfare parasite suck g on the government teat."[34] The jury, too, disregarded Jeantel's testimony, th one juror later reporting that she was "hard to understand" and "not cre le," and another acknowledging that, during their over 16 hours of deliber ons, "no one mentioned Jeantel. . . . Her testimony played no role whatsoe r in their decision."[35]

It's not only marginalized dialects that taken less seriously in a courtroom; researchers writing in the *Duke Law urnal* as far back as 1978 found that listeners rated speakers that used gen red speech patterns as less convincing, less competent, less intelligent, le trustworthy, and less likely to be telling the truth—and this held true wheth the speakers were actually male or female.[36] To determine this, the researc rs identified two distinct speaking styles used by witnesses, "powerless" nd "powerful." The "powerless" style used several of the types of gendere speech patterns we discussed in Chapter 5—uptalk, intensifiers such as *de itely*, tag questions such as *you know*—as well as other patterns that are ty cally used more by women than by men, including hedges such as *I thin* and politeness markers such as *please*. The "powerful" style was simply)C without these features, as in the following example:

> Q. Approximately how long did you stay th before the ambulance arrived?
>
> A. (Powerless): Oh, it seems like it was ab t, uh, twenty minutes. Just long enough to help my friend, Mrs. Davis, you k w, get straightened out.
>
> A. (Powerful): Twenty minutes. Long enou to help get Mrs. Davis straightened out.[37]

The researchers then recorded four spe ers, two men and two women, giving the same testimony taken from a r trial in both the powerless and the powerful styles. The respondents, 96 llege undergraduates, rated the powerful male speaker the highest for bein convincing and trustworthy and for telling the truth, and the powerful fem speaker the highest for competence and intelligence. In all cases, the po rful speakers were rated higher than the powerless speakers, and in some ases, quite significantly so. For instance, on the question, "To what exten lid you believe the witness was telling the truth?," the students rated the p erful male highest at 4.24 (on a 10-point scale from +5 to -5), the powerfu female second at 3.70, the powerless male third at 2.86, and the powerle female last at a dismal 1.88. In fact, the powerless female scored lowest on every metric except competence. Her lowest score was for intelligence at -0.23.[38] There is clearly gender bias at play here in that the powerless female speaker was penalized more harshly for her speech than the powerless male, but *both* speakers' credibility suffered when using the gendered speech patterns.

THE EFFECTS OF MEDIA STEREOTYPES ON PEOPLE'S ATTITUDES

Linguistic discrimination has real, tangible consequences for speakers, and what's more, research has shown that stereotypical portrayals of marginalized groups in the media have real effects on viewers' attitudes toward those groups. In a 1997 study, for example, Thomas E. Ford showed videos of comedy sketches—some neutral and some depicting Black people in negative stereotypes such as being "poor, uneducated, and prone to acts of crime and violence"—to undergraduate students. He then asked those students to rate the likelihood that a hypothetical individual named either Tyrone or Todd was guilty of an accusation of physical assault. The students were equally likely to assign guilt to Todd whether they watched the neutral comedy sketch or the stereotype-filled sketch, but their guilt ratings for Tyrone increased significantly after watching the stereotype-filled sketch. Ford hypothesized that watching TV portrayals of negative Black stereotypes has real-world effects on viewers' attitudes toward Black people.[39]

Similarly, in a 2007 study, Qingwen Dong and Arthur Phillip Murrillo found that White American young adults whose primary exposure to other races was through TV were considerably more likely to hold negative, stereotypical views of Hispanic people, indicating that 1) TV portrayals of Hispanics are still quite negative and stereotypical, and 2) people's attitudes are influenced by viewing those portrayals.[40] Narissra M. Punyanunt-Carter, too, in her 2008 survey of over 400 undergraduates found that, in general, they believed the negative representations of Black people on TV to be true to life, but not the positive stereotypes.[41] And as we discussed in Chapter 4, a 2012 study of over 3,000 non-Latinx people by the National Hispanic Media Coalition on *The Impact of Media Stereotypes on Opinions and Attitudes Towards Latinos* determined that viewers of negative representations of Latinx people in media reported more negative beliefs about real-world Latinx people, such as that they are more likely to rely on welfare, be involved with drugs, and take American jobs.[42]

Ediberto Román links such stereotyping not only to tangible external consequences such as violence and discrimination, but to internal consequences. "[S]tereotyping serves the hegemonic function of having the stigmatized accept the stigma," he writes. "In light of the fact that Latinas and Latinos are inundated with negative reinforcement from film, television and print media, there is good reason to believe that this group will become complicit in embodying the characterizations the dominant culture has assigned. In effect Latinas and Latinos will become experts in their discrediting attributions, believing that the dominant gaze accurately depicts them."[43] In other words, just as negative teacher attitudes w[ill] create self-fulfilling prophesies of low-performing students, the negative attitudes that marginalized people internalize about themselves may create self-fulfilling prophesies as they live down to the expectations of the dominant White society. And though the research linking stereotypical portrayals of marginalized *linguistic* groups directly to real-world attitudes is as yet sparse, based on the bounty of evidence above, it's reasonable to believe that the effects would be the same.

SOLUTIONS

Linguistic discrimination will not be eradicated until racism, sexism, and classism are eradicated, and obviously that day is still far over the horizon. But that doesn't mean there is no space to make inroads in the meantime.

Like other forms of prejudice, linguistic discrimination is learned, and my research suggests that our schools and our media constitute two of the major places in which it is learned. As I discussed in the introduction, our public schools still largely teach that EDC is the "correct" way to speak English and that all other dialects are aberrations—at best, appropriate for the home or the playground but not the classroom,[44] at worst, inappropriate and "wrong" in any context. To correct this we must simply begin with better teacher education, specifically training that provides future teachers with a basic understanding of the history of English and the formation of its many dialects, the roots of dialect and gendered speech prejudices, and the structure of the most widely spoken stigmatized dialects such as Black English and Chicano English. As Cross, DeVaney, and Jones put it, "Teachers of all subjects and grades should be made aware of linguistic implications of differences in dialect and understand that 'different' is not necessarily 'wrong.'"[45] Ball and Lardner observe that the best Black teachers working in community organizations "build on the language practices of their African American students." Instead of "correcting" their uses of Black English or attempting to replace their native dialects with EDC, they "work explicitly to make students metacognitively aware of their oral and written uses of African American English and of alternative ways of expressing their ideas" in various genres of writing.[46] As a teacher of composition at both a community college and a state university, I can attest that these are skills that benefit *all* writers, regardless of their native dialects, and that it *is* possible to teach alternate modes of communication without leading students to believe that their native dialect is incorrect or inferior.

School board policies, too, must be revised to acknowledge the wide range of dialects with which students are likely to enter the system and those students' right to keep their dialects. The intentions of the Oakland school board's 1996 resolution acknowledging the legitimacy of "Ebonics," were promising, though its execution was poor, but as far back as 1974 the Conference on College Composition and Communication instituted a similar resolution, which read

> We affirm the students' right to their own patterns and varieties of language—the dialects of their nurture or whatever dialects in which they find their own identity and style. Language scholars long ago denied that the myth of a standard American dialect has any validity. The claim that any one dialect is unacceptable amounts to an attempt of one social group to exert its dominance over another. Such a claim leads to false advice for speakers and writers, and immoral advice for humans. A nation proud of its diverse heritage and its cultural and racial variety will preserve its heritage of dialects. We affirm strongly that teachers must have the experiences and training that will enable them to respect diversity and uphold the right of students to their own language.[47]

The first draft of this statement was to the CCCC in 1972, fifty years previous to the time of this writing, yet these issues persist, and they will continue to do so until school boards and local governments nationwide recognize the real harm that linguistic discrimination causes to their students and to marginalized groups across the country.

In addition to learning inaccurate and essentialist messages about English in school, children and people of all ages see those messages reinforced in their media, including mainstream film: Black English speakers are criminals or comedians; Southern speakers are ignorant and racist; SIE speakers are drug dealers; GSP users are vapid and self-absorbed. And since, as Lippi-Green points out, media are so many citizens' primary source of exposure to speakers of stigmatized dialects, then the messages coming from media might be even louder than those they hear at school.

Today, decisions about which movies get produced, which get big budgets and broad marketing and exposure, are made almost entirely by major studios for whom profit is the first and only motivator. As Augusto Boal wrote in his classic *Theatre of the Oppressed*, "[T]he dominant art will always be that of the dominant class, since it is the only class that possesses the means to disseminate it."[48] Individual actors and creators may have idealist visions for their projects, but without major studio funding, those visions remain exactly that. Knowing that studios are driven by p fit, do we as consumers have an obligation to support those films whose v ues align with our own? In the case of linguistic prejudice, does this mean eking out those films with more equitable and accurate portrayals of mar nalized speakers, and shunning those films without? What about the doz s of films in our set with broad racial and gender diversity but no linguis diversity at all, such as 2019's *Shazam!*, which features a rainbow coaliti of orphans-turned-superheroes, yet every one of those diverse, working c s, inner city children somehow speaks EDC? Obviously these are questio that moviegoers and consumers must answer for themselves, but those wh ave found the arguments in this book convincing might keep these points i mind with the next movie ticket they purchase. At a minimum we can and hould view the media we enjoy with a critical eye, and be cognizant of the ejudices and unconscious biases that films may be reinforcing in us withou ur knowledge.

LIMITATIONS AND S GGESTIONS FOR FURTHER R SEARCH

This study examined only the highest-gr sing films at the domestic box office released during a specific period of me. By necessity, many popular films were omitted from this list, includin those that were more successful through in-home-viewing options and thos "cult classics" that became better known after their release. And of course, si e the COVID-19 pandemic, studios and theaters have been forced to adap often releasing big budget movies in theaters and on streaming services si ultaneously, or even foregoing a theatrical release completely. When more liable methods are developed to track in-home viewing, my film set can an should be reconfigured to better reflect Americans' actual film consumptio abits.

Television and streaming media, too, sh ld be included in future studies provided the time and resources are avail e. The combination of network, cable, and streaming shows constitutes a n ssive corpus of data ripe for collection and analysis, but this is too great a ndertaking for one individual.

Other stigmatized dialects also need f her study. Though the dialects discussed here likely fall at the interse on of "most stigmatized" and "most widely spoken," other marginalize peakers fall prey to stereotypes that undoubtedly appear in mainstream edia. For example, indigenous Americans are one of the most underrep ented groups in modern media; in fact, the new (as of 2021) Hulu series *servation Dogs*, which features a primarily indigenous cast and writers' r m, may be the first of its kind. How are this demographic and its margin zed speakers portrayed in other media? What evidence in media do we fi of the egregiously understudied

Rez dialects, and does it prop up previously held prejudices about Native people? What about East Coast and Midwestern blue collar dialects and foreign-accented English? How are English speakers from other parts of the world depicted beyond the trope of the British villain?

I hope that this book will serve as a starting point for research of this nature, and that future scholars in this field will find it incomplete but useful.

NOTES

1. C. Mason Weaver, "Funding Ebonics Isn't a New Idea, It's Just a Bad One," The National Center for Public Policy Research, April 1, 1997, https://nationalcenter.org/project21/1997/04/01/funding-ebonics-isnt-a-new-idea-its-just-a-bad-one/.

2. Martin Luther King Jr., etc. v. Ann Arbor Sch. Dist., 473 F. Supp. 1371, 1381 (E.D. Mich. 1979), https://law.justia.com/cases/federal/district-courts/FSupp/473/1371/2148458/.

3. Martin Luther King Jr., etc. v. Ann Arbor Sch. Dist., 473 F. Supp. at 1378.

4. Rosina Lippi-Green, *English with an Accent: Language, Ideology, and Discrimination in the United States* (New York: Routledge, 2012), 306.

5. Lippi-Green, *English with an Accent*, 310.

6. Weaver, "Funding Ebonics."

7. Jonathan Capehart, "DEA: the E is for 'Ebonics,'" *Washington Post*, August 24, 2010, http://voices.washingtonpost.com/postpartisan/2010/08/dea_the_e_is_for_ebonics.html.

8. John B. Cross, Thomas DeVaney, and Gerald Jones, "Pre-Service Teacher Attitudes Toward Differing Dialects," *Linguistics and Education* 12, no. 4 (2001): 216–17, https://doi.org/10.1016/S0898-5898(01)00051-1.

9. Cross, DeVaney, and Jones, "Pre-Service Teacher Attitudes," 221.

10. Cross, DeVaney, and Jones, "Pre-Service Teacher Attitudes," 218.

11. Cross, DeVaney, and Jones, "Pre-Service Teacher Attitudes," 220.

12. Cross, DeVaney, and Jones, "Pre-Service Teacher Attitudes," 215.

13. Cross, DeVaney, and Jones, "Pre-Service Teacher Attitudes," 223.

14. Brandi L. Newkirk-Turner, et al., "Pre-Service Teachers' Attitudes toward Students' Use of African American English," *The Researcher: An Interdisciplinary Journal* 26, no. 2 (2013): 55–56, https://www.jsums.edu/researcher/files/2014/02/Special-Issue-CUR-Complete-Summer-2013.pdf.

15. Newkirk-Turner, et al., "Pre-Service Teachers' Attitudes," 50.

16. Arnetha Ball and Ted Lardner, "Dispositions Toward Language: Constructs of Teacher Knowledge and the Ann Arbor Black English Case," *College Composition and Communication* 48, no. 4 (1997): 478, http://dx.doi.org/10.2307/358453.

17. Ball and Lardner, "Dispositions Toward Language," 472.

18. Ball and Lardner, "Dispositions Toward Language," 483.

19. Ball and Lardner, "Dispositions Toward Language," 483.

20. Lippi-Green, *English with an Accent*, 327–28.

21. Lippi-Green, *English with an Accent*, 32

22. Lippi-Green, *English with an Accent*, 32

23. Anita Henderson, "Is Your Money Whe Your Mouth Is?: Hiring Managers' Attitudes Toward African-American Vernacula English," (PhD diss., University of Pennsylvania, 2001), 168.

24. Henderson, "Is Your Money," 199.

25. Henderson, "Is Your Money," 204.

26. Henderson, "Is Your Money," 237.

27. Henderson, "Is Your Money," 214.

28. Rindy C. Anderson et al., "Vocal Fry M Undermine the Success of Young Women in the Labor Market," *PLOS ONE* 9, . 5 (2014), https://doi.org/10.1371/journal.pone.0097506.

29. Ikuko Patricia Yuasa, "Creaky Voice: A N Feminine Voice Quality for Young Urban-Oriented Upwardly Mobile American men?," *American Speech* 85, no. 3 (2010): 325, https://doi.org.10.1215/00031283- 10-018.

30. Anderson et al., "Vocal Fry May Underm e."

31. John Baugh, *Out of the Mouths of Slav* (Austin: University of Texas Press, 1999), 76.

32. Baugh, *Out of the Mouths of Slaves*, 75.

33. John R. Rickford and Sharese King, "Lan age and Linguistics On Trial: Hearing Rachel Jeantel (and Other Vernacular Spea rs) in the Courtroom and Beyond," *Language* 92, no. 4 (2016): 954–55.

34. Rickford and King, "Language and Ling stics on Trial," 957.

35. Rickford and King, "Language and Ling stics on Trial," 950.

36. John M. Conley, William M. O'Barr, an E. Allan Lind, "The Power of Language: Presentational Style in the Courtroom *Duke Law Journal* (1978): 1385, https://scholarship.law.duke.edu/cgi/viewconte cgi?article=2686&context=dlj.

37. Conley, O'Barr, and Lind, "The Power o anguage," 1380.

38. Conley, O'Barr, and Lind, "The Power o anguage," 1384–5.

39. Thomas E. Ford, "Effects of Ster typical Television Portrayals of African-Americans on Person Perception," *S al Psychology Quarterly* 60, no. 3 (1997): 269–71.

40. Qingwen Dong and Arthur Phillip Murril , "The Impact of Television Viewing on Young Adults' Stereotypes Towards Hispani mericans," *Human Communication* 10, no. 1 (2007): 39–41, https://www.researc ate.net/publication/228984764_The_impact_of_television_viewing_on_young_a ts'_stereotypes_towards_Hispanic_Americans.

41. Narissra M. Punyanunt-Carter, "The Pe ived Realism of African American Portrayals on Television," *The Howard Journa f Communications* 19, no. 3 (2008): 251, https://doi.org/10.1080/10646170802218 .

42. *The Impact of Media Stereotypes on Op ons and Attitudes Towards Latinos*, National Hispanic Media Coalition, 2012, 12– https://www.chicano.ucla.edu/files/news/NHMCLatinoDecisionsReport.pdf.

43. Ediberto Román, "Who Exactly Is Livin a Vida Loca: The Legal and Political Consequences of Latino-Latina Ethnic and acial Stereotypes in Film and Other

Media," *The Journal of Gender, Race & Justice* 4, no. 37 (2000): 63–65, https://ecollections.law.fiu.edu/faculty_publications/313/.

44. H. Samy Alim and Geneva Smitherman, *Articulate While Black: Barack Obama, Language, and Race in the U.S.* (New York: Oxford University Press, 2012), 172–75.

45. Cross, DeVaney, and Jones, "Pre-Service Teacher Attitudes," 223.

46. Ball and Lardner, "Dispositions Toward Language," 480–81.

47. *Students' Right to Their Own Language*, Conference on College Composition and Communication, April 1974, https://prod-ncte-cdn.azureedge.net/nctefiles/groups/cccc/newsrtol.pdf.

48. Augusto Boal, *Theatre of the Oppressed* (New York: Theatre Communications Group, 1985), 53.

Appendix A

List of Films by Estimated Number of Tickets Sold

Film	*Adj. Lifetime Gross*	*Lifetime Gross*	*Est. Num Tickets*	*Year*
Star Wars: Episode VII - The Force Awakens	$989,072,973	$936,662,225	108,115,100	2015
Avatar	$890,220,657	$760,507,625	97,309,600	2009
Avengers: Endgame	$871,551,653	$858,373,000	95,268,900	2019
The Avengers	$703,334,845	$623,357,910	76,881,200	2012
Jurassic World	$702,496,857	$652,270,625	76,789,600	2015
Black Panther	$698,123,039	$700,426,566	76,311,500	2018
The Dark Knight	$681,605,723	$535,234,033	74,506,000	2008
Avengers: Infinity War	$662,519,555	$678,815,482	72,419,700	2018
Shrek 2	$649,997,317	$441,226,247	71,050,900	2004
Spider-Man	$646,112,934	$407,022,860	70,626,300	2002
Star Wars: Episode VIII - The Last Jedi	$618,377,017	$620,181,382	67,594,500	2017
Incredibles 2	$606,527,181	$608,581,744	66,299,200	2018
Pirates of the Caribbean: Dead Man's Chest	$591,242,146	$423,315,812	64,628,400	2006
The Lord of the Rings: The Return of the King	$563,900,522	$377,845,905	61,639,700	2003
Finding Nemo	$563,413,831	$380,843,261	61,586,500	2003
Rogue One: A Star Wars Story	$552,939,904	$532,177,324	60,441,600	2016
The Lion King	$551,852,167	$543,638,043	60,322,700	2019
Spider-Man 2	$550,351,840	$373,585,825	60,158,700	2004
The Passion of the Christ	$546,199,412	$370,782,930	59,704,800	2004
Star Wars: Episode III - Revenge of the Sith	$542,721,216	$380,270,577	59,324,600	2005
The Lord of the Rings: The Two Towers	$528,091,201	$342,551,365	57,725,400	2002
The Dark Knight Rises	$526,777,500	$448,139,099	57,581,800	2012

Film	Adj. Lifetime Gross	time Gross	Est. Num Tickets	Year
Beauty and the Beast	$520,064,453	04,481,165	56,848,000	2017
Finding Dory	$513,753,018	86,295,561	56,158,100	2016
Harry Potter and the Sorcerer's Stone	$513,616,708	18,087,620	56,143,200	2001
Star Wars: Episode IX - The Rise of Skywalker	$503,014,704	15,202,542	54,984,300	2019
The Lord of the Rings: The Fellowship of the Ring	$501,323,178	15,544,750	54,799,400	2001
Transformers: Revenge of the Fallen	$493,103,400	02,111,870	53,900,900	2009
Star Wars: Episode II - Attack of the Clones	$489,147,661	10,676,740	53,468,500	2002
Avengers: Age of Ultron	$488,076,391	59,005,868	53,351,400	2015
Toy Story 3	$487,966,611	15,004,880	53,339,400	2010
The Hunger Games: Catching Fire	$467,613,399	24,668,047	51,114,600	2013
Frozen II	$466,080,138	77,373,578	50,947,000	2019
The Hunger Games	$465,314,423	08,010,692	50,863,300	2012
Pirates of the Caribbean: The Curse of the Black Pearl	$463,353,020	05,413,918	50,648,900	2003
Monsters, Inc.	$452,157,290	90,642,256	49,425,100	2001
Frozen	$448,643,415	00,738,009	49,041,000	2013
Spider-Man 3	$447,484,321	36,530,303	48,914,300	2007
Iron Man 3	$446,889,679	09,013,994	48,849,300	2013
Harry Potter and the Deathly Hallows: Part 2	$441,015,535	81,409,310	48,207,200	2011
Toy Story 4	$440,663,324	34,038,008	48,168,700	2019
How the Grinch Stole Christmas	$440,097,042	60,044,825	48,106,800	2000
Captain Marvel	$433,383,080	26,829,839	47,372,900	2019
Shrek	$432,630,172	67,665,011	47,290,600	2001
Shrek the Third	$429,120,872	22,719,944	46,907,000	2007
Despicable Me 2	$429,002,858	68,065,385	46,894,100	2013
Captain America: Civil War	$427,732,155	08,084,349	46,755,200	2016
The Matrix Reloaded	$427,189,658	31,576,461	46,695,900	2003
Transformers	$424,501,878	19,246,193	46,402,100	2007
Wonder Woman	$421,879,966	12,563,408	46,115,500	2017
Jurassic World: Fallen Kingdom	$420,312,856	17,719,760	45,944,200	2018
Harry Potter and the Goblet of Fire	$415,273,954	90,417,905	45,393,400	2005
The Chronicles of Narnia: The Lion, the Witch and the Wardrobe	$413,286,936	91,710,957	45,176,200	2005
Harry Potter and the Chamber of Secrets	$412,959,426	62,450,136	45,140,400	2002

Film	Adj. Lifetime Gross	Lifetime Gross	Est. Num Tickets	Year
Pirates of the Caribbean: At World's End	$411,436,228	$309,420,425	44,973,900	2007
Iron Man	$406,110,984	$319,034,126	44,391,800	2008
Transformers: Dark of the Moon	$404,913,467	$352,390,543	44,260,900	2011
Meet the Fockers	$404,109,328	$279,261,160	44,173,000	2004
Indiana Jones and the Kingdom of the Crystal Skull	$404,031,567	$317,101,119	44,164,500	2008
Jumanji: Welcome to the Jungle	$403,733,332	$404,540,171	44,131,900	2017
Guardians of the Galaxy Vol. 2	$398,469,381	$389,813,101	43,556,500	2017
Spider-Man: Far from Home	$396,491,511	$390,532,085	43,340,300	2019
The Secret Life of Pets	$395,883,147	$368,384,330	43,273,800	2016
American Sniper	$394,110,200	$350,126,372	43,080,000	2014
Harry Potter and the Order of the Phoenix	$390,214,840	$292,353,413	42,654,200	2007
Inside Out	$389,376,852	$356,921,711	42,562,600	2015
Deadpool	$386,910,462	$363,070,709	42,293,000	2016
Alice in Wonderland	$385,163,130	$334,191,110	42,102,000	2010
The Incredibles	$384,504,450	$261,441,092	42,030,000	2004
Cast Away	$383,262,106	$233,632,142	41,894,200	2000
The Jungle Book	$381,583,387	$364,001,123	41,710,700	2016
My Big Fat Greek Wedding	$378,919,392	$241,438,208	41,419,500	2002
Guardians of the Galaxy	$376,706,411	$333,176,600	41,177,600	2014
Furious 7	$375,299,397	$353,007,020	41,023,800	2015
The Hunger Games: Mockingjay - Part 1	$372,583,257	$337,135,885	40,726,900	2014
Minions	$372,467,073	$336,045,770	40,714,200	2015
Harry Potter and the Half-Blood Prince	$372,177,071	$302,305,431	40,682,500	2009
Harry Potter and the Prisoner of Azkaban	$369,640,238	$249,975,996	40,405,200	2004
Bruce Almighty	$368,405,213	$242,829,261	40,270,200	2003
Mission: Impossible II	$365,610,397	$215,409,889	39,964,700	2000
Rush Hour 2	$365,552,763	$226,164,286	39,958,400	2001
Iron Man 2	$362,898,831	$312,433,331	39,668,300	2010
Zootopia	$362,329,805	$341,268,248	39,606,100	2016
Aladdin	$361,011,530	$355,559,216	39,462,000	2019
Up	$359,289,814	$293,004,164	39,273,800	2009
Signs	$358,922,051	$227,966,634	39,233,600	2002
The Twilight Saga: New Moon	$358,707,065	$297,816,253	39,210,100	2009
The Twilight Saga: Eclipse	$356,589,226	$300,531,751	38,978,600	2010
Batman v Superman: Dawn of Justice	$350,020,722	$330,360,194	38,260,600	2016
Suicide Squad	$349,275,133	$325,100,054	38,179,100	2016
Inception	$346,932,245	$292,576,195	37,923,000	2010

Film	Adj. Lifetime Gross	time Gross	Est. Num Tickets	Year
Skyfall	$346,191,230	04,360,277	37,842,000	2012
The Hobbit: An Unexpected Journey	$346,115,299	03,003,568	37,833,700	2012
Spider-Man: Homecoming	$342,314,166	34,201,140	37,418,200	2017
Cars	$340,908,982	44,082,982	37,264,600	2006
Harry Potter and the Deathly Hallows: Part 1	$340,342,700	96,347,721	37,202,700	2010
The Hangover	$340,006,042	77,322,503	37,165,900	2009
Aquaman	$339,898,091	35,061,807	37,154,100	2018
Night at the Museum	$338,868,904	50,863,268	37,041,600	2006
I Am Legend	$335,963,393	56,393,010	36,724,000	2007
Austin Powers in Goldmember	$335,870,995	13,307,889	36,713,900	2002
War of the Worlds	$334,364,265	34,280,354	36,549,200	2005
It	$333,992,842	28,828,874	36,508,600	2017
The Twilight Saga: Breaking Dawn - Part 2	$332,345,227	92,324,737	36,328,500	2012
The Twilight Saga: Breaking Dawn - Part 1	$328,543,180	81,287,133	35,912,900	2011
Joker	$327,515,822	35,451,311	35,800,600	2019
X-Men: The Last Stand	$327,331,941	34,362,462	35,780,500	2006
The Mummy Returns	$326,526,887	02,019,785	35,692,500	2001
X2: X-Men United	$326,107,894	14,949,694	35,646,700	2003
Man of Steel	$322,483,324	91,045,518	35,250,500	2013
Pearl Harbor	$320,907,066	98,542,554	35,078,200	2001
Gladiator	$318,490,077	87,705,427	34,814,000	2000
Deadpool 2	$317,510,290	24,591,735	34,706,900	2018
Star Trek	$316,056,620	57,730,019	34,548,000	2009
Thor: Ragnarok	$313,981,778	15,058,289	34,321,200	2017
Jumanji: The Next Level	$312,783,346	20,314,960	34,190,200	2019
Men in Black II	$310,273,958	93,735,288	33,915,900	2002
The Perfect Storm	$309,954,682	32,618,434	33,881,000	2000
King Kong	$308,914,706	18,080,025	33,770,600	2005
The Amazing Spider-Man	$308,096,655	62,030,663	33,677,900	2012
The Blind Side	$304,660,541	55,959,475	33,302,300	2009
The Da Vinci Code	$303,830,787	17,536,138	33,211,600	2006
Monsters University	$303,728,326	68,492,764	33,200,400	2013
What Women Want	$302,715,605	82,811,707	33,089,700	2000
The Bourne Ultimatum	$302,468,600	27,471,070	33,062,700	2007
Gravity	$301,325,974	74,092,705	32,937,800	2013
Wedding Crashers	$298,649,171	09,255,921	32,645,200	2005
Despicable Me	$298,185,351	51,513,985	32,594,500	2010
The Hunger Games: Mockingjay - Part 2	$296,420,637	81,723,902	32,401,600	2015
The Lego Movie	$295,631,136	57,760,692	32,315,300	2014
Batman Begins	$294,839,805	06,852,432	32,228,800	2005

Film	Adj. Lifetime Gross	Lifetime Gross	Est. Num Tickets	Year
Charlie and the Chocolate Factory	$294,657,753	$206,459,076	32,208,900	2005
Ocean's Eleven	$293,430,047	$183,417,150	32,074,700	2001
Jurassic Park III	$292,830,831	$181,171,875	32,009,200	2001
Planet of the Apes	$290,940,786	$180,011,740	31,802,600	2001
Hancock	$290,435,798	$227,946,274	31,747,400	2008
The Hangover Part II	$288,972,064	$254,464,305	31,587,400	2011
The Hobbit: The Desolation of Smaug	$288,310,640	$258,366,855	31,515,100	2013
Captain America: The Winter Soldier	$285,385,918	$259,766,572	31,195,400	2014
National Treasure: Book of Secrets	$285,176,421	$219,964,115	31,172,500	2007
WALL·E	$285,161,783	$223,808,164	31,170,900	2008
The Hobbit: The Battle of the Five Armies	$284,320,137	$255,119,788	31,078,900	2014
Alvin and the Chipmunks	$283,148,235	$217,326,974	30,950,800	2007
Meet the Parents	$281,700,969	$166,244,045	30,792,600	2000
Sing	$280,546,449	$270,395,425	30,666,400	2016
300	$280,054,269	$210,614,939	30,612,600	2007
Superman Returns	$279,451,394	$200,081,192	30,546,700	2006
Transformers: Age of Extinction	$277,886,114	$245,439,076	30,375,600	2014
Ice Age	$277,736,996	$176,387,405	30,359,300	2002
Shrek Forever After	$277,478,098	$238,736,787	30,331,000	2010
Madagascar	$276,298,878	$193,595,521	30,202,100	2005
The Day After Tomorrow	$275,099,532	$186,740,799	30,071,000	2004
Happy Feet	$274,557,035	$198,000,317	30,011,700	2006
Ratatouille	$274,510,379	$206,445,654	30,006,600	2007
Kung Fu Panda	$274,493,912	$215,434,591	30,004,800	2008
Dr. Seuss' the Grinch	$274,188,358	$270,620,950	29,971,400	2018
Brave	$274,061,196	$237,283,207	29,957,500	2012
Pirates of the Caribbean: On Stranger Tides	$273,786,746	$241,071,802	29,927,500	2011
Ice Age: The Meltdown	$272,817,022	$195,330,621	29,821,500	2006
The Polar Express	$271,173,982	$187,224,490	29,641,900	2004
Despicable Me 3	$271,018,460	$264,624,300	29,624,900	2017
A Beautiful Mind	$269,095,480	$170,742,341	29,414,700	2001
Oz the Great and Powerful	$267,761,653	$234,911,825	29,268,900	2013
X-Men	$266,981,301	$157,299,718	29,183,600	2000
Hannibal	$266,840,416	$165,092,268	29,168,200	2001
Maleficent	$266,712,340	$241,410,378	29,154,200	2014
Scary Movie	$266,506,502	$157,019,771	29,131,700	2000
Mr. & Mrs. Smith	$265,938,391	$186,336,279	29,069,600	2005
What Lies Beneath	$263,855,315	$155,464,351	28,841,900	2000
Elf	$262,970,671	$174,626,840	28,745,200	2003
Fast & Furious 6	$261,148,323	$238,679,850	28,546,000	2013

Film	Adj. Lifetime Gross	time Gross	Est. Num Tickets	Year
The Bourne Supremacy	$259,632,444	76,241,941	28,380,300	2004
Chicago	$258,956,383	70,687,518	28,306,400	2002
Alvin and the Chipmunks: The Squeakquel	$258,933,512	19,614,612	28,303,900	2009
Moana	$258,601,427	48,757,044	28,267,600	2016
X-Men: Days of Future Past	$257,370,062	33,921,534	28,133,000	2014
Ted	$257,265,771	18,815,487	28,121,600	2012
Hitch	$256,175,289	79,495,555	28,002,400	2005
National Treasure	$253,708,899	73,008,894	27,732,800	2004
How to Train Your Dragon	$252,669,648	17,581,231	27,619,200	2010
Die Another Day	$252,347,627	60,942,139	27,584,000	2002
Catch Me If You Can	$250,812,536	64,615,351	27,416,200	2002
Star Trek Into Darkness	$250,530,768	28,778,661	27,385,400	2013
Twilight	$246,885,157	93,962,473	26,986,900	2008
The Lorax	$246,348,150	14,030,500	26,928,200	2012
Madagascar 3: Europe's Most Wanted	$246,151,460	16,391,482	26,906,700	2012
Big Hero 6	$245,910,859	22,527,828	26,880,400	2014
Sherlock Holmes	$245,795,590	09,028,679	26,867,800	2009
The Simpsons Movie	$243,514,911	83,135,014	26,618,500	2007
Fantastic Beasts and Where to Find Them	$243,495,699	34,037,575	26,616,400	2016
Monsters vs. Aliens	$243,242,290	98,351,526	26,588,700	2009
Mission: Impossible - Ghost Protocol	$243,234,057	09,397,903	26,587,800	2011
Doctor Strange	$242,106,982	32,641,920	26,464,600	2016
Scooby-Doo	$241,374,201	53,294,164	26,384,500	2002
Ice Age: Dawn of the Dinosaurs	$241,026,564	96,573,705	26,346,500	2009
The Martian	$240,250,785	28,433,663	26,261,700	2015
Fast Five	$238,204,303	09,837,675	26,038,000	2011
Shark Tale	$236,955,556	60,861,908	25,901,500	2004
Dawn of the Planet of the Apes	$236,083,720	08,545,589	25,806,200	2014
American Pie 2	$234,533,077	45,103,595	25,636,700	2001
Logan	$233,907,331	26,277,068	25,568,300	2017
Dinosaur	$233,796,636	37,748,063	25,556,200	2000
The Fast and the Furious	$233,611,840	44,533,925	25,536,000	2001
Casino Royale	$232,630,224	67,445,960	25,428,700	2006
The Fate of the Furious	$231,018,287	26,008,385	25,252,500	2017
Tangled	$230,234,275	00,821,936	25,166,800	2010
Lilo & Stitch	$229,565,532	45,794,338	25,093,700	2002
Madagascar: Escape 2 Africa	$229,068,778	80,010,950	25,039,400	2008
World War Z	$229,055,055	02,359,711	25,037,900	2013
Justice League	$228,244,513	29,024,295	24,949,300	2017

Film	Adj. Lifetime Gross	Lifetime Gross	Est. Num Tickets	Year
Terminator 3: Rise of the Machines	$228,133,818	$150,371,112	24,937,200	2003
Mission: Impossible - Fallout	$228,059,716	$220,159,104	24,929,100	2018
Thor: The Dark World	$226,338,000	$206,362,140	24,740,900	2013
The Longest Yard	$225,667,427	$158,119,460	24,667,600	2005
Ant-Man and the Wasp	$224,441,551	$216,648,740	24,533,600	2018
Wild Hogs	$223,753,596	$168,273,550	24,458,400	2007
xXx	$223,746,277	$142,109,382	24,457,600	2002
The Amazing Spider-Man 2	$222,883,589	$202,853,933	24,363,300	2014
The Pursuit of Happyness	$222,790,276	$163,566,459	24,353,100	2006
Cinderella	$222,365,794	$201,151,353	24,306,700	2015
Fantastic Four	$220,782,217	$154,696,080	24,133,600	2005
X-Men Origins: Wolverine	$220,593,762	$179,883,157	24,113,000	2009
Godzilla	$220,546,190	$200,676,069	24,107,800	2014
Bohemian Rhapsody	$219,564,574	$216,668,042	24,000,500	2018
Cars 2	$219,056,842	$191,452,396	23,945,000	2011
The Santa Clause 2	$218,903,150	$139,236,327	23,928,200	2002
A Star Is Born	$218,142,923	$215,288,866	23,845,100	2018
Night at the Museum: Battle of the Smithsonian	$217,352,507	$177,243,721	23,758,700	2009
Sherlock Holmes: A Game of Shadows	$217,286,639	$186,848,418	23,751,500	2011
Over the Hedge	$216,514,520	$155,019,340	23,667,100	2006
Teenage Mutant Ninja Turtles	$216,321,490	$191,204,754	23,646,000	2014
Venom	$216,314,171	$213,515,506	23,645,200	2018
Mission: Impossible - Rogue Nation	$216,137,608	$195,042,377	23,625,900	2015
Wreck-It Ralph	$215,481,673	$189,422,889	23,554,200	2012
Quantum of Solace	$214,524,757	$168,368,427	23,449,600	2008
It Chapter Two	$214,179,865	$211,593,228	23,411,900	2019
I, Robot	$213,315,348	$144,801,023	23,317,400	2004
Erin Brockovich	$213,169,889	$125,595,205	23,301,500	2000
22 Jump Street	$212,818,593	$191,719,337	23,263,100	2014
Charlie's Angels	$212,438,937	$125,305,545	23,221,600	2000
Lara Croft: Tomb Raider	$212,008,966	$131,168,070	23,174,600	2001
The Matrix Revolutions	$211,284,418	$139,313,948	23,095,400	2003
Spectre	$210,429,048	$200,074,609	23,001,900	2015
Bad Boys II	$210,288,164	$138,608,444	22,986,500	2003
Coco	$209,793,239	$210,460,015	22,932,400	2017
Nutty Professor II: The Klumps	$209,290,081	$123,309,890	22,877,400	2000
Solo: A Star Wars Story	$209,021,120	$213,767,512	22,848,000	2018
The Croods	$208,333,165	$187,168,425	22,772,800	2013
Minority Report	$207,959,913	$132,072,926	22,732,000	2002
Lincoln	$207,959,913	$182,207,973	22,732,000	2012
Crouching Tiger, Hidden Dragon	$207,738,524	$128,078,872	22,707,800	2000

Film	Adj. Lifetime Gross	etime Gross	Est. Num Tickets	Year
Interstellar	$207,570,194	38,020,017	22,689,400	2014
Talladega Nights: The Ballad of Ricky Bobby	$207,008,487	48,213,377	22,628,000	2006
The Karate Kid	$206,457,757	76,591,618	22,567,800	2010
Anger Management	$205,793,588	35,645,823	22,495,200	2003
Thor	$205,535,605	81,030,624	22,467,000	2011
Cheaper by the Dozen	$204,546,670	38,614,544	22,358,900	2003
Ralph Breaks the Internet	$203,798,336	01,091,711	22,277,100	2018
Rise of the Planet of the Apes	$203,705,938	76,760,185	22,267,000	2011
Captain America: The First Avenger	$203,566,884	76,654,505	22,251,800	2011
The Ring	$203,169,846	29,128,133	22,208,400	2002
Men in Black 3	$202,297,095	79,020,854	22,113,000	2012
Bringing Down the House	$201,349,328	32,716,677	22,009,400	2003
The Proposal	$201,028,221	63,958,031	21,974,300	2009
Traffic	$200,619,291	24,115,725	21,929,600	2000
Hulk	$200,530,552	32,177,234	21,919,900	2003
Sweet Home Alabama	$200,196,638	27,223,418	21,883,400	2002
Ant-Man	$199,690,735	30,202,163	21,828,100	2015
Big Momma's House	$199,531,554	17,559,438	21,810,700	2000
2012	$199,497,705	66,112,167	21,807,000	2009
Mr. Deeds	$198,860,066	26,293,452	21,737,300	2002
True Grit	$197,922,362	71,243,005	21,634,800	2010
Knocked Up	$197,818,071	48,768,917	21,623,400	2007
TRON: Legacy	$197,808,923	72,062,763	21,622,400	2010
Horton Hears a Who!	$196,892,260	54,529,439	21,522,200	2008
How to Train Your Dragon 2	$196,671,785	77,002,924	21,498,100	2014
Troy	$196,487,903	33,378,256	21,478,000	2004
Remember the Titans	$196,105,503	15,654,751	21,436,200	2000
Pitch Perfect 2	$196,036,890	84,296,230	21,428,700	2015
The Revenant	$195,764,270	83,637,894	21,398,900	2015
The Help	$195,747,803	69,708,112	21,397,100	2011
Sex and the City	$194,494,481	52,647,258	21,260,100	2008
Dunkirk	$194,262,114	89,740,665	21,234,700	2017
Chicken Little	$193,093,872	35,386,665	21,107,000	2005
Spider-Man: Into the Spider-Verse	$192,970,369	90,241,310	21,093,500	2018
2 Fast 2 Furious	$192,910,905	27,154,901	21,087,000	2003
The Patriot	$192,352,857	13,330,342	21,026,000	2000
Bridesmaids	$192,279,670	69,106,725	21,018,000	2011
Grown Ups	$192,200,079	62,001,186	21,009,300	2010
Click	$191,843,294	37,355,633	20,970,300	2006
The Bourne Identity	$191,566,100	21,661,683	20,940,000	2002
Fast & Furious	$190,158,171	55,064,265	20,786,100	2009
Ice Age: Continental Drift	$189,594,634	61,321,843	20,724,500	2012

Film	Adj. Lifetime Gross	Lifetime Gross	Est. Num Tickets	Year
Clash of the Titans	$189,503,151	$163,214,888	20,714,500	2010
Home	$188,630,400	$177,397,510	20,619,100	2015
Kung Fu Panda 2	$187,734,778	$165,249,063	20,521,200	2011
The Sum of All Fears	$187,228,875	$118,907,036	20,465,900	2002
Mission: Impossible III	$187,198,686	$134,029,801	20,462,600	2006
Fifty Shades of Grey	$187,098,054	$166,167,230	20,451,600	2015
Django Unchained	$187,016,634	$162,805,434	20,442,700	2012
Rush Hour 3	$186,325,020	$140,125,968	20,367,100	2007
The Heat	$186,154,861	$159,582,188	20,348,500	2013
Something's Gotta Give	$185,595,898	$124,728,738	20,287,400	2003
Gone Girl	$184,969,237	$167,767,189	20,218,900	2014
G.I. Joe: The Rise of Cobra	$184,107,464	$150,201,498	20,124,700	2009
The Departed	$184,071,785	$132,384,315	20,120,800	2006
8 Mile	$183,696,704	$116,750,901	20,079,800	2002
Juno	$183,687,555	$143,495,265	20,078,800	2007
Mamma Mia!	$183,682,066	$144,169,664	20,078,200	2008
Ocean's Twelve	$183,661,025	$125,544,280	20,075,900	2004
A Quiet Place	$183,444,210	$188,024,361	20,052,200	2018
The SpongeBob Movie: Sponge Out of Water	$183,418,594	$162,994,032	20,049,400	2015
Robots	$182,966,667	$128,200,012	20,000,000	2005
Dr. Dolittle 2	$182,566,884	$112,952,899	19,956,300	2001
Seabiscuit	$182,475,401	$120,277,854	19,946,300	2003
Spy Kids	$182,189,058	$112,719,001	19,915,000	2001
Get Out	$181,855,144	$176,040,665	19,878,500	2017
The Lego Batman Movie	$181,832,273	$175,750,384	19,876,000	2017
Gran Torino	$181,702,367	$148,095,302	19,861,800	2008
Chicken Run	$181,328,200	$106,834,564	19,820,900	2000
Crazy Rich Asians	$180,527,721	$174,532,921	19,733,400	2018
The Chronicles of Narnia: Prince Caspian	$180,445,386	$141,621,490	19,724,400	2008
Paul Blart: Mall Cop	$179,454,621	$146,336,178	19,616,100	2009
Borat: Cultural Learnings of America for Make Benefit Glorious Nation of Kazakhstan	$179,250,614	$128,505,958	19,593,800	2006
The Boss Baby	$178,884,680	$175,003,033	19,553,800	2017
Live Free or Die Hard	$178,883,765	$134,529,403	19,553,700	2007
Straight Outta Compton	$178,655,972	$161,197,785	19,528,800	2015
Hotel Transylvania 2	$178,462,942	$169,700,110	19,507,700	2015
50 First Dates	$178,117,135	$120,908,074	19,469,900	2004
Taken	$177,817,070	$145,000,989	19,437,100	2009
Us	$177,769,498	$175,084,580	19,431,900	2019
S.W.A.T.	$177,405,395	$116,934,650	19,392,100	2003
Van Helsing	$177,040,376	$120,177,084	19,352,200	2004

Film	Adj. Lifetime Gross	time Gross	Est. Num Tickets	Year
Fast & Furious Presents: Hobbs & Shaw	$176,563,748	73,956,935	19,300,100	2019
Pirates of the Caribbean: Dead Men Tell No Tales	$176,404,567	72,558,876	19,282,700	2017
Marley & Me	$176,239,897	43,153,751	19,264,700	2008
Snow White and the Huntsman	$175,700,145	55,332,381	19,205,700	2012
Fahrenheit 9/11	$175,593,110	19,194,771	19,194,000	2004
Hidden Figures	$175,497,967	69,607,287	19,183,600	2016
Fantastic 4: Rise of the Silver Surfer	$175,416,547	31,921,738	19,174,700	2007
The Princess Diaries	$174,959,130	08,248,956	19,124,700	2001
Miss Congeniality	$174,837,458	06,807,667	19,111,400	2000
We're the Millers	$174,719,444	50,394,119	19,098,500	2013
Jason Bourne	$174,585,878	62,434,410	19,083,900	2016
Mary Poppins Returns	$174,439,505	71,958,438	19,067,900	2018
Puss in Boots	$174,331,555	49,260,504	19,056,100	2011
The Devil Wears Prada	$174,223,604	24,740,460	19,044,300	2006
Slumdog Millionaire	$174,028,745	41,319,928	19,023,000	2008
The Greatest Showman	$173,980,259	74,340,174	19,017,700	2017
John Wick: Chapter 3 - Parabellum	$173,641,770	71,015,687	18,980,700	2019
Kong: Skull Island	$173,545,713	68,052,812	18,970,200	2017
Hotel Transylvania 3: Summer Vacation	$173,518,268	67,510,016	18,967,200	2018
American Gangster	$172,999,557	30,164,645	18,910,500	2007
A Series of Unfortunate Events	$172,993,154	18,634,549	18,909,800	2004
Gone in 60 Seconds	$172,525,674	01,648,571	18,858,700	2000
The Incredible Hulk	$171,762,703	34,806,913	18,775,300	2008
Wanted	$171,383,047	34,508,551	18,733,800	2008
Little Fockers	$171,094,874	48,438,600	18,702,300	2010
Black Hawk Down	$171,061,026	08,638,745	18,698,600	2001
Les Misérables	$170,829,573	48,809,770	18,673,300	2012
Star Trek Beyond	$170,741,749	58,848,340	18,663,700	2016
American Hustle	$170,346,541	50,117,807	18,620,500	2013
Walk the Line	$169,649,438	19,519,402	18,544,300	2005
Megamind	$169,613,759	48,415,853	18,540,400	2010
Spy Kids 3-D: Game Over	$169,549,721	11,761,982	18,533,400	2003
Divergent	$169,307,290	50,947,895	18,506,900	2014
Enchanted	$168,631,228	27,807,262	18,433,000	2007
Hotel Transylvania	$168,606,528	48,313,048	18,430,300	2012
Dodgeball	$168,421,731	14,326,736	18,410,100	2004
The Village	$168,231,446	14,197,520	18,389,300	2004
Bee Movie	$168,212,235	26,631,277	18,387,200	2007
Freaky Friday	$167,223,300	10,230,332	18,279,100	2003
Scary Movie 3	$166,850,963	10,003,217	18,238,400	2003

Film	Adj. Lifetime Gross	Lifetime Gross	Est. Num Tickets	Year
The Last Samurai	$166,610,361	$111,127,263	18,212,100	2003
X-Men: First Class	$166,361,527	$146,408,305	18,184,900	2011
Get Smart	$166,044,994	$130,319,208	18,150,300	2008
The Break-Up	$165,791,586	$118,703,275	18,122,600	2006
San Andreas	$165,745,844	$155,190,832	18,117,600	2015
A Christmas Carol	$165,673,572	$137,855,863	18,109,700	2009
Neighbors	$165,034,104	$150,157,400	18,039,800	2014
Road to Perdition	$164,472,396	$104,454,762	17,978,400	2002
The Smurfs	$164,384,572	$142,614,158	17,968,800	2011
Mad Max: Fury Road	$164,077,188	$154,058,340	17,935,200	2015
Angels & Demons	$163,561,222	$133,375,846	17,878,800	2009
How to Train Your Dragon: The Hidden World	$163,268,475	$160,799,505	17,846,800	2019
Rio	$163,074,531	$143,619,809	17,825,600	2011
X-Men: Apocalypse	$162,968,410	$155,442,489	17,814,000	2016
The Grudge	$162,576,861	$110,359,362	17,771,200	2004
Fantastic Beasts: The Crimes of Grindelwald	$161,655,624	$159,555,901	17,670,500	2018
Superbad	$161,509,251	$121,463,226	17,654,500	2007
Knives Out	$161,451,616	$165,363,234	17,648,200	2019
Halloween	$161,430,575	$159,342,015	17,645,900	2018
The Pacifier	$161,397,641	$113,086,868	17,642,300	2005
The Secret Life of Pets 2	$161,289,691	$158,874,395	17,630,500	2019
The King's Speech	$161,120,447	$138,797,449	17,612,000	2010
The Italian Job	$161,011,581	$106,128,601	17,600,100	2003
Vanilla Sky	$160,728,898	$100,618,344	17,569,200	2001
Unbreakable	$160,688,645	$95,011,339	17,564,800	2000
How to Lose a Guy in 10 Days	$160,533,124	$105,813,373	17,547,800	2003
The Conjuring	$160,284,289	$137,400,141	17,520,600	2013
Trolls	$159,949,460	$153,707,064	17,484,000	2016
I Now Pronounce You Chuck & Larry	$159,642,991	$120,059,556	17,450,500	2007
Daddy's Home	$159,362,137	$150,357,137	17,419,800	2015
Taken 2	$158,955,036	$139,854,287	17,375,300	2012
American Wedding	$158,639,419	$104,565,114	17,340,800	2003
The Great Gatsby	$158,334,779	$144,840,419	17,307,500	2013
Daddy Day Care	$158,233,233	$104,297,061	17,296,400	2003
21 Jump Street	$158,205,788	$138,447,667	17,293,400	2012
Hairspray	$158,063,988	$118,871,849	17,277,900	2007
Blades of Glory	$157,695,311	$118,594,548	17,237,600	2007
The Curious Case of Benjamin Button	$156,935,084	$127,509,326	17,154,500	2008
La La Land	$156,507,857	$151,101,803	17,107,800	2016
Cars 3	$156,371,547	$152,901,115	17,092,900	2017
The Last Airbender	$156,355,080	$131,772,187	17,091,100	2010
The 40-Year-Old Virgin	$156,205,962	$109,449,237	17,074,800	2005

Film	Adj. Lifetime Gross	time Gross	Est. Num Tickets	Year
The Others	$156,011,102	6,522,687	17,053,500	2001
Legally Blonde	$156,007,443	6,520,674	17,053,100	2001
Grown Ups 2	$155,814,413	33,668,525	17,032,000	2013
Ocean's Thirteen	$155,780,564	17,154,724	17,028,300	2007
Daredevil	$155,572,897	02,543,518	17,005,600	2003
1917	$155,460,373	59,227,644	16,993,300	2019
Fun with Dick and Jane	$155,430,183	10,332,737	16,990,000	2005
Argo	$155,008,445	36,025,503	16,943,900	2012
Ride Along	$155,001,126	34,938,200	16,943,100	2014
Alvin and the Chipmunks: Chipwrecked	$154,741,314	33,110,742	16,914,700	2011
Identity Thief	$154,632,449	34,506,920	16,902,800	2013
The Wolverine	$154,569,325	32,556,852	16,895,900	2013
Ghost Rider	$153,982,917	15,802,596	16,831,800	2007
Me, Myself & Irene	$153,724,019	0,570,999	16,803,500	2000
Terminator Salvation	$153,685,596	25,322,469	16,799,300	2009
Space Cowboys	$153,496,226	0,464,773	16,778,600	2000
The Cat in the Hat	$153,219,946	01,149,285	16,748,400	2003
Four Christmases	$153,082,721	20,146,040	16,733,400	2008
Charlie's Angels: Full Throttle	$152,972,941	00,830,111	16,721,400	2003
Kung Fu Panda 3	$152,969,282	43,528,619	16,721,000	2016
Panic Room	$151,785,487	6,397,334	16,591,600	2002
Silver Linings Playbook	$151,570,501	32,092,958	16,568,100	2012
Scream 3	$151,300,626	9,143,175	16,538,600	2000
America's Sweethearts	$151,299,711	3,607,673	16,538,500	2001
Cats & Dogs	$150,940,181	3,385,515	16,499,200	2001
Cloudy with a Chance of Meatballs	$150,919,140	24,870,275	16,496,900	2009
The Meg	$150,584,311	45,443,742	16,460,300	2018
War for the Planet of the Apes	$150,455,320	46,880,162	16,446,200	2017
Collateral	$148,797,642	01,005,703	16,265,000	2004
Inglourious Basterds	$147,608,358	20,540,719	16,135,000	2009
Shutter Island	$147,417,158	28,012,934	16,114,100	2010
The Aviator	$147,372,331	02,610,330	16,109,200	2004
The Emperor's New Groove	$147,268,040	9,302,687	16,097,800	2000
Save the Last Dance	$147,176,557	1,057,006	16,087,800	2001
Red Dragon	$146,672,484	3,149,898	16,032,700	2002
G-Force	$146,415,416	19,436,770	16,004,600	2009
Pokémon Detective Pikachu	$146,317,528	44,105,346	15,993,900	2019
Safe House	$145,880,238	26,373,434	15,946,100	2012
Maid in Manhattan	$145,180,391	4,011,225	15,869,600	2002
Super 8	$144,607,705	27,004,179	15,807,000	2011
Bolt	$144,602,216	14,053,579	15,806,400	2008
Rio 2	$144,591,238	31,538,435	15,805,200	2014

Film	Adj. Lifetime Gross	Lifetime Gross	Est. Num Tickets	Year
Once Upon a Time . . . In Hollywood	$144,494,266	$142,502,728	15,794,600	2019
The Vow	$144,349,722	$125,014,030	15,778,800	2012
Into the Woods	$143,831,926	$128,002,372	15,722,200	2014
Kingsman: The Secret Service	$143,758,740	$128,261,724	15,714,200	2015
Lone Survivor	$143,755,995	$125,095,601	15,713,900	2013
Million Dollar Baby	$143,457,759	$100,492,203	15,681,300	2004
Lucy	$143,364,446	$126,663,600	15,671,100	2014
The Scorpion King	$143,361,702	$91,047,077	15,670,800	2002
Rango	$143,311,386	$123,477,607	15,665,300	2011
Two Weeks Notice	$143,213,499	$93,354,851	15,654,600	2002
Prometheus	$143,141,227	$126,477,084	15,646,700	2012
Split	$143,102,804	$138,291,365	15,642,500	2017
Anchorman 2: The Legend Continues	$142,955,516	$127,352,707	15,626,400	2013
Life of Pi	$142,608,794	$124,987,023	15,588,500	2012
Shazam!	$142,526,459	$140,371,656	15,579,500	2019
The Divergent Series: Insurgent	$142,506,333	$130,179,072	15,577,300	2015
Master and Commander: The Far Side of the World	$141,867,779	$93,927,920	15,507,500	2003
District 9	$141,741,532	$115,646,235	15,493,700	2009
The Other Guys	$141,373,769	$119,219,978	15,453,500	2010
Cold Mountain	$141,086,511	$95,636,509	15,422,100	2003
Tropic Thunder	$140,812,061	$110,515,313	15,392,100	2008
Salt	$140,337,263	$118,311,368	15,340,200	2010
The Princess Diaries 2: Royal Engagement	$140,201,868	$95,170,481	15,325,400	2004
Dreamgirls	$138,984,224	$103,365,956	15,192,300	2006
Ocean's 8	$138,793,939	$140,218,711	15,171,500	2018
Ghostbusters	$137,948,633	$128,350,574	15,079,100	2016
The Fault in Our Stars	$137,822,386	$124,872,350	15,065,300	2014
The Peanuts Movie	$136,915,786	$130,178,411	14,966,200	2015
Legally Blonde 2	$136,825,218	$90,186,328	14,956,300	2003
The Legend of Tarzan	$136,142,752	$126,643,061	14,881,700	2016
Atlantis: The Lost Empire	$135,861,898	$84,056,472	14,851,000	2001
Bedtime Stories	$135,526,154	$110,101,975	14,814,300	2008
Lee Daniels' The Butler	$135,496,880	$116,632,095	14,811,100	2013
Horrible Bosses	$135,433,756	$117,538,559	14,804,200	2011
Spy Kids 2: Island of Lost Dreams	$135,163,880	$85,846,429	14,774,700	2002
Mystic River	$135,124,543	$90,135,191	14,770,400	2003

Source: IMDb

Appendix B

Further Reading

Baldwin, James. "If Black English Isn't a Language, Then Tell Me, What Is?" *The New York Times*, July 29, 1979. https://archive.nytimes.com/www.nytimes.com/books/98/03/29/specials/baldwin-english.html?,%2522%2520&st=cse.

Baugh, John. *Beyond Ebonics: Linguistic Pride and Racial Prejudice*. New York: Oxford University Press, 2000.

Baugh, John. *Linguistics in Pursuit of Justice*. New York: Cambridge University Press, 2018.

Birnbaum, Michele. "Dark Dialects: Scientific And Literary Realism in Joel Chandler Harris's Uncle Remus Series." *New Orleans Review* 18, no. 1 (Spring 1991): 36–45.

Blot, Richard K., ed. *Language and Social Identity*. Westport: Praeger Publishers, 2003.

Bogle, Donald. *Toms, Coons, Mulattoes, Mammies, and Bucks: An Interpretive History of Blacks in American Films*. 5th ed. New York: Bloomsbury Publishing, 2016.

Bucholtz, Mary. "Race and the Re-embodied Voice in Hollywood Film." *Language and Communication* 31, no. 3 (July 2011): 255–65. https://doi.org/10.1016/j.langcom.2011.02.004.

Bucholtz, Mary. *White Kids: Language, Race, and Styles of Youth Identity*. Cambridge: Cambridge University Press, 2011.

Cramer, Jennifer, Susan Tamasi, and Paulina Bounds. "Southernness and Our Linguistic Planets of Belief: The View From Kentucky." *American Speech* 93, no. 3–4 (August-November 2018): 445–70. https://doi.org/10.1215/00031283-7271272.

de Klerk, Vivian and Barbara Bosch. "Linguistic Stereotypes: Nice Accent—Nice Person?" *International Journal of the Sociology of Language* 116 (January 1995): 17–38. http://dx.doi.org/10.1515/ijsl.1995.116.17.

Dunstan, Stephany Brett. "The Influence of Speaking a Dialect of Appalachian English on the College Experience." PhD diss., North Carolina State University, 2013.

Dunstan, Stephany Brett, Walt Wolfram, Audr J. Jaeger, and Rebecca E. Crandall. "Educating the Educated: Language Div ity in the University Backyard." *American Speech* 90, no. 2 (May 1, 201 : 266–280. https://doi.org/10.1215/00031283-3130368.

Duranti, Alessandro, ed. *A Companion to Lingu c Anthropology*. Malden: Blackwell Publishing, 2006.

Eberhardt, Maeve. "Gendered Representation Through Speech: The Case of the Harry Potter Series." *Language and Literat : International Journal of Stylistics* 26, no. 3 (August 8, 2017). https://doi:10.11 /0963947017701851.

Eckert, Penelope. "Three Waves of Variation dy: The Emergence of Meaning in the Study of Sociolinguistic Variation." *Ann Review of Anthropology* 41 (2012): 87–100. https://doi.org/10.1146/annurev-ant -092611-145828.

Ellis, Michael. "Literary Dialect as Linguisti vidence: Subject-Verb Concord in Nineteenth-Century Southern Literature." *erican Speech* 69, no. 2 (Summer 1994). https://doi:10.2307/455697.

Fox-Kales, Emily. *Body Shots: Hollywood a the Culture of Eating Disorders*. Albany: State University of New York Press 011.

Godley, Amanda J., Julie Sweetland, Rebec S. Wheeler, Angela Minnici, and Brian D. Carpenter. "Preparing Teachers Dialectally Diverse Classrooms." *Educational Researcher* 35, no. 8 (Noven r 2006): 30–37. https://doi.org/10.3102/0013189X035008030.

Guerrero, Jr., Armando. "'You Speak Good glish for Being Mexican' East Los Angeles Chicano/a English: Language and I tity." *Voices* 2, no. 1 (2014): 53–62. https://escholarship.org/uc/item/94v4c08k.

Hamilton, Karen C. "Y'all Think We're Stupi Deconstructing Media Stereotypes of The American South." PhD diss., Geor Southern University, 2009. https://digitalcommons.georgiasouthern.edu/etc 91/?utm_source=digitalcommons.georgiasouthern.edu%2Fetd%2F491&u _medium=PDF&utm_campaign=PDFCoverPages.

Jones, Taylor, Jessica Rose Kalbfeld, Ryan H ock, and Robin Clark. "Testifying While Black: An Experimental Study of Co Reporter Accuracy in Transcription of African American English." *Language* 95, . 2 (June 2019): 216–52. https://doi.org/10.1353/lan.2019.0042.

Koenecke, Allison, Andrew Nam, Emily Lak Joe Nudell, Minnie Quartey, Zion Mengesha, Connor Toups, John R. Rickf , Dan Jurafsky, and Sharad Goel. "Racial Disparities in Automated Speech Re gnition." *PNAS* 117, no. 14 (March 23, 2020): 7684–89. https://doi.org/10.1073/ as.1915768117.

Lakoff, Robin. "Language and Woman's Place *Language in Society* 2, no. 1 (April 1973): 45–80. https://www.jstor.org/stable/4 707.

Lakoff, Robin. *The Language War*. Berkeley: iversity of California Press, 2000.

Landecker, Heidi. "Discrimination's 'Back or': Tackling Language Bias on Campus." *The Chronicle of Higher Edu on*, September 18, 2016. https://www.chronicle.com/article/discriminations- ck-door-tackling-language-bias-on-campus/.

Lopez, Johana P. "Speaking With Them or Speaking for Them: A Conversation About the Effect of Stereotypes in the Latina/Hispanic Women's Experiences in the United States." *New Horizons in Adult Education and Human Resource Development* 25, no. 2 (March 2013): 99–106. http://dx.doi.org/10.1002/nha.20020.

McWhorter, John. *Our Magnificent Bastard Tongue: The Untold History of English*. New York: Gotham Books, 2008.

McWhorter, John. *What Language Is (And What It Isn't and What It Could Be)*. New York: Gotham Books, 2011.

Minnick, Lisa Cohen. *Dialect and Dichotomy: Literary Representations of African American Speech*. Tuscaloosa: University of Alabama Press, 2007.

Newmark, Kalina, Nacole Walker, and James Stanford. "'The Rez Accent Knows No Borders': Native American Ethnic Identity Expressed Through English Prosody." *Language in Society* 45, no. 5 (September 2016): 633–64. http://dx.doi.org/10.1017/S0047404516000592.

Rickford, John R. "The Ebonics Controversy in My Backyard: A Sociolinguist's Experiences and Reflections." *Journal of Sociolinguistics* 3, no. 2 (May 1999): 267–75. https://doi.org/10.1111/1467-9481.00076.

Ronkin, Maggie and Helen E. Karn. "Mock Ebonics: Linguistic Racism in Parodies of Ebonics on the Internet." *Journal of Sociolinguistics* 3, no. 3 (December 16, 2002): 360–80. https://doi.org/10.1111/1467-9481.00083.

Savini, Catherine. "10 Ways to Tackle Linguistic Bias in Our Classrooms." *Inside Higher Ed*, January 27, 2021. https://www.insidehighered.com/advice/2021/01/27/how-professors-can-and-should-combat-linguistic-prejudice-their-classes-opinion.

Sledd, James. "Bi-Dialectalism: The Linguistics of White Supremacy." *English Journal* 58, no. 9 (December 1969): 1307–1315+1329. https://doi.org/10.2307/811913.

Smitherman, Geneva. *Talkin and Testifyin: The Language of Black America*. Boston: Houghton Mifflin, 1977.

Soares, Telma O. "Animated Films and Linguistic Stereotypes: A Critical Discourse Analysis of Accent Use in Disney Animated Films." Master's thesis, Bridgewater State University, August 2017.

Tannen, Deborah. *You Just Don't Understand: Women and Men in Conversation*. New York: Quill, 2001.

Tannen, Deborah. "Who Does the Talking Here?" *The Washington Post*, July 15, 2007. https://www.washingtonpost.com/wp-dyn/content/article/2007/07/13/AR2007071301815.html.

Temple Adger, Carolyn, Walt Wolfram, and Donna Christian. *Dialects in Schools and Communities*. 2nd ed. New York: Routledge, 2007. https://vc.bridgew.edu/theses/53/?utm_source=vc.bridgew.edu%2Ftheses%2F53&utm_medium=PDF&utm_campaign=PDFCoverPages.

Young, Vershawn Ashanti. "'Nah, We Straight': An Argument Against Code Switching." *jac* 29, no. 1–2 (2009): 49–76. https://www.jstor.org/stable/20866886.

Bibliography

Alim, H. Samy and Geneva Smitherman. *Articulate While Black: Barack Obama, Language, and Race in the U.S.* New York: Oxford University Press, 2012.

Alim, H. Samy. "Sorry to Bother You: Deepening the Political Project of Raciolinguistics." In *Raciolinguistics: How Language Shapes Our Ideas About Race*, edited by H. Samy Alim, John R. Rickford, and Arnetha F. Ball, 347–65. New York: Oxford University Press, 2020.

Anderson, Rindy C., Casey A. Klofstad, William J. Mayew, and Mohan Venkatachalam. "Vocal Fry May Undermine the Success of Young Women in the Labor Market." *PLOS ONE* 9, no. 5 (May 28, 2014). https://doi.org/10.1371/journal.pone.0097506.

Association of American Medical Colleges. "Diversity in Medicine: Facts and Figures 2019." 2021. https://www.aamc.org/data-reports/workforce/interactive-data/figure-18-percentage-all-active-physicians-race/ethnicity-2018.

Bailey, Richard W. *Speaking American: A History of English in the United States*. New York: Oxford University Press, 2012.

Ball, Arnetha and Ted Lardner. "Dispositions Toward Language: Constructs of Teacher Knowledge and the Ann Arbor Black English Case." *College Composition and Communication* 48, no. 4 (December 1997). http://dx.doi.org/10.2307/358453.

Baugh, John. *Out of the Mouths of Slaves*. Austin: University of Texas Press, 1999.

Bernstein, Cynthia Goldin. "Misrepresenting the American South." *American Speech* 75, no. 4 (Winter 2000): 339–42.

Boal, Augusto. *Theatre of the Oppressed*. New York: Theatre Communications Group, 1985.

Branham, Dana. "SMU Stands By Survey Asking 'Why Are Black People So Loud?'" *The Dallas Morning News*, last modified May 18, 2018. https://www.nbcdfw.com/news/local/smu-stands-by-survey-asking-why-are-black-people-so-loud/237077/.

Bucholtz, Mary and Qiuana Lopez. "Performing Blackness, Forming Whiteness: Linguistic Minstrelsy in Hollywood Film." *Journal of Sociolinguistics* 15, no. 5 (November 25, 2011): 680–706. https://doi.org/10.1111/j.1467-9841.2011.00513.x.

Capehart, Jonathan. "DEA: the E is for 'Ebonics.'" *The Washington Post*, August 24, 2010. http://voices.washingtonpost.com/postpartisan/2010/08/dea_the_e_is_for_ebonics.html.

Chun, Elaine Wonhee. "Listening to the outhern Redneck: Pathways Of Contextualization On Youtube." *American* *ech* 93, no. 3-4 (August 1, 2018): 425–44. https://doi.org/10.1215/00031283-7 1261.

Clouse, Lindsey. "Django Unbleached: The La uages of Power and Authenticity in Mainstream Film." *Journal of Popular Filn nd Television* 47, no. 4 (November 18, 2019): 207–14. https://doi.org/10.1080/0 56051.2018.1562415.

Conference on College Composition and Con unication. *Students' Right to Their Own Language.* April 1974, https://prod-nc cdn.azureedge.net/nctefiles/groups/cccc/newsrtol.pdf.

Conley, John M., William M. O'Barr, and E. an Lind. "The Power of Language: Presentational Style in the Courtroom." *L e Law Journal* (1978): 1375–99. https://scholarship.law.duke.edu/cgi/viewcor nt.cgi?article=2686&context=dlj.

Coupland, Nikolas. "The Mediated Perfori nce of Vernaculars." *Journal of English Linguistics* 37, no. 3 (Septer er 2009): 284–300. https://doi.org/10.1177/0075424209341188.

Crockett, Zachary. "'Gang Member' and 'Thug oles in Film are Disproportionately Played by Black Actors." *Vox*, Septe er 13, 2016. https://www.vox.com/2016/9/13/12889478/black-actors-typec ting.

Cross, John B., Thomas DeVaney, and Gerald nes. "Pre-Service Teacher Attitudes Toward Differing Dialects." *Linguistics and ducation* 12, no. 4 (Summer 2001): 211–27. https://doi.org/10.1016/S0898-5898)00051-1.

Crystal, David. *A Dictionary of Language*. C ago: University of Chicago Press, 1999.

Crystal, David. *The Fight for English*. Oxford: xford University Press, 2006.

Dallaston, Katherine and Gerard Docherty "The Quantitative Prevalence of Creaky Voice (Vocal Fry) in Varieties of I glish: A Systematic Review of the Literature." *PLOS ONE* 15, no. 3 (Marc 11, 2020). https://doi.org/10.1371/journal.pone.0229960.

Dictionary of American Regional English, Vol e II. Cambridge: Belknap Press of Harvard University Press, 1991.

Dong, Qingwen and Arthur Phillip Murrillo. The Impact of Television Viewing on Young Adults' Stereotypes Towar Hispanic Americans." *Human Communication* 10, no. 1 (January 2007): –44. https://www.researchgate.net/publication/228984764_The_impact_of_tel ision_viewing_on_young_adults'_stereotypes_towards_Hispanic_Americans.

Dragojevic, Marko, Dana Mastro, Howard G s, and Alexander Sink. "Silencing Nonstandard Speakers: A Content Analysi of Accent Portrayals on American Primetime Television." *Language in Societ* 45, no. 1 (February 2016): 59–85. https://doi.org/10.1017/S004740451500074

Eisenhauer, Karen. "Field Report: The Prin ss Problem." Interview by Carrie Neill. Dscout. Accessed March 26, 20 https://dscout.com/people-nerds/field-report-the-princess-problem.

Ellis, Michael. "The Treatment of Dialect in ppalachian Literature." In *Talking Appalachian: Voice, Identity, and Communit* edited by Amy D. Clark and Nancy M. Hayward, 163–82. Lexington: University f Kentucky Press, 2013.

Ford, Thomas E. "Effects of Stereotypical Television Portrayals of African-Americans on Person Perception." *Social Psychology Quarterly* 60, no. 3 (September 1997): 266–78.

Fought, Carmen. "Talkin' with mi Gente (Chicano English)." In *American Voices: How Dialects Differ from Coast to Coast*, edited by Walt Wolfram and Ben Ward, 233–7. Malden: Blackwell Publishing, 2006.

Fridland, Valerie and Kathryn Bartlett. "Correctness, Pleasantness, and Degree of Difference Ratings Across Regions." *American Speech* 81, no. 4 (November 1, 2006): 358–86. https://doi.org/10.1215/00031283-2006-025.

Fridland, Valerie, Kathryn Bartlett, and Roger Kreuz. "Making Sense Of Variation: Pleasantness and Education Ratings Of Southern Vowel Variants." *American Speech* 80, no. 4 (November 1, 2005): 366–87. https://doi.org/10.1215/00031283-80-4-366.

Funk, Cary and Kim Parker. "Diversity in the STEM Workforce Varies Widely Across Jobs." Pew Research Center. January 8, 2019. https://www.pewresearch.org/social-trends/2018/01/09/diversity-in-the-stem-workforce-varies-widely-across-jobs/.

Gilmour, Paisley. "Captain Marvel's Directors on Carol Danvers' Sexuality." *Cosmopolitan*, May 23, 2019. https://www.cosmopolitan.com/uk/love-sex/relationships/a27566789/captain-marvel-queer-sexuality/.

Greer, Sarah. "The Perception of Coolness: Voice Quality and Its Social Uses and Interpretations." Master's thesis, University of Calgary, 2015. https://prism.ucalgary.ca/handle/11023/2238.

Greer, Sarah and Stephen Winters. "The Perception of Coolness: Differences in Evaluating Voice Quality in Male and Female Speakers." *Proceedings of the 18th International Congress on Phonetic Sciences*. Glasgow, August 2019. http://www.internationalphoneticassociation.org/icphs-proceedings/ICPhS2015/Papers/ICPHS0883.pdf.

Grose, Jessica, Penny Eckert, and Susan Sankin. Interview by Terry Gross. "From Upspeak To Vocal Fry: Are We 'Policing' Young Women's Voices?" *Fresh Air*, NPR, July 23, 2015. https://www.npr.org/2015/07/23/425608745/from-upspeak-to-vocal-fry-are-we-policing-young-womens-voices.

Hadler, Jeffrey. "Remus Orthography: The History of the Representation of the African-American Voice." *Journal of Folklore Research* 35, no. 2 (1998): 99–126.

Henderson, Anita. "Is Your Money Where Your Mouth Is?: Hiring Managers' Attitudes Toward African-American Vernacular English." PhD diss., University of Pennsylvania, 2015.

Herrin, Roberta T. "'Shall We Teach 'Em or Learn 'Em?' Attitudes Toward Language in Appalachian Children's Literature." *Journal of the Appalachian Studies Association* 3 (1991): 192–8. https://jstor.org/stable/41445612.

Hildebrand-Edgar, Nicole. "Creaky Voice: An Interactional Resource for Indexing Authority." Master's thesis, University of Victoria, 2014. https://dspace.library.uvic.ca/bitstream/handle/1828/7437/Hildebrand-Edgar_Nicole_MA_2016.pdf?sequence=1&isAllowed=y.

Hill, Jane H. "Language, Race, and White Public Space." *American Anthropologist* 100, no. 3 (September 1998): 680. http://www.jstor.org/stable/682046.

Hill, Jane H. *The Everyday Language of White R ism*. West Sussex: Wiley-Blackwell, 2008. Kindle.

Hinojos, Sara Veronica. "Lupe Vélez ar Her Spicy Visual 'Accent' in English-Language Print Media." *Latino Stu* 17, no. 3 (July 19, 2019): 338–61. https://doi:10.1057/s41276-019-00194-y.

Huber, Patrick. "A Short History of Redneck: ie Fashioning of a Southern White Masculine Identity." *Southern Cultures* 1, no (Winter 1995): 145–66. https://doi.org/10.1353/scu.1995.0074.

Human Rights Watch. "Decades of Disparity: rug Arrests and Race in the United States." March 2, 2009. https://www.hrw.or port/2009/03/02/decades-disparity/drug-arrests-and-race-united-states.

IMDb. "The Lion King (2019) Quotes." 2( ). https://imdb.com/title/tt6105098/quotes/?tab=qt&ref_=tt_trv_qu.

IMDb. "How Are Grosses Adjusted For Ticke Price Inflation?" 2021. https://help.imdb.com/article/imdbpro/industry-resear box-office-mojo-by-imdbpro-faq/GCWTV4MQKGWRAUAP?ref_=mojo_cs nd#inflation.

IMDb. "Larry the Cable Guy." 2(. https://www.imdb.com/name/nm1249256/?ref_=tt_cl_t_4.

IMDb. "Where Does Box Office Mojo by IMD ro Get Its Data?" 2021. https://help.imdb.com/article/imdbpro/industry-resear box-office-mojo-by-imdbpro-faq/GCWTV4MQKGWRAUAP?ref_=mojo_cs nd#data.

Irvine, Judith T. and Susan Gal. "Language Ide gy And Linguistic Differentiation." In *Regimes of Language: Ideologies, Pol s, and Identities*, edited by P. V. Kroskrity, 35–84. Santa Fe: School of Ameri n Research Press, 2000.

King, Sharese. "From African American Ver ular English to African American Language: Rethinking the Study of Race l Language in African Americans' Speech." *Annual Review of Linguistics* 6 (nuary 2020): 285–300. https://doi.org/10.1146/annurev-linguistics-011619-030 6.

Labov, William. *Principles of Linguistic Cha e: Internal Factors*. Oxford: Basil Blackwell, 1994. Quoted in Guy Bailey an an Tillery. "Sounds of the South." In *American Voices: How Dialects Differ m Coast to Coast*, edited by Walt Wolfram and Ben Ward, 11–16. Malden: Bl well Publishing, 2006.

Labov, William. "The Organization of Di ct Diversity in North America." University of Pennsylvania. Accessed Septe er 8, 2021. https://www.ling.upenn.edu/phono_atlas/ICSLP4.html.

Labov William, Sharon Ash, and Charles Bob , "A National Map of The Regional Dialects of American English." University o ennsylvania. July 15, 1997. https://www.ling.upenn.edu/phono_atlas/NationalM /NationalMap.html#Heading2.

Levine, Lawrence W. *Black Culture and Blac onsciousness: Afro-American Folk Thought from Slavery to Freedom*. New Y k: Oxford University Press, 1977. KINDLE.

Library of Congress. "A Note on th Language of the Narratives." Accessed October 5, 2020. https:// .gov/collections/slave-narratives-from-the-federal-writers-project-193 -to-1938/articles-and-essays/note-on-the-language-of-the-narratives/.

Lie, Nadia. "From Latin to Latino Lover: Hispanicity and Female Desire in Popular Culture." *Journal of Popular Romance Studies* 4, no. 1 (February 8, 2014). http://www.jprstudies.org/2014/02/from-latin-to-latino-lover-hispanicity-and-female-desire-in-popular-cultureby-nadia-lie/.

Lippi-Green, Rosina. *English with an Accent: Language, Ideology and Discrimination in the United States*. New York: Routledge, 2012.

Logan, John. Quoted in Jordan Zakarin, "New Bond Goes Old School: Exploring 007's Past and Playing With 'Sexual Intimidation,'" *The Hollywood Reporter*, November 6, 2012, https://www.hollywoodreporter.com/movies/movie-news/james-bond-gay-flirtation-parental-386864/.

Lomax, John. Quoted in "A Note on the Language of the Narratives." Library of Congress. Accessed October 5, 2020. https://loc.gov/collections/slave-narratives-from-the-federal-writers-project-1936-to-1938/articles-and-essays/note-on-the-language-of-the-narratives/.

Lopez, Qiuana. "Imitation or Influence: White Actors and Black Language in Film." *Proceedings of the Seventeenth Annual Symposium About Language and Society*. Austin, April 10-11, 2009. 110–20. https://www.academia.edu/1385768/Imitation_or_Influence_White_actors_and_Black_language_in_film.

Lopez, Qiuana. "Minstrelsy Speaking: Metaparodic Representations of Blackface and Linguistic Minstrelsy in Hollywood Films." *Discourse, Context, and Media* 23 (June 2018): 16–24. https://doi.org/10.1016/j.dcm.2017.09.011.

Lopez, Qiuana and Mary Bucholtz. "'How My Hair Look?' Linguistic Authenticity and Racialized Gender and Sexuality on *The Wire*." *Journal of Language and Sexuality* 6, no. 1 (January 2017): 1–29. https://doi.org/10.1075/jls.6.1.01lop.

Mastro, Dana E. and Elizabeth Behm-Morawitz. "Latino Representation on Primetime Television." *Journalism and Mass Communication Quarterly* 82, no. 1 (Spring 2005): 110–30.

McCarroll, Meredith. "On and On: Appalachian Accent and Academic Power." *Southern Cultures* 22, no. 2 (Summer 2016). https://www.southerncultures.org/article/on-and-on-appalachian-accent-and-academic-power/.

Monteilhet, Hubert. *Neropolis: Roman des Temps Néroniens*. Paris: Éditions du Juillard, 1984.

National Hispanic Media Coalition. *The Impact of Media Stereotypes on Opinions and Attitudes Towards Latinos*. 2012. https://www.chicano.ucla.edu/files/news/NHMCLatinoDecisionsReport.pdf.

Newkirk-Turner, Brandi L., Melody Cooper Williams, Tracy Harris, and Preselfannie E. Whitfield McDaniels. "Pre-Service Teachers' Attitudes toward Students' Use of African American English." *The Researcher: An Interdisciplinary Journal* 26, no. 2 (Summer 2013): 41–57. https://www.jsums.edu/researcher/files/2014/02/Special-Issue-CUR-Complete-Summer-2013.pdf.

NPR. "Letters: Reactions To 'Bad English.'" *All Things Considered*. June 4, 2014. https://www.npr.org/2014/06/04/318888320/letters-reactions-to-bad-english.

Penfield, Joyce and Jacob Ornstein-Galicia. *Chicano English: An Ethnic Contact Dialect*. Amsterdam: John Benjamins Publishing, 1985.

Podesva, Robert J. "Gender and the Social Mea ig of Non-Modal Phonation Types." *Proceedings of the 37th Annual Meeting* *the Berkeley Linguistics Society*. Berkeley, 2013, 427–48. http://journals.li iisticsociety.org/proceedings/index.php/BLS/article/viewFile/832/615.

Preston, Dennis R. "Where the Worst Englis s Spoken." In *Focus on the USA*, edited by Edgar W. Schneider, 297–369. Am rdam: Benjamins, 1996.

Preston, Dennis R. "Changing Research on tl Changing Perceptions of Southern U.S. English." *American Speech* 93, no. 3-4 ugust 1, 2018): 471–96. https://doi.org/10.1215/00031283-7271283.

Punyanunt-Carter, Narissra M. "The Perce d Realism of African American Portrayals on Television." *The Howard Jour* *of Communications* 19, no. 3 (July 25, 2008): 241–57. https://doi.org/10.1080/1 46170802218263.

Rickford, John R. and Sharese King. "Langua and Linguistics On Trial: Hearing Rachel Jeantel (and Other Vernacular Spea s) in the Courtroom and Beyond." *Language* 92, no. 4 (2016): 948–88.

Rodriguez, Jose I., Aaron Castelan Cargile, and larc D. Rich. "Reactions to African-American Vernacular English: Do More onological Features Matter?" *The Western Journal of Black Studies* 28, no. September 2004): 407–14. https://www.researchgate.net/publication/2815265 _Reactions_to_African-American_Vernacular_English_Do_More_Phonologica eatures_Matter.

Román, Ediberto. "Who Exactly Is Living La ida Loca: The Legal and Political Consequences of Latino-Latina Ethnic and cial Stereotypes in Film and Other Media." *The Journal of Gender, Race & Ju ce* 4, no. 37 (2000): 37–68. https://ecollections.law.fiu.edu/faculty_publications 13/.

Russell, Margaret M. "Race and the Dominant ze: Narratives of Law and Inequality in Popular Film." *Legal Studies Forum* 15, r 3 (1991): 243–54.

Saad, Linda. "Gallup Vault: Black Americans' eferred Racial Label." Gallup. July 13, 2020. https://news.gallup.com/vault/3 566/gallup-vault-black-americans-preferred-racial-label.aspx.

Schofield, Alexandra and Leo Mehr. "Gen -Distinguishing Features in Film Dialogue." *Proceedings of the Fifth Works* *on Computational Linguistics for Literature*. San Diego, June 2016. Strouds rg: Association for Computational Linguistics, 2020. https://doi:10.18653/v1/W -02.

Serrano, Julia. "Trans Woman Manifesto." *Wh ing Girl: A Transsexual Woman on Sexism and the Scapegoating of Femininity*. w York: Seal Press, 2007.

Shea, Ammon. Interview by Robert Siegel. *Things Considered*. NPR. June 3, 2014. https://www.npr.org/transcripts/31857 07.

Slade, Alison and Amber J. Narro, "An Accep le Stereotype: The Southern Image in Television Programming." In *Mediated* *ages of the South: The Portrayal of Dixie in Popular Culture*, edited by Alis Slade, Dedria Givens-Carroll, and Amber J. Narro, 5–19. New York: Lexingto Books, 2012.

Slade, Alison, Dedria Givens-Carroll, and Am r J. Narro. *Mediated Images of the South: The Portrayal of Dixie in Popular* *ture*. New York: Lexington Books, 2012.

Slobe, Tyanna. "Style, Stance, and Social Meaning in Mock White Girl." *Language in Society* 47 (June 28, 2018): 541–67. https://doi.org/10.1017/S004740451800060X.

Smith, Stacy L., Marc Choueiti, and Katherine Pierper. *Inclusion or Invisibility? Comprehensive Annenberg Report on Diversity in Entertainment.* Institute for Diversity and Empowerment at Annenberg (IDEA). USC Annenberg School for Journalism and Communication, February 22, 2016.

Spungen, Lauren. "When Can Homophobia Live and Let Die?: An Examination of Sexual Deviance in the James Bond Franchise." *Film Matters* (Spring 2017): 12–17. https://fms.wustl.edu/files/fms/imce/fm_spungen_article.pdf.

Stewart, Catherine A. *Long Past Slavery: Representing Race in the Federal Writers' Project*. Chapel Hill: University of North Carolina Press, 2016.

TV Tropes. "Drill Sergeant Nasty." Accessed September 8, 2021. https://tvtropes.org/pmwiki/pmwiki.php/Main/DrillSergeantNasty.

United States Bureau of Labor Statistics. *Occupational Employment and Wage Statistics*. May 2020. https://www.bls.gov/oes/current/oes330000.htm.

United States Bureau of Labor Statistics. "Data for Occupations Not Covered in Detail." *Occupation Outlook Handout*. Accessed September 8, 2021. https://www.bls.gov/ooh/about/data-for-occupations-not-covered-in-detail.htm#Transportation%20and%20material%20moving%20occupations.

United States Bureau of Labor Statistics. *Labor Force Statistics from the Current Population Survey*. Accessed September 8, 2021. https://www.bls.gov/cps/cpsaat13.htm.

United States Census Bureau. *Language Spoken at Home*. Accessed September 8, 2021. https://data.census.gov/cedsci/table?q=%22spanish%20at%20home%22&tid=ACSST1Y2019.S1601&hidePreview=false.

United States Census Bureau. *Population Estimates, July 1, 2019, (V2019)*. Accessed September 8, 2021. https://www.census.gov/quickfacts/fact/table/US/PST045219.

United States Department of Defense. Office of the Under Secretary of Defense, Personnel, and Readiness. *Population Representation in the Military Services: Fiscal Year 2016 Summary Report*. 2016. https://www.cna.org/pop-rep/2016/summary/summary.pdf.

United States Department of Health and Human Services. Substance Abuse and Mental Health Services Administration. *2019 National Survey of Drug Use and Health (NSDUH) Releases*. Accessed September 8, 2021. https://www.samhsa.gov/data/release/2019-national-survey-drug-use-and-health-nsduh-releases.

United States Federal Writers' Project. Work Projects Administration. *Slave Narratives: A Folk History of Slavery in the United States from Interviews with Former Slaves*. Washington, DC: Library of Congress, 1941. https://hdl.loc.gov/loc.mss/mesn.001.

United States Federal Writers' Project. "Volume II Arkansas Narratives Part 4." *Slave Narratives: A Folk History of Slavery in the United States from Interviews with Former Slaves*. Washington, DC: Library of Congress, 1941. https://hdl.loc.gov/loc.mss/mesn.024.

United States National Center for Education atistics. *Race/Ethnicity of College Faculty*. Accessed September 8, 2021. tps://nces.ed.gov/fastfacts/display.asp?id=61.

Vélez, Lupe. 1933. Quoted in Sara Veronica nojos, "Lupe Vélez and Her Spicy Visual 'Accent' in English-Language Print M dia," *Latino Studies* 17, no. 3 (July 19, 2019): 338–61, https://doi:10.1057/s412 -019-00194-y.

Warren, Paul. *Uptalk: The Phenomenon of Risi Intonation*. Cambridge: Cambridge University Press, 2016.

Weaver, C. Mason. "Funding Ebonics Isn't a w Idea, It's Just a Bad One." The National Center for Public Policy Research pril 1, 1997. https://nationalcenter.org/project21/1997/04/01/funding-ebonics-is -a-new-idea-its-just-a-bad-one/.

Whitelock, James. "NASCAR Most & Le Popular States [MAP]." World Sports Network. Rebel Penguin ApS. July 2020. https://www.wsn.com/nascar/most-popular-states/.

Wilkinson, Crystal. "Holler." *Slice Magazine*, r 6 (2010). Quoted in Michael Ellis, "The Treatment of Dialect in Appalachian terature," in *Talking Appalachian: Voice, Identity, and Community*, eds. Amy). Clark and Nancy M. Hayward (Lexington: University of Kentucky Press, 2 3), 177.

Wilson, John Paul, Kurt Hugenberg, and Nicho O. Rule. "Racial Bias in Judgments of Physical Size and Formidability: From S to Threat." *Journal of Personality and Social Psychology* 113, no. 1 (201 59–80. http://dx.doi.org/10.1037/pspi0000092.

Wilson, Theresa. "Ebonics is Actually Just Ba English." *Iowa State Daily*, January 16, 1997. https://www.iowastatedaily.com oonics-is-actually-just-bad-english/article_2486872c-0b88-5d6a-8c0c-e63b963b 39.html.

Yuasa, Ikuko Patricia. "Creaky Voice: A New Feminine Voice Quality for Young Urban-Oriented Upwardly Mobile American omen?" *American Speech* 85, no. 3 (August 1, 2010): 315–37. https://doi.org.10 15/00031283-2010-018.

Zirkel, Sabrina. "Is There a Place for Me? Role odels and Academic Identity among White Students and Students of Color." *Teac s College Record* 104, no. 2 (2002). https://doi.org.10.1111/1467-9620.00166.

Index

Page references for figures are italicized.

About the Author

Lindsey Clouse (she/her) teaches writing at Western Dakota Technical College and Black Hills State University in Rapid City, South Dakota. Her previously published work includes a scholarly analysis of Black English in modern action film, and she was a contributor to the third edition of *Reading Popular Culture: An Anthology for Writers*. When she's not thinking, talking, or writing about language and movies, she enjoys hiking with her dogs in the beautiful Black Hills.